ONE WEEK LOAN
UNIVERSITY OF GLAMORGAN
TREFOREST LEARNING RESOURCES CENTRE
Pontypridd, CF37 1DL
Telephone: (01443) 482626
Books are to be returned on or before the last date below

THE REDISCOVERY OF AMERICA

Geo. Washington
President of the United States
From his Profile taken in 1791.

The Rediscovery of America

Transatlantic Crosscurrents in an Age of Revolution

Stuart Andrews

First published in Great Britain 1998 by
MACMILLAN PRESS LTD
Houndmills, Basingstoke, Hampshire RG21 6XS and London
Companies and representatives throughout the world

A catalogue record for this book is available from the British Library.

ISBN 0–333–72618–9

First published in the United States of America 1998 by
ST. MARTIN'S PRESS, INC.,
Scholarly and Reference Division,
175 Fifth Avenue, New York, N.Y. 10010

ISBN 0–312–21405–7

Library of Congress Cataloging-in-Publication Data
Andrews, Stuart.
The rediscovery of America : transatlantic crosscurrents in an age
of revolution / Stuart Andrews.
p. cm.
Includes bibliographical references and index.
ISBN 0–312–21405–7 (cloth)
1. United States—History—Revolution, 1775–1783—Participation,
Foreign. 2. United States—History—Revolution, 1775–1783—Causes.
3. United States—History—Revolution, 1775–1783—Influence.
4. United States—Intellectual life—18th century. 5. Rhetoric–
–Political aspects—United States—History—18th century. 6. United
States—Relations—Europe. 7. Europe—Relations—United States.
I. Title.
E269.F67A53 1998
973.3'1—dc21 97–52924
CIP

earning Resources
Centre

12161934

This book is printed on paper suitable for recycling and made from fully managed and
sustained forest sources.

10   9   8   7   6   5   4   3   2   1
07   06   05   04   03   02   01   00   99   98

Printed and bound in Great Britain by
Antony Rowe Ltd, Chippenham, Wiltshire

To the staff of Bristol Reference Library

The Rediscovery of America

'This continent, which had been unknown for possibly the whole of antiquity and many centuries in modern times; the first wild destiny of that continent and its second destiny after the arrival of Christopher Columbus; the supremacy of the European monarchies shaken in this new world; a republic of unfamiliar type foreshadowing a change in the human mind; the part which my country had played in these events; these seas and shores owing their independence in part to the French flag and blood; a great man issuing from the midst of discord and wilderness; Washington living in a flourishing city on the spot where William Penn bought a plot of forest land; the United States passing on to France the revolution which France had supported with her arms...'

Chateaubriand

Contents

Contents

Preface

Two images. First the *Matthew*, which carried John Cabot to mainland America 500 years ago. As I write, a replica of Cabot's ship sails out of Bristol to re-enact that historic voyage. Second the key of the Bastille, which hangs in George Washington's home at Mount Vernon to symbolize the political impact of the New World on Europe during the American and French Revolutions.

The Rediscovery of America features some twenty representatives of England, France and America, whose careers in some sense spanned the Atlantic in the last quarter of the eighteenth century. Among these transatlantic figures are men of action with a role in one or other (or both) of the revolutions. There are also propagandists, political exiles, and speculators in real estate; two are naturalists and yet others are poets or novelists who dream of crossing the Atlantic, but never do so. Each revolutionary figure is presented through his or her writings and correspondence, much of which is not easily accessible but is offered here in digestible form – sometimes after translation from the French.

The introduction offers a brief survey of the interaction between Europe and America from the time of Columbus himself to the Columbiads of late eighteenth-century poets. The other chapters focus on individuals, but collectively illustrate the three-fold impact of Revolutionary America: as an embodiment of Enlightenment ideals, as an asylum for the 'friends of liberty' and as a stimulus to the Romantic imagination. No attempt is made to establish causal connections between the American and French Revolutions. The study concerns the subjective responses of individuals and the recurrence of transatlantic imagery in revolutionary rhetoric. It thus presents a series of case studies which illuminate the still reverberating debate on the Palmer–Godechot thesis of the 1960s. The contested concept of an 'Atlantic Revolution' is here partly corroborated in the language and experience of representatives of the Revolutionary generation.

More generally the book is an approach to intellectual history which recognizes that, although political philosophers do not themselves cause revolutions, their ideas supply politicians with slogans to justify and rationalize actions dictated by *Realpolitik*. Abstract political ideas can colour the surface, even when not shaping the substance of political debate.

More generally still, the book is aimed beyond academia to an audience that will find interest and amusement in the sheer proliferation of personal transatlantic links during the Revolutionary period, and in the interlocking relationships of the individuals involved.

I wish to record my personal thanks: to the Information Department of the United States Embassy, which 30 years ago sent me as a young schoolmaster to America, where my visits to Mount Vernon and Monticello sowed the seeds of this book; to the staff of Bristol Reference Library and its magnificent collection of eighteenth-century works on America; to Repton School Library which is unusually rich in eighteenth-century texts; and to the Library of my alma mater, the University of Cambridge. I am also grateful to the readers and successive editors of *History Today* and to my lunchtime audiences at the National Portrait Gallery, on whom I have so often tested my material; to Professor Christopher Frayling, who tracked down the text of Rousseau's three-act play on Columbus; to Andrew Fairbairn for the London links between Locke and Montesquieu; to Reggie Watters and The Friends of Coleridge for their encouragement when it most mattered; to the patience of my other friends and family, particularly my wife; and to my pupils at Repton, Norwich and Clifton. All have contributed willingly or unwittingly to the *Rediscovery*. The responsibility for any imperfections in concept or execution remains my own.

Stuart Andrews

List of Illustrations

Acknowledgments

Early versions of chapters 2, 6, 7 and 13 were first published in *History Today*, and here appear in an expanded form; similarly chapters 3 and 5 combine material from four separate articles, which I wrote for the same journal. All such previously published material is reproduced with the permission of the Editor of *History Today*.

I have generally used the original eighteenth-century texts, except where modern editions are indicated in the notes. Of these, I have particularly relied on *Richard Price and the Ethical Foundations of the American Revolution*, edited with an introduction by Bernard Peach (Duke University Press, Durham, North Carolina, 1979) and *The Life and Selected Writings of Thomas Jefferson*, edited by Adrienne Koch and William Peden (Random House, New York, 1944).

In quoting from texts, I have modernized spelling and punctuation, and have not followed the author's use of capitals for the initial letter of nouns, or of italics for place names. In doing so, I am guided by a wish to avoid giving the impression that eighteenth-century men and women spoke, wrote or thought in a quaintly archaic form of English.

Cover picture (reproduced with permission): *Figurehead*, Index of American Design, © 1997 Board of Trustees, National Gallery of Art, Washington. All other illustrations are reproduced from eighteenth- or nineteenth-century texts.

Introduction

W. T. RAYNAL, F.R.S

Member of the Academy of Sciences
& Belle Lettres of Prussia.

1 Discovery and Rediscovery: Planters, Puritans and Philosophes

The propaganda success of the American Declaration of Independence is shown by the change in European attitudes to America between 1770 and 1790. In 1768 the Dutchman Cornelius de Pauw could boldly assert: 'It is certain that the conquest of the New World, so renowned and so unjust, was the greatest of the misfortunes that humanity has suffered.' Twenty years later, but before the fall of the Bastille, Abbé Genty made a contrasting claim in his *Influence of the Discovery of America on the Happiness of the Human Race*. For the Frenchman, 'the independence of the Anglo-Americans is the event most suited to hastening the revolution which must restore happiness on earth.' The shift in European perceptions during those 20 years, was indeed a rediscovery of America.[1]

It was more than a century after Columbus that the British tried to make their first firm settlement in America. The Spanish, the Portuguese and the French were all established in the New World before England planted her first tentative colony at Jamestown in 1607. Cabot's voyages out of Bristol, in the late 1490s, carried him beyond Columbus's landfall and on to the mainland, where he sighted Newfoundland and sailed down the coast of Nova Scotia. In the 1560s, Sir John Hawkins apparently resupplied the French foothold in Florida – thus making common cause with France against the monopolistic claims of Spain. As Richard Hakluyt the younger wrote: 'Whoever is conversant with Portuguese and Spanish writers shall find that they account all other nations for pirates, rovers and thieves which visit any heathen coast that they have sailed by or looked on.' The expansionist aims of Spain and Portugal were reinforced by Pope Alexander VI's division of the New World between them in 1493, with the result that, under Elizabeth I, Protestant principles became identified with English patriotism.[2]

Five years before Hakluyt wrote his more famous *Principal Navigations of the English Nation* (1589), he had written his *Discourse on Western Planting*. Ostensibly composed at the request of Walter Raleigh, this memoir advocated the planting of English colonies in those parts of the New World that Spaniards and Portuguese had not reached. This view of America, not simply as a staging post, or base for privateers, but as a continent ripe for settlement, had been promoted by Humphrey Gilbert, Raleigh's half-brother. Before his early death in 1583, Gilbert had devised plans aimed at providing an asylum for religious refugees, and at encouraging the emigration of the poor by means of government subsidies. The planting of colonies became crown policy under the Stuarts – quite apart from the private emigration provoked by the religious policies of James I and Charles I. The first settlement at Jamestown, promoted by London merchants under royal charter, was an unpromising beginning. Nearly half the 140 or so would-be settlers who had landed in 1607 were dead by the time the second wave arrived in the following year. Not until tobacco was successfully cultivated would Virginia's fortunes seem secure, and despite further reinforcements, the population was still well under 1000 in 1620.

In that year the *Mayflower* sailed into Massachusetts Bay, and William Bradford stepped ashore into what he later described as a 'hideous and desolate wilderness, full of wild beasts and wild men'. Before landing, the male settlers had signed the Mayflower Compact to 'covenant and combine ourselves together into a civil body politic' and to enact such laws 'from time to time, as shall be thought most meet and convenient for the general good of the colony'. The foundation of America's reputation as an asylum for the persecuted had been laid. The end of the English Civil War prompted a new phase of colonial settlement: between March 1663 and June 1664, Carolina, New York and New Jersey were all chartered. Political philosophy and practical politics seemed for a time to coalesce in Carolina's 'Fundamental Constitutions', drawn up by Lord Ashley, the future first Earl of Shaftesbury. John Locke, a member of Ashley's circle and tutor to his grandson, has been credited with drawing up the constitutions. In the 1761 edition of *Essay on Manners*, Voltaire would write of Carolina: 'The greatest glory of this colony is to have received its laws from the philosopher Locke. Complete freedom of conscience, toleration of all religions was the basis of these laws.'[3]

By the end of the seventeenth century, commercial profit had become a more powerful impulse than freedom from persecution; and the duty of monitoring the management of colonies, and advising the Privy Council on colonial policy, was firmly vested in the newly created Board of Trade and Plantations. Two pamphlets, soon to be published in London, and promoting Carolina as a place of settlement, would reflect the change in emphasis. *A Letter from South Carolina* (1710), purporting to have been written by 'a Swiss Gentleman' (but actually written by a Englishman), supplies an account of the climate, agriculture and social institutions of Carolina, 'together with the manner and necessary charges of SETTLING A PLANTATION there, and the annual profit it will produce.' The second pamphlet, published in 1712 and entitled *Profitable Advice for Rich and Poor*, reinforces Carolina's appeal by offering, in dialogue form, 'propositions for the advantageous settlement of people in general, but especially of the laborious poor, in that fruitful, pleasant and profitable country...'. It thus echoes the first author's claim for Carolina that 'there is no place in the continent of America where people can transport themselves to greater advantage'.[4]

The *Letter from South Carolina* includes good government among the colony's attractions, but there is no talk yet of Nature, Nature's God or the Rights of Man. There is an admission (which reappears verbatim in *Profitable Advice*) that Carolina's appeal is to those 'who affect solitude, contemplation, gardening, groves, woods, and the like innocent delights of plain simple Nature'. The main message of both pamphlets, however, is that land is cheap, and that 'One hundred pounds sterling, well manag'd in a plantation in Carolina, affords far greater profit than six times as much here.' Yet both authors have an eye on poorer emigrants, and suggest government grants 'for transporting annually a few supernumeraries of our nation'.[5]

The attraction of exporting one's social problems had prompted the foundation of Georgia in 1732. It arose from a House of Commons Committee on overcrowded gaols, chaired by the retired army officer James Oglethorpe. The result of the committee's report was that General Oglethorpe was charged with the task of establishing a colony of poor debtors, released from English prisons. The committee had argued that the debtors and their families would 'increase so fast as to become a security and defence of our possessions against the French and Indians of those parts; that they may be employed in cultivating flax and hemp, which being allowed to make into yarn, would be returned to England and Ireland and greatly promote our manufactures.' It was an optimistic vision, almost as romantic as John Wesley's notion of what awaited him as chaplain to the new colony: 'Towards mortifying the desire of the flesh, the desire of sensual pleasures, it will be no small thing to be able, without fear of giving offence, to live on water and the fruits of the earth.'[6]

The Scots (and Scottish-Irish from Ulster) are usually thought to have spearheaded eighteenth-century transatlantic migration. The Act of Union (1707) had officially recognized Scotland's trade with North America. When Defoe toured Britain in the 1720s, he noted Glasgow's advantage in the colonial trade compared with London. The *Scots Magazine*, published in Edinburgh from 1739 to 1826, carried American news from the first, and reprinted extracts from American newspapers. Although Scottish emigration to America in the decade or so after the Seven Years War was probably not more than 25 000 in total, the *Scots Magazine* regularly reported the sailing of ships carrying emigrants, while American employers advertised in the Scottish press. Many such emigrants went as indentured servants, who bound themselves for a term of years in return for passage money. Such transatlantic connections were severed by the War of Independence. And even when the war was virtually over, a statute of the Georgia Assembly of August 1782 declared that 'the people of Scotland have in general manifested a decided inimicality to the civil liberties of America', and that therefore no Scotsman was to be allowed to settle or carry on his trade in Georgia, unless he supported the patriot side.[7]

Thomas Jefferson's first draft of the Declaration of Independence had included the complaint that George III's invading army contained 'not only soldiers of our common blood, but Scotch and foreign mercenaries.' This was omitted from the final text, to avoid offending Scotsmen resident in America. Jefferson's tutor was a graduate of Edinburgh – according to Jefferson the finest university in the world. Benjamin Franklin received an honorary doctorate from St Andrews University, and described his first visit to Scotland in 1759 as 'Six weeks of the *densest* happiness I have met with in any part of my life.' In Edinburgh, he met the leading figures of the Scottish Enlightenment, and on his second visit in 1771, David Hume gave a dinner party in his honour. By the 1770s the Edinburgh medical school had attracted over 100 American students – including Benjamin Rush. Scottish cultural colonization was also fostered by appeals from the Presbyterian synods of New York and Philadelphia to the General Assembly of the Church of Scotland. In the 1750s the Assembly authorized a collection 'at all church doors in Scotland' for the recently founded College of New Jersey (later Princeton University), and in 1768 the Scottish Presbyterian minister John Witherspoon became the College President.[8]

Witherspoon, one of two Scottish signatories of the Declaration of Independence and a member of the Continental Congress, has been credited with importing the Scottish Enlightenment into America; and he undoubtedly gave greater colonial currency to the ideas of the Edinburgh school. Yet Robertson's *Charles V* seems to have been the only work of the Scottish Enlightenment published in America before the Revolution. Even Adam Smith's *Wealth of Nations* had to wait for the Philadelphia edition of 1789, while Hugh Blair's influential Lectures on *Rhetoric and Belles Lettres* (which went through 56 complete or abridged editions between 1805 and 1823) appeared first at Philadelphia in 1784 – though in time to influence the drafting of the Federal Constitution.[9]

It was the war which wrought a change in the tone of books published on America. The scientific impulses of the European Enlightenment had ensured an interest in the natural history of North America from at least the 1750s. Peter Kalm's expedition to North America was sponsored by the University of Uppsala (where Linnaeus was Professor of Botany) and Kalm's *Travels*, appearing in Swedish in 1753, was the result. The two-volume work, published in English in 1771 and in Dutch a year later, claims to embrace not only natural history, but also 'the civil, ecclesiastical and commercial state of the country, the manners of the inhabitants and several curious and important matters on various subjects.' Kalm notes the 'good clear water of Philadelphia'; he provides a table of the 'value of goods shipped annually from England to Pennsylvania'; he commends the religious liberty accorded to every law-abiding citizen 'be his religion ever so strange'; and he applauds the security of persons and property in Philadelphia, enabling each inhabitant 'to live in his house like a king'. But it is clear where Kalm's emphasis lies. Listing 58 trees which 'grow spontaneously in the woods which are nearest to Philadelphia', he devotes 16 pages to trees before noting that 'coals have not yet been found in Pennsylvania'.[10]

He does not pause to describe methods of wine-making from red and white currants 'for in Sweden this art is in higher perfection than in North America'. He notices that there are no hares to be seen, but finds 'some animals which are a medium between our hares and rabbits and make a great devastation whenever they get into fields of cabbages and turnips'. As for rattlesnakes, Kalm refers his readers to his own report in the Memoirs of the Swedish Academy of Sciences for the years 1752 and 1753. He records encouragingly that 'everyone is of the opinion that the American savages were a very good-natured people, if they were not attacked', and he is more than half convinced by the claims of local people that 'giants had formerly lived in these

parts'. Kalm the scientist nevertheless takes daily meteorological read-
ings to illustrate differences in climate, and is given a stone by Franklin which is notable for 'its indestructibility in the fire'. When he
reaches New York, en route for Canada, Kalm lists nine places of
worship in the city, including the Jewish synagogue; and in his second
volume he devotes a paragraph to the Moravians – though he quickly
reverts to discussing cherries and yams. This volume has none of the
engraved plates that enliven volume one – 'mocking-bird and red-
breasted thrush' or 'racoon and American pole-cat'. But the plates
remind us that Kalm's book is overwhelmingly a work of natural
history, with minimal political or sociological comment.[11]

By the time Kalm's *Travels* appeared in English, the anonymous
Account of the European Settlements in America (first published during
the Seven Years War) had reached its fifth edition (1770). It was one
of a dozen books on Britain's American colonies that Voltaire had in
his library. The preface to the first edition claims that, before Pitt's
'Year of Glorious Victories' there were few Englishmen who made
North America 'any part of their study; though the matter is certainly
very curious in itself, and extremely interesting to us as a trading
people'. Indeed the author focuses primarily on trade, explaining: 'I
have but little considered their civil, and yet less their natural history.'
For our anonymous author, 'the people of America' are the Indians.
He remarks that 'liberty in its fullest extent is the darling passion of
the Americans', but this is not apparently meant as a compliment. He
goes on to describe their varieties of torture, not only 'to give a true
idea of their character', but also to show 'in the strongest light to
what an inconceivable degree of barbarity the passions of men let
loose will carry them'.[12]

Contemporary views of the Indians certainly fell somewhat short of
Rousseau's idealized 'noble savage'. De Pauw, writing in 1768, was
influenced by the claim of Buffon, the French naturalist, that nature
was degenerate in the New World, and that 'to be precise the savage is
weak and small in his generative organs'. De Pauw's conviction of the
ethnic inferiority of the Indians gained greater currency through his
contribution to the article on America in the 1776 *Supplement* to the
Encyclopédie, where he describes the Americans as 'less industrious,
less inventive than the inhabitants of our hemisphere'. De Pauw writes
mainly of the Indians of the Amazon, whom he reports as seeming to
live 'in an eternal childhood', but he adds confidently that 'there is not
in the whole of the new world the smallest American tribe that is free,
or which thinks of learning to read or write.' The second half of the

Encyclopédie article, written by the Swiss Samuel Engel, does somewhat redress the balance in favour of the savages, by rejecting the epithet 'barbarous' in describing them.[13]

Less surprisingly, the same equivocal attitude is seen in an account of Canadian Indians written half a century earlier by the Jesuit priest, Pierre Charlevoix. His *Journal of Travels in North America* was published as early as 1721, but republished in English translations in 1761 and 1763. Father Charlevoix tries to be fair to the Indians. He describes how they go bear-hunting 'equipp'd as for war, and their faces smeared with black', but omits their barbaric treatment of prisoners and 'the particulars of all that passes in these horrible executions'. He insists that, though warlike, the Indians are skilled treaty-makers and reveal in their negotiations 'a dexterity, and a nobleness of sentiments, which would do honour to the most polished nations'. After describing their method of electing their chiefs, Charlevoix remarks admiringly, 'Thus it is reason that governs.' And he concludes: 'These Americans are entirely convinced that man is born free, that no power on earth has any right to make any attempts against his liberty, and that nothing can make amends for its loss.'[14]

The advertisement to the English edition of the *Journal*, while asserting that it had shown the importance of Canada – when ministers were talking of exchanging it for Guadeloupe – claimed that the author afforded his readers 'much entertainment' by his account of 'the manners, customs, etc of the various inhabitants of these vast countries'. Among the curiosities recorded are the fruit of the vinegar tree and the nesting habits of penguins and of 'many other birds that can't fly'. The bodies of the Indians, he notices in some puzzlement, are completely devoid of hair except for their eye-brows and their head, attributing this peculiarity to 'the constant custom the Americans have of smoking, and which is common to both sexes'. Writing of the sugary substance drawn from ash trees, he expresses his surprise at finding in Canada 'what Virgil says in foretelling the golden age, that honey should flow from the trees'. But his classical allusions sometimes have a political thrust, as when he points to the way in which the Indians conduct themselves in their assemblies 'with such prudence, maturity, ability and I will also say, for the most part, such probity, as would have done honour to the Areopagus of Athens and the Senate of Rome in the most flourishing times of those republics'. This comparison is echoed by Abbé Raynal in his history of the European settlements in North America, first published in 1770.[15]

Voltaire, who dismissed Raynal's massive work as 'a re-hash with rhetoric' (*un réchauffé avec de la declamation*), had focused attention on the New World as early as the 1730s. His drama *Alzire or the Americans* (1736) has nothing essentially American about it, though it is set in Peru. It does, however, contain the famous lines claiming that the American Indian 'equals us in courage, and surpasses us in happiness.' Voltaire's eulogies were more often reserved for the Quakers. In his *Letters on the English* (*Lettres philosophiques*) of 1733, he wrote that 'William Penn could boast of having established on earth the golden age which is so much talked about, and which has existed only in Philadelphia'. And 30 years later, he wrote in his *Philosophical Dictionary* (1764): 'If it were not that the sea makes me intolerably sick, it would be into your bosom, Pennsylvania, that I would go to finish the remainder of my career – what there is of it.' Although Voltaire did not himself cross the Atlantic, his writings did. An English translation of his works in 35 volumes appeared in America about 1760, while in 1758 the New York Society was proposing to its members his *Letters on the English, History of the War of 1741, Essay on Manners* and the *Age of Louis XIV*.[16]

The fact that Voltaire and Raynal were writing before the Declaration of Independence, raises the question of how far French influence shaped the rhetoric, if not the political principles of the American Revolution. Some American historians, notably Daniel Boorstin, indignantly repudiate any such suggestion. For them the ideas of the Founding Fathers were the product of 'plantation necessities', and nothing more than 'an index to the problems of a Virginian planter'. An interest in history and a knowledge of medical remedies, a familiarity with mechanics and meteorology, and, above all, a sufficient knowledge of law to survive in a highly litigious society – all were the stock-in-trade of a successful planter. To seek to explain the political ideals of Jefferson by 'looking to the bookish prospectuses of English and French political theorists' was to miss the obvious point that these political principles already existed within the colonial tradition. The philosophers of the European Enlightenment were 'as irrelevant as the guilty cousin who suddenly appears in the last scene of a bad mystery play'. To Jacques Godechot, however, 'the Enlightenment is unquestionably one of the important causes of the Atlantic Revolution', and he claims that revolutionary ideas crossed the Atlantic more rapidly than they percolated through the frontiers of European states. For other historians the American Revolution is a Puritan Revolution – a reassertion of protestant values against the designs of an established church.[17]

The apparent contradictions are partly explained by the undoubted fact that the Protestant Reformation contained within itself the seeds of the Enlightenment. The Puritan insistence on the appeal to conscience, on individuals' ability to interpret the Bible for themselves, on the duty to elect suitably dedicated ministers, on the need to destroy superstition and repudiate tradition – all these emphases established critical habits that would have secular repercussions, particularly when scientific methodology began to oust dogmatic theology. The Calvinistic piety of New England was not just a matter of predestination and church discipline. In opposing the evangelistic fervour of George Whitefield and Jonathan Edwards, Charles Chauncy, writing in the 1740s, had condemned what he called 'the prevalence of *enthusiasm, superstition* and *intemperate zeal*', adding: 'Tis not enough that they have *heat* in their *affections*, but they must have *light* in their *minds.*' Chauncy was for 60 years minister of the First Church in Boston, and had graduated from Harvard, a Puritan foundation. And even Edwards, a Yale graduate but briefly President of Princeton, appealed (like John Wesley) to reason and experience, as well as to Scripture – though he did not go as far as Chauncy's declaration that 'the voice of reason is the voice of God'.[18]

Edwards shared the belief, conspicuous among colonial Presbyterians, Congregationalists and Baptists, that the biblical portrayal of the thousand-year reign of Christ and his saints was a firm prediction of an earthly millenium. Edwards saw the millenium as a time when 'the absolute and despotic powers of the kings of the earth shall be taken away, and liberty shall reign throughout the earth'; and in 1742 he even predicted that the millenium would probably begin in America. By the 1770s, Samuel West, a New Hampshire minister who joined Washington's army after Bunker Hill, could circulate a sermon which interpreted the Revolution as the fulfilment of the millenial prophecies of Isaiah, while Joel Barlow's *Prospect of Peace* (1778) took its imagery from Daniel, and looked towards a scriptural millenium:

> Then Love shall rule, and Innocence adore
> Discord shall cease, and Tyrants be no more;
> 'Till yon bright orb, and those celestial spheres
> In radiant circles, mark a thousand years.

Barlow's lines show what a short step it was from the millenial tradition of New England to the secular Utopia of the *philosophes*, so eagerly embraced by the Virginian Founding Fathers.[19]

The Founding Fathers, like the friends of the American Revolution in England, tended to be Unitarians, who rejected orthodox Christian teaching on the Trinity and the salvation theology it implied. Unitarians thus reinforced the belief in a purely man-made millenium – despite having their roots in Calvinistic Presbyterianism. And it was eighteenth-century Ulster Presbyterians, crossing the Atlantic for economic rather than religious reasons, who brought with them a covenanting tradition which converged with the contractual theories of John Locke. Indeed Witherspoon specifically stressed the link between such contractual theories and the Scottish Covenanters of the 1640s. Locke, like three-quarters of the population of the American colonies, came from a dissenting background. His father had fought on the Parliamentary side in the English Civil War, and John was at Oxford during the Commonwealth. The master of his college was a noted Puritan, while the professor of history whose lectures Locke attended was a Dutch Huguenot. Forty years later, when well into his fifties, Locke spent five years in Holland – a Calvinist country that welcomed political exiles. And it was in Holland that the *philosophes* published (or purported to publish) many of their books. Montesquieu's history of the Roman Empire, Diderot's *Philosophical Thoughts*, Rousseau's *Emile* and the *Social Contract*, and the early editions of Raynal's history of the Indies all carry Amsterdam or The Hague as the place of publication. It was the Dutch who not only coined the word 'democrat', but also attempted a democratic revolution with a 'Free Corps', modelled on the American militia and foreshadowing the Paris National Guard. Diderot decided that the Dutch were unlikely to be converts to the Enlightenment because they remained *superstitieux*. Yet Priestley's *History of the Corruptions of Christianity* (1784) was immediately translated into Dutch; and Pieter Paulus, one of the leaders of the Patriot Revolt and author of *Treatise on Equality* (1793), not only called Jesus the 'architect of eternal civil rights', but emphasized that Christ himself preached equality.[20]

Throughout the century, Calvinist Switzerland also offered political asylum to the *philosophes*. Montesquieu's *De l'esprit des lois* was published in Geneva, where Voltaire took refuge and first printed *Candide*. Voltaire's *Idées républicaines*, though couched in general terms, was based on his admiration for Geneva. D'Alembert's lengthy and laudatory account of the city in the *Encyclopédie* not only contained a defence of theatres – which provoked a furious riposte from Rousseau – but also paid tribute to the enlightened face of Calvinism. Rousseau was himself born in Geneva, and in 1754 announced his reconversion to Reformed Protestantism in order to claim citizenship of Calvin's city. In the 1760s the attempt by Geneva's ruling oligarchy to suppress both *Emile* and the *Social Contract* would persuade Rousseau to renounce his citizenship – and led indirectly to the burgher revolt of 1768. But he had prefaced his *Discourse on the Origin and Foundation of Inequality among Men* (1755) with a long dedication to the Genevan Republic.[21]

It was in a footnote to his prize-winning essay for the Dijon Academy, *Discourse on the Moral Effects of the Arts and Sciences*, that Rousseau wrote: 'The American savages, who go naked, and live entirely on the chase, have always been impossible to subdue. What yoke, indeed, can be imposed on men who stand in need of nothing?' The freedom enjoyed by the American Indian, as celebrated by Charlevoix and Rousseau, and the self-reliant independence of the Pennsylvania Quaker, as extolled by Voltaire, could indeed be contrasted with the European's lack of liberty, in order to make a political point. But it was the political impact of the War of Independence, the new constitutions of the 13 states and the Philadelphia debates on the federal constitution in the months before the Bastille fell, that turned 'free America' into a revolutionary model. In Peter Gay's phrase, the war made America an exporter rather than an importer of Enlightenment principles. The 18 years that separate the Declaration of Independence from the fall of Robespierre saw the publication of 20 full-scale books on the United States. Of these more than a quarter appeared first in French, and ten more were quickly published in French translations. And the list does not include Adam Smith's seminal *Inquiry into the Nature and Causes of the Wealth of Nations*, published in 1776, but describing a colonial America that was already doomed.[22]

In part of book IV, Smith devotes a dozen pages to a brief history of colonial settlement from Columbus onwards. He ridicules the Spanish explorers for their obsession with gold, describing the search for gold mines as 'perhaps the most disadvantageous lottery in the world'. He thinks that there are no colonies where progress has been faster than in the British colonies of North America, but warns his readers that it is unlikely the colonists will ever voluntarily submit. He points to the growing self-confidence of the colonists' Continental Congress, whose members 'feel in themselves at this moment a degree of importance which, perhaps, the greatest subjects in Europe scarce feel'. And in words that reproduce almost verbatim (though without acknowledgment) a sentence from the introduction to Raynal's history of the

Indies, Smith writes: 'The discovery of America, and that of a passage to the East Indies by the Cape of Good Hope, are the two greatest and most important events recorded in the history of mankind.' The consequences, he admits, are incalculable, but, like his French counterparts, Smith pins his faith on 'that mutual communication of knowledge and of all sorts of improvements which an extensive commerce from all countries to all countries naturally, or rather necessarily, carries along with it'.[23]

The year 1776, which saw the appearance of the *Wealth of Nations* was also the year in which Rousseau chose to publish a three act play he had written 35 years earlier as the libretto for his half-finished opera *La Découverte du Nouveau Monde* (*Discovery of the New World*). It features Columbus as the civilizing conqueror who (in the closing words of the chorus) will unite 'Two worlds separated by the unfathomed deep.' The poet Philip Freneau had responded even more swiftly to the topicality of the New World. In 1772, before the American war had begun, he published his Princeton graduation address as *The Rising Glory of America*. He went on to write a poem in 18 stanzas entitled *The Pictures of Columbus, the Genoese*. The title implies the need to 'place' Columbus for American readers, and Joel Barlow, who dedicated his own narrative poem *Vision of Columbus* (1787) to Louis XVI, thought it necessary to preface his nine books of rhymed couplets with a biographical essay on the explorer. Among the book's subscribers were Louis XVI himself (25 copies), George Washington (20 copies), Alexander Hamilton, Benjamin Franklin and Tom Paine.[24]

Barlow's 'vision' comes to Columbus in a Spanish prison, when an angel offers to show him the future of the New World, where:

> Freedom's unconquered sons, with healthy toil,
> Shall lop the grove and warm the furrowed soil,
> From iron ridges break the rugged ore,
> Smooth the pale marble, spire the bending shore.

After watching scene after scene from the War of Independence, Columbus is shown the scientific fruits of enlightenment – achievements that will eclipse those of the ancient world. Thus, concludes the angel:

> Let thy delighted soul no more complain
> Of dangers braved and griefs endured in vain,
> Of courts insidious, envy's poison'd stings,

The loss of empire and the frown of kings;
While these bright scenes thy glowing thoughts compose,
To spurn the vengeance of insulting foes,
And all the joys descending ages gain,
Repay thy labours and remove thy pain.

By the time of the poem's publication in 1787, the new capital of South Carolina had already been christened 'Columbia', while gold, silver and copper coins, bearing a female personification of Columbia, had been struck on the orders of the Confederation treasurer, Gouverneur Morris. In 1791 it was decided that the new federal capital on the banks of the Potomac should be sited in 'the Territory of Columbia' – hence today's Washington DC. Freneau's poetic use of 'Columbia' as an alternative to 'America' was never adopted, though the possibility was still being debated in the 1820s, and the Smithsonian Institution in Washington started life as the Columbia Institute for the Promotion of Arts and Sciences.[25]

In 1792, the tercentenary of Columbus's landfall in the New World was celebrated in New York with the erection of a temporary obelisk, and with what the local press called an 'evening's entertainment' of speeches and toasts. In Baltimore the world's first permanent public monument to the explorer was raised in the form of a 44 ft brick and cement column, decorated with a marble slab given by the French consul. By now Joel Barlow was in Paris, where he was friendly with the Girondins, and with such English expatriates as Mary Wollstonecraft and Tom Paine. Before arriving in Paris, Barlow had spent two years in London, where he was a prominent member of the London Society for Constitutional Information, and managed to find a publisher for Paine's *Age of Reason*. Barlow had himself written radical pamphlets. His *Letter to the National Convention of France* offered gratuitous advice on how to remedy the 'defects' in the 1791 Constitution, and earned him honorary French citizenship, while his *Advice to the Privileged Orders*, though praised by Charles James Fox in Parliament, was suppressed by the British Government and led to his enforced departure for France.

In Paris, Barlow wrote a verse philippic entitled *The Conspiracy of Kings*, translated Brissot's American travelogue into English and published (in French) an appeal to the inhabitants of Piedmont to consider the advantages and necessity of introducing French revolutionary principles into Italy. He even persuaded the voters of Savoy to adopt him as a candidate for election to the National Convention;

and, disappointed in his hopes of becoming a deputy, in 1795 he accepted the post of consul to Algiers. There was a bizarre postscript. Back in America, and working (at Jefferson's suggestion) on a history of the United States, Barlow was appointed Minister to France, with instructions to negotiate with Napoleon for more generous treatment of American commerce. Napoleon, in the throes of invading Russia, summoned Barlow to Vilna; but Bonaparte's defeat at Beresina prevented their meeting, and Barlow, on his way back to France, died amid the extremities of a Polish winter.[26]

The importance of the history of ideas does not depend on any extravagant claim that philosophic principles cause political events. The *philosophes* were not the architects of either the American or the French Revolution. But the traffic in ideas can create a climate of opinion that regards established institutions as outmoded, and therefore no longer worth defending; and it can supply the slogans that politicians use to justify their actions in the pursuit of personal power or national interests. In terms of symbols and slogans, the American Revolution was a European event. America was indeed 'rediscovered' by eighteenth-century Europe. To the lure of the wilderness and the distant enchantment of the noble savage was now added the attraction of a new republic embodying the ideals of the Enlightenment. The idea of an 'Atlantic Revolution' may seem too abstract, but most of the 'heroes of two worlds' featured in the following chapters spoke and wrote as if the abstraction was a reality. And slogans and symbols are as much part of history as the political actualities that underly them. The Statue of Liberty presented by the French people in celebration of the first centenary of the American Revolution, symbolizes a political kinship that is something more than propaganda.

Founding Fathers in Europe

IOHN ADAMS, L.L.D.

2 Porcelain and Revolutionary Principles: Franklin and the French

In 1790, the year that Benjamin Franklin died, Gouverneur Morris was buying porcelain in Paris for shipping back to America. Morris, who had put the United States Constitution into its final literary form and would soon succeed Thomas Jefferson as American minister to France, was engaged on a commission for George Washington. As he wrote to the President: 'I was violently tempted to send out two dozen cups and saucers with the needful accompaniments for Mrs Washington...100 to 150 guineas will procure a very handsome set of tea china and a very large and neat table set.' He was impressed by the quality of the porcelain produced by the 'Manufacture of Angoulême', and recorded in his diary: 'I think I shall purchase for General Washington here.' He did, and a butter dish, two soup plates and nine dinner plates (all with the Angoulême mark) survive to this day.[1]

The Washingtons already had a Sèvres dinner service (bought from the French ambassador), and a Polish visitor to Mount Vernon in 1798 noticed that 'the table was laid in the great hall for twenty persons with a service of porcelain of Sèvres'. This fashion for French porcelain in the new American Republic reminds us that the Atlantic was not as great an obstacle before the age of steam as we tend to suppose. The width of the Atlantic is used to excuse the British Government's misunderstanding of the grievances of its North American subjects, and also to explain the sort of muddle that led to General Burgoyne's surrender at Saratoga. Yet the truth is that the Atlantic was not regarded as an obstacle by men who lived at a time when travel by sea was faster and hardly more hazardous than travel by road. The Lunar Society of Birmingham – so called because it held its meetings on the night of the full moon when its members could travel more safely – had close links with Benjamin Franklin in spite of the War of Independence. Franklin visited Birmingham several times, and was responsible for introducing Jefferson's old tutor, Dr William Small, to Matthew Boulton, one of the leading figures of the Society. Franklin, though not himself a member of the Lunar Society, was a Fellow of the Royal Society and of the Royal Society for the Encouragement of Arts, Manufactures and Commerce founded in London in 1754.[2]

Apart from living in London for 18 months when still in his teens, Franklin spent two longer spells in Britain. The first was from 1757 to 1762 when he came to negotiate with the British Government and the Penn family on behalf of the Pennsylvania Assembly. During these years he received an honorary doctorate from the universities of Oxford and St Andrews, and the freedom of the cities of Edinburgh and Glasgow; he took his seat for the first time as a member of the Council of the Royal Society; he visited Holland and Flanders, and returned in time to see the coronation procession of George III. His second and longer mission lasted from 1764 to 1775, during the crucial years leading up to the War of Independence. In this period he visited France, where he was presented to Louis XV, and was elected a member of both the French Academy of Sciences and the Royal Society of Sciences at Göttingen.

It was during this second visit that Franklin started writing his autobiography, though it was not published until 1791 and then first in French. Franklin recounts how his 'bookish inclinations' as a youth 'determin'd my father to make me a printer', and how the trade of printing did enable him to borrow books overnight from booksellers' apprentices. Part one of the autobiography ends with Franklin aged 25, having just founded the first subscription library in North America. In his own words: 'These libraries have improv'd the general conversation of the Americans, made the common tradesmen and farmers as intelligent as most gentleman from other countries, and perhaps have contributed in some degree to the stand so generally made throughout the colonies in defence of their privileges.' It was a mark of the eighteenth-century Enlightenment to believe in the power of libraries, museums and encyclopedias.[3]

By the time the second part of the autobiography could be started, the War of Independence had been fought, the British had been defeated and Franklin was one of three commissioners charged by Congress with the task of concluding a satisfactory peace. His diplomatic mission had started with the objective of obtaining treaties of commerce and alliance with France. Franklin landed in Brittany on 3 December 1776, travelling overland to Nantes – a port that was already being used for the shipment of arms to the American rebels. A grand dinner to welcome Congress's commissioner was given by friends of America, and a ball was held in his honour. He arrived in Paris on 20 December. Twelve months earlier, the Comte de

Vergennes, the French foreign minister, had already embarked on transatlantic diplomacy. He had sent Achard Bonvouloir as emissary to Philadelphia, where Franklin was introduced to him by a French bookseller in the city. Bonvouloir made an informal offer of French recognition of American independence in return for trade between the states and France. On the strength of this contact, Franklin had written in December 1775 to the physiocrat Barbeu Dubourg, translator and editor of Franklin's works in France, asking him to air the possibility of a Franco-American alliance, to emphasize the value of American trade and to recommend much-needed military engineers to assist the rebel army.

At the same time Vergennes had also encouraged Beaumarchais in his scheme to supply the rebels with arms and munitions. Even before the Declaration of Independence, France and Spain had promised to back Beaumarchais with one million *livres* each, thus enabling him to establish Roderigue Hortalez and Company – his dummy export business for gun-running. But when Franklin arrived in Paris, Vergennes was beginning to hesitate about backing the rebels, and was unwilling to commit himself as long as it looked as if Washington's army might be beaten. Saratoga would soon remove the French minister's misgivings. Meanwhile Franklin was in no particular hurry. He allowed himself to be fêted as a Quaker – though he was a free-thinker – and he continued to wear his fur hat which he had needed for his winter crossing of the Atlantic.

Franklin was already well known in France for his studies in electricity. As early as 1754 Diderot, in *Thoughts on the Interpretation of Nature*, chose Franklin's work as a model for the experimental method. By 1770 Franklin had embraced (or pretended to embrace) the doctrines of the physiocrats. Thus the *Ephémérides du Citoyen* cited Franklin as 'having adopted the principles of the French economists', and reported, on the basis of his testimony, that 'there is not a single artisan is Pennsylvania who does not read the newspapers at the dinner table'. And in 1775, before Franklin had been despatched to Paris, the *Mercure de France* had already decided that the American colonies were ripe for independence. The *Mercure* welcomed the prospect of free trade between America and Europe, and proclaimed: 'Then America will congratulate herself on having taken Europeans to her bosom. Then and only then will Europe receive the prize of the discovery of America.'[4]

Franklin had hardly arrived in the French capital before engravings of him were to be found hanging in Parisian homes, and two years later he could tell his daughter that his portrait had been turned into medallions: 'some to be set in the lids of snuffboxes and some so small as to be worn in rings; and the numbers sold are incredible. These, with the pictures, busts and prints (of which copies upon copies are spread everywhere), have made your father's face as well known as that of the moon'. John Adams, arriving in Paris in the summer of 1778 to replace the discredited Deane (who was believed to have misappropriated Congressional funds), was not an admirer of Franklin's approach to diplomacy. 'The life of Dr Franklin,' he later complained, 'was a scene of continual dissipation. I could never obtain the favour of his company in a morning before breakfast.' Franklin's self-indulgent habits made him popular with Parisians, but Adams was convinced that it led to the favouring of French rather than American interests.[5]

The year that brought the formal end of the War of Independence, with a treaty signed in Paris (1783), also saw the publication in French (at Franklin's suggestion) of the new constitutions of the 13 ex-colonies. They were bound in one volume, together with the text of the Declaration of Independence, and were entitled *The Constitutions of the Thirteen States of America*. The volume was published by Louis XVI's printer. Meanwhile French learned societies introduced competitions for the best papers on the effect of America on the world, and the Chevalier Quesnay de Beaurepaire, grandson of the famous physiocrat, planned to found a French academy in America. It was to be an academy of arts and sciences, centred on Richmond, Virginia, but with branches in Baltimore, Philadelphia and New York. The cornerstone of the main academy was laid on 1 July 1786. Quesnay then returned to Paris to solicit more support – notably from the King and Queen. But Louis XVI had graver financial preoccupations, and the academy never opened its doors. Americans did not, however, need a French academy to introduce them to the writings of the European Enlightenment. James Otis, in his *Rights of the British Colonies Asserted and Approved* (Boston 1764), quoted at length not only from Locke and the seventeenth-century jurists Grotius and Pufendorf, but also from the earlier works of Rousseau. Josiah Quincy Jr similarly referred with approval to Montesquieu, Rousseau and the Italian jurist Beccaria. And when it came to a clash with the ecclesiastical establishment, the pamphleteers turned to Voltaire.

More often, it is true, they relied on English sources. Jonathan Mayhew describes how, having been 'initiated, in youth, in the doctrines of civil liberty, as they were taught by such men ... as Sidney and Milton, Locke and Hoadly, among the moderns, I liked them; they seemed rational'. And John Adams in *Thoughts on Government* (1776) expressed the view that the root principles of good government could be found only in 'Sidney, Harrington, Locke, Milton, Nedham, Neville, Burnet and Hoadly.' It was this tradition of 'English Liberty' that was embodied in the person of John Wilkes and excited the cry of 'Wilkes and Liberty' on both sides of the Atlantic. In February 1769 William Palfrey was writing to Wilkes that 'the fate of Wilkes and America must stand or fall together'. Meanwhile the arrival of troops in Boston revived the spectre of a standing army, which had haunted the parliamentary debates of the seventeenth century. The Virginian Bill of Rights (1776) was closely modelled on the English Bill of Rights (1689) and quoted one article verbatim: 'That excessive bail ought not to required, nor excessive fines imposed, nor cruel and unusual punishments inflicted.' The same clause would appear as the eighth amendment to the Federal Constitution.[6]

The political principles of the 1689 Revolution had, of course, been widely advertised through the writings of John Locke, who is traditionally regarded as the philosopher of the American, no less than of the English, Revolution. In August 1770 Samuel Adams invoked Locke in his attack on Lieutenant–Governor Hutchinson for summoning the General Court of Massachusetts to meet in Cambridge instead of Boston: 'We beg leave to recite to your Honour what the Great Mr Locke has advanced in his Treatise of Civil Government, upon the like Prerogative of the Crown.' Locke's influence on the Revolution was taken for granted by contemporaries. The *Boston Gazette* for 1 March 1773 warmly commended the first American edition of the *Second Treatise of Civil Government*: 'It should be early and carefully explained by every father to his son, by every preceptor in our public and private schools to his pupils, and by every mother to her daughter.'[7]

The year 1773 was a little late for the appearance in America of a book that was supposed to have inspired the Revolution. There had, of course, been earlier English editions circulating in America. Copies of the *Collected Works of Locke* in three folio volumes appeared in the library of Harvard in the 1720s, at Yale in 1733 and at the College of New Jersey in 1755. The first separate edition of the *Two Treatises* to be frequently found in American libraries is the English edition of 1728. But there is no evidence that it figured in the curriculum of any American college before the Revolution. It was, however, on a recommended reading list at the College of Philadelphia in 1756. In his autobiography, John Adams wrote: 'I had read Harrington, Sidney, Hobbes, Nedham and Locke, but with very little application to any particular views till these debates in Congress'. He meant the debates of November to December 1775. But ten years earlier, at the age of 30, Adams had written that a native of America – he does not yet call him an American – knows that 'rulers are no more than attorneys, agents and trustees for the people; and if the cause, the interest and trust, is insidiously betrayed, or wantonly trifled away, the people have a right to revoke the authority that they themselves have deputed, and to constitute abler and better agents, attorneys and trustees.' Thus, 11 years before the Declaration of Independence, did Adams rehearse its arguments and foreshadow its language.[8]

Adams's language and arguments came from Locke. By early 1775, in the articles he wrote for the *Boston Gazette* under the pseudonym 'Novanglus', the similarities are even more striking. Adams argued that there was no provision either in common law or in the British constitution, for the case of the colonies: 'It is not a conquered but a discovered country. It came not by marriage to the king, but was purchased by the settlers of the savages. It was not granted of the king by his grace, but was dearly, very dearly earned by the planters in the labour, blood and treasure which they expended to subdue it to cultivation.' In chapter V of his *Second Treatise of Civil Government* Locke had written:

> The labour of his body and the work of his hands we may say are properly his. Whatsoever, then, he removes out of the state that nature hath provided and left it in, he hath mixed his labour with, and joined to it something that is his own, and thereby makes it his property...at least where there is enough and as good left in common for others.[9]

In the vastness of America there was indeed 'enough and as good left in common for others'. That was what made it a place where the social contract could become an historical reality. That was how the plantation experience shaped political ideas. As Max Beloff wrote in his introduction to the collected issues of the *Federalist*: 'The social contract was not an anthropological figment or a logical abstraction; it was a document drawn up and signed at Philadelphia.' Yet Franklin's autobiography contains only one reference to Locke, and that simply a record of reading the *Essay Concerning Human Understanding*. The Modern Library edition of Jefferson's collected writings contains five references to Locke of which four are merely the mention of his name, while the fifth is confined to one sentence in a letter of 1790: 'Locke's little book on government is perfect as far as it goes.' The same letter devotes no less than 13 lines to Montesquieu; and we know that in his younger days he had copied out substantial extracts from *De l'esprit des lois* – perhaps from the three volume French edition of Montesquieu's works which he acquired in December 1769 at the age of 26.[10]

In 1772 an attempt was made to launch an American edition of *De l'esprit des lois*. The *Massachusetts Gazette and the Boston Post Boy and Advertiser* for 19 October carried a full-page advertisement proposing a subscription edition of what it called '*Spirit of Laws* (which ought to be in every man's hands) translated from the French original and which has been translated and published in most of the civilized nations of Europe.' Not enough subscribers were forthcoming, and Americans had to wait until 1802 for an edition of their own; but there were no less than ten English editions in circulation by 1773. The debates at Philadelphia, on the proposed federal constitution of the United States, show clearly enough that Montesquieu's theories had become the common currency of American political discussion. Alexander Hamilton and James Madison both quoted from him frequently. James Wilson of Pennsylvania referred to Montesquieu in support of a 'confederated republic'; Edmund Randolph of Virginia, defending the introduction of a regular census on which representation could be based, cited Montesquieu to prove that 'what relates to suffrage' was a 'fundamental article in Republican governments'. Similarly the debates at the various state conventions held to ratify the Federal Constitution contain frequent references to Montesquieu.[11]

But the most convincing testimony to Montesquieu's influence comes from the collected volumes of the *Federalist*, a series of political essays, chiefly by Madison and Hamilton, which were addressed to the people of New York State in an effort to win them over to the new Federal Constitution. Of the half dozen or so references to Montesquieu, two (*Federalist* no. 9 and no. 47) are detailed examinations of his theories. In no. 47, which Madison devoted to a discussion of the separation of powers, at least half the pamphlet's eight pages are concerned with Montesquieu, whom Madison describes as 'the oracle who is always consulted and cited on this subject'. In no. 9, Hamilton had called for a strong federal government – what he calls in a phrase borrowed from Montesquieu a 'Confederate Republic'. Yet the index to the 85 issues of the *Federalist* contains not a single reference to Locke.[12]

Did Montesquieu himself perhaps draw on Locke? His own writings make no acknowledgment to the Englishman. The footnotes in *De l'esprit des lois* contain references to Cicero and Tacitus, Plato, Aristotle and Plutarch, 'the anonymous author of the life of Louis the Debonair', the Charter of Louis the Fat, the Capitulary of Charles the Bald, Burnet's *History of the Reformation*, Perry's *State of Russia* (published in Paris in 1717) and the 1660 Navigation Acts. Sidney is also cited, but not Locke. Of course, Montesquieu's famous section, in book XI, on the Constitution of England amounts to a surprisingly small proportion of the work as a whole. In the Hafner edition of 1949 it occupies only 11 pages out of 600, though despite the lack of acknowledgment, Locke's influence is clearly evident.[13]

Although the first edition of Locke's *Two Treatises* to be printed in France did not appear until 1749 – the year after the publication of *De l'esprit des lois* – anonymous editions in French had been printed in Amsterdam in 1691 and in Geneva in 1724. While Montesquieu was in London between 1729 and 1731, he met several Frenchmen who were interested in Locke. One of them, Pierre Coste, had not only known Locke personally, but helped him to translate his works into French for the Amsterdam edition, which was subsequently smuggled into France. It was in this 1691 French edition that the word *confédératif* appeared for the first time in French. Its second appearance was in *De l'esprit des lois*. We know that James Madison had studied Montesquieu in his student days at Princeton, where by the 1760s *De l'esprit des lois* was already a textbook. John Adams annotated his copy with 'a sort of index to every paragraph', and Franklin also had a copy of his own. French political ideas, as well as French porcelain and French war supplies, had found their way to America before Franklin was given a hero's welcome in Paris. So the American Declaration of Independence was couched in terms already familiar to the French.

The Countess d'Houdetot, Rousseau's mistress and the 'Sophie' of his *Confessions*, hailed Franklin as 'legislator of one world and benefactor of two'. Yet he had actually played little part in American constitution-making. As Adams somewhat waspishly told Barbé Marbois, secretary to the Chevalier de la Luzerne, Franklin's contribution as a law-maker had been exaggerated:

It is universally believed in France, England and all Europe that his electric wand has accomplished this Revolution. But nothing is more groundless. He has done very little. It is believed that he made all the American constitutions and their confederation; but he made neither. He did not even make the constitution of Pennsylvania, bad as it is.

Yet the importance of Franklin lay less in his achievements than in his image. He was regarded in France, and throughout Europe, as the authentic representative of independent America. Even Adams admitted as much:

> Franklin's reputation was more universal than that of Leibnitz or Newton, Frederick or Voltaire...His name was familiar to government and people, to kings, courtiers, nobility, clergy and philosophers, as well as plebeians, to such an extent that there was scarcely a peasant or a citizen, a *valet de chambre*, coachman or footman, a lady's chamber-maid or a scullion in a kitchen who was not familiar with it and who did not consider him a friend to humankind...[14]

If Montesquieu had helped to shape American revolutionary thinking, Franklin's American example lent weight to the political campaign of the French *philosophes*. Montesquieu had died some 20 years before Franklin's official embassy to France, but Voltaire returned to Paris to spend the last few months of his life in the capital. During those months the American folk-philosopher met the French *philosophe* on more than one occasion. At their first meeting, Voltaire insisted on demonstrating his ability to speak English and on blessing Franklin's grandson, Temple. When Voltaire was initiated into the Masonic Lodge of the Nine Sisters, it was Franklin who escorted the frail 84-year-old; and three weeks later, amid popular acclamation, the two men embraced at a session of the *Académie des Sciences*. Solon embracing Sophocles, Adams called it. Barely a month later Voltaire was dead. In this same year (1778) Houdon, sculptor of both Voltaire and Rousseau, executed his marble bust of Franklin; and Turgot bestowed on Franklin his famous epitaph: *Eripuit coelo fulmen sceptrumque tyrannis*. ('He snatched the thunderbolt from heaven and the sceptre from tyrants.') Thus were Franklin's twin roles of practical scientist and practical revolutionary celebrated.[15]

The year 1778 had begun with the successful negotiation of the 'treaty of amity and commerce' which Franklin and the other commissioners had been working for. By the end of the year, the three-man commission was superseded by a minister plenipotentiary – a post which unsurprisingly fell to Franklin. The instrument of appointment, together with Congress's instructions, was brought to Paris by Lafayette, on leave from his American command. When the marshal was temporarily attached to the general staff of the French army preparing to invade England, Franklin despatched his grandson to Le Havre with a presentation sword for Lafayette. A covering letter explained that Congress 'sensible of your merit towards the United States, but unable to adequately reward it', had commissioned the sword and directed it 'to be ornamented with suitable devices'. Franklin had encouraged the French ministry of marine in its plans for a joint invasion of England, with John Paul Jones commanding the fleet and Lafayette leading the land forces. Paul Jones's flagship was called *Bonhomme Richard*, after the Richard of Franklin's best-selling *Poor Richard's Almanac*. Franklin himself considered that the proposed invasion fell into the category of wartime operations which 'thought to be impossible do often, for that very reason, become possible and practicable because nobody expects them and no precautions are taken to guard against them'. In the event the invasion was called off, and it was left to Paul Jones to harass the British, while Lafayette returned across the Atlantic to share in the final Franco-American victory at Yorktown.[16]

French naval intervention was crucial in the defeat of Britain. John Adams realized that French support was not entirely disinterested, but was tactless enough to lecture Louis XVI's ministers on the advantages France derived from the American alliance. Vergennes, tiring of unwelcome letters, told Adams tartly that he preferred to communicate only with Franklin – 'the sole person who has letters of credence to the King from the United States'. Franklin also had more tact. As he wrote to Congress, he thought Adams was misguided to stress the benefits to France: Louis liked to see himself as a benefactor, and it was Congress's duty (and interest) 'to increase the pleasure by our thankful acknowledgments'.[17]

The end of the American War provided a stimulus for transatlantic emigration, which was encouraged by a spate of publications: Crèvecoeur's *Letters of an American Farmer* (1782), Jefferson's *Notes on Virginia* (1784), *Travels in North America* by the Marquis de Chastellux (1787) and the continued popularity of Raynal's history of the Indies (which reached its thirtieth edition in 1789). Then, in the early 1790s, came the trio of books (which Coleridge read in 1794) by Brissot, Imlay and Cooper. Franklin was sufficiently prescient to foresee this flood, and to sense the danger of exaggerated expectations. He therefore published in 1782 his *Information to Those Who Would Remove to*

America. In this 13-page pamphlet, Franklin explains that he 'thinks it may be useful, and prevent inconvenient, expensive and fruitless removals and voyages of improper persons', if he gives clearer and truer impressions of life in the New World 'than appears hitherto to have prevailed'.[18]

America, according to Franklin, is emphatically 'the land of labour and by no means what the English call *Lubberland* and the French *Pays de Cocagne*.' What are needed are 'hearty young labouring men' who 'understand the husbandry of corn and cattle'; and Franklin adds reassuringly that 'the acre in America is the same with the English acre, or the acre in Normandy'. He advises a careful reading of the individual state constitutions, together with the Articles of Confederation (which at this stage were all that bound the states together), in order to understand that Congress has no power to bribe desirable immigrants with suitable inducements. Nevertheless, he continues encouragingly: 'Artisans are so eager for apprentices, that many of them will even give money to the parents to have boys from ten to fifteen years of age bound apprentice to them, till the age of twenty-one.' Young people will be less at risk than in Europe since 'bad examples are more rare in America, which must be a comfortable consideration to parents'. Indeed Franklin comes close to calling America God's own country: 'The Divine Being seems to have manifested his approbation of the mutual forbearance and kindness with which the different sects trust each other, by the remarkable prosperity with which he has been pleased to favour the whole country.' One sees why Thomas Cooper – campaigner against the slave trade, friend of Brissot and co-champion with Joseph Priestley of the rights of Dissenters in England – printed Franklin's pamphlet as an appendix to his own *Some Information Respecting America*.[19]

After the first publication of his advice to emigrants Franklin remained in France for a further three years. He was now installed at the Hotel Valentinois, where he had room not only for his household, his guests and his servants, but for a printing-press, a cellar of some 1200 bottles and a science laboratory-cum-workshop, where he invented bifocal spectacles. His interest in invention led him to follow the new development of balloon travel. As if to mark the dawn of a new era, the first ascent of a Montgolfier balloon took place from the *Champ de Mars* in August 1783, and Franklin was there to see it. When asked with characteristic eighteenth-century earnestness what was the *use* of the new invention, he is supposed to have replied: 'What is the use of a new-born baby?' He evidently thought that balloons might usefully deter the kings of the earth from waging war. Five thousand balloons, Franklin thought, 'could not cost more than five ships of the line'; and what prince could afford to defend his country against 'ten thousand men descending from the clouds'? More prosaically, the American John Jeffries crossed the English Channel in December 1783, in company with Jean-Pierre Blanchard, and delivered to Franklin a letter from England – 'the first through the air'.[20]

Franklin busied himself with the social life of the *salons* as well as with the military potential of balloons. In explaining why he kissed the necks of so many ladies, he wrote: 'As to the kissing of lips or cheeks, it is not the mode here; the first is reckoned rude, and the other may rub off the paint.' It seems that Franklin the widower even contemplated acquiring a French wife. It may just have been gallantry that led him to pay court to Mme Helvétius, widow of the famous *philosophe*. Her apparent determination to reject his marriage proposal, out of loyalty to her husband's memory, did not prevent her from reproaching Franklin for neglecting her – a censure to which he archly replied: 'Madame, I am waiting until the nights are longer.'[21]

Franklin finally left for home in July 1785. Jefferson had arrived the previous August to take part in the negotiation of commercial treaties with other European powers, and in May 1785 was appointed minister to France in Franklin's place. Crossing the Atlantic with Franklin was the sculptor Houdon, on his way to Mount Vernon to model a portrait bust of Washington. Between Paris and Le Havre, Franklin wrote two letters to Mme Helvétius, and three years later he was still writing to her from Philadelphia: 'Often in my dreams, I have breakfast with you. I sit beside you on one of your hundred sofas, I walk with you in your beautiful garden.' Apart from such regrets, his last journey on French soil was a painful one, as he was suffering from a stone in the kidneys. To ease the discomfort, he travelled in one of Marie Antoinette's litters slung between two Spanish mules. It was a touching token of royal regard for the American Republic and its accredited representative. Franklin could not have foreseen the connection between his mission to France and the Queen's journey to the guillotine a short eight years later.[22]

3 American *Encyclopédiste*: Jefferson at Home and Abroad

In 1809, a few days before he retired as President of the United States after eight years in the post, Thomas Jefferson wrote to the French physiocrat, Dupont de Nemours: 'Nature intended me for the tranquil pursuits of science, by rendering them my supreme delight. But the enormities of the times in which I have lived have forced me to take a part in resisting them, and to commit myself on the boisterous ocean of political passions.' And when Jefferson came to design his own tombstone, he stipulated a plain cube surmounted by an obelisk with this inscription, '& not a word more':

Here was buried
Thomas Jefferson
author of the Declaration of American Independence
of the Statute of Virginia for religious freedom
& Father of the University of Virginia

He did not record that he had also been President of the United States.[1]

The three achievements that Jefferson chose to commemorate – equality of rights, religious toleration and the expansion of education – were three of the main objectives of the European Enlightenment. In 1759, the year of Voltaire's *Candide*, Jefferson was 16 and working to gain admission to William and Mary College, Virginia. That same year, Jean D'Alembert, mathematician and co-editor with Diderot of the *Encyclopédie*, wrote what has often been regarded as the epitome of the Enlightenment:

If one considers without bias the present state of our knowledge, one cannot deny that philosophy among us has shown progress. Natural science from day to day accumulates new riches. Geometry, by extending its limits, has borne its torch into the regions of physical science which lay nearest at hand. The true system of the world has been recognised, developed and perfected...everything has been discussed and analysed, or at least mentioned.

31

Sixty years later, Jefferson expressed comparable faith in the march of progress when writing to Dr Benjamin Waterhouse:

> When I contemplate the immense advances in science and discoveries in the arts which have been made within the period of my life, I look forward with equal confidence to equal advances by the present generation, and have no doubt that they will be as much wiser than we have been, as we than our fathers were, and they than the burners of witches.

And only ten days before he died, Jefferson wrote to another correspondent: 'All eyes are opened, or opening, to the rights of man. The general spread of the light of science has already laid open to every view the palpable truth that the mass of mankind has not been born with saddles on their backs, nor a favoured few booted and spurred, ready to ride them legitimately by the grace of God.'[2]

It is not perhaps very surprising that such sentiments should have come from the author of the Declaration of Independence; but they were penned 50 years after the Declaration was drafted, and it is rather more surprising that a man of 83 should still cherish the ideals he held at 33. Elsewhere Jefferson admittedly makes clear that the evidence of the French Revolution and the Napoleonic Wars had somewhat tempered the idealism of 1776, but he seems still to have regarded America as the citadel of the Enlightenment. He wrote to John Adams in 1821:

> Yet I will not believe our labours are lost... And even should the cloud of barbarism and despotism again obscure the science and liberties of Europe, this country remains to preserve and restore light and liberty to them. In short, the flames kindled on the 4th of July, 1776, have spread over too much of the globe to be extinguished by the feeble engines of despotism...[3]

Jefferson owed much of his formal education, at both primary and college level, to Scotsmen rather than Frenchmen. In his autobiography he records his particular debt to 'Dr William Small of Scotland', then Professor of Mathematics and Natural Philosophy at William and Mary College, but later a member of the Birmingham Lunar Society. Jefferson was the only Founding Father to have read Newton's *Principia*, but he also studied Law. His personal library contained 450 law books, including Blackstone's *Commentaries*, Coke's *Reports* and at least one commentary on Montesquieu's *De l'esprit des Lois*. If these were his chief legal authorities, it is hardly surprising his

Summary View of the Rights of British America (1774) claimed that the people's rights are 'derived from the laws of nature, and not as the gift of their Chief Magistrate'. The author of the Declaration of Independence had announced himself.[4]

Jefferson should have gone to France in 1776, the year the Declaration of Independence was signed. Congress had nominated him as one of the commissioners appointed to negotiate treaties of alliance and commerce with the French government, but as he explains: 'Such was the state of my family that I could not leave it, nor could I expose it to the dangers of the sea, and of capture by the British ships, then covering the ocean.' After the death of his wife in 1782, he expected to travel to Paris for the peace negotiations, but in the event, he was not needed: the resident commissioners signed the treaty without him.[5]

In May 1784 Congress resolved to recall Benjamin Franklin and appoint Jefferson as Minister Plenipotentiary in his place. He accordingly set off for Paris with his small daughter and his violin – having spent nearly two months travelling through some of the New England states 'informing myself of the commerce of each'. He had already been asked (in 1781) by M. de Marbois, of the French legation in Philadelphia, to answer some questions on Virginia. The resulting pamphlet, intended at first for a limited circulation, was *Notes on the State of Virginia* (1784). It made its first public appearance in a pirated French edition, leading Jefferson to publish the English text 'to let the world see that it was not really so bad as the French translation had made it appear.' This was to be, apart from his autobiography, his only full-length book. Jefferson reached Paris too late to meet any of the French *encyclopédistes* – except for Buffon. Rousseau and Voltaire had both died in 1778, D'Alembert in 1783 and Diderot in 1784, a few months after Jefferson's arrival.[6]

He did not in any case share the atheism of Diderot and D'Alembert, but was himself a Deist. As he would write in 1822: 'The pure simple unity of the Creator of the universe is now all but ascendant in the Eastern States; it is dawning in the West and advancing towards the South; and I confidently expect that the present generation will see Unitarianism become the general religion of the United States.' Equally characteristic of Jefferson's rationalistic cast of mind is his letter to a Philadelphia bookseller in 1814 over a magistrate's inquiry into the sale of a book supposed to be damaging to religion: 'Is this then our freedom of religion?' he asked. 'It is an insult to our citizens to question whether they are rational beings or not, and blasphemy against religion to suppose it cannot stand the test of truth and reason.'[7]

Jefferson's religious views and his hostility to censorship were but two aspects of his intellectual kinship with the French *philosophes*. Once when Alexander Hamilton, his great political rival, was dining with him at Monticello, his guest pointed to the portraits of Francis Bacon, John Locke and Isaac Newton and asked who they were. Jefferson tells us he replied that 'they were my trinity of the three greatest men the world had ever produced'. Bacon, Locke and Newton – these were the very seventeenth-century figures whose influence did so much to shape the attitudes of the *philosophes*. Montesquieu's theories owed much to those of Locke, it was Voltaire who popularized Newton's natural philosophy in France, while Diderot, in the prospectus to the *Encyclopédie* of 1751, paid tribute to 'the Chancellor Bacon who sketched the plan of a universal dictionary of sciences and arts...'. Jefferson would use Bacon's *Advancement of Learning* to classify his library.[8]

The eighteenth century was an age of collectors and observers rather than of mathematicians – an age of Baconians. The very fact that we keep the French term *philosophe*, when speaking of Voltaire and his fellow *encyclopédistes*, is a reminder that they were not true philosophers in the sense that Locke and Newton were. It was an age of encyclopaedias, dictionaries and museums. Thus if American men of science were empirical and descriptive rather than philosophical in their approach, they were well in tune with their European counterparts. To collect, to classify, to categorize – these were the chief ambitions of the *philosophes*. The *Encyclopédie*, in spite of its evident political bias, was a compendium of facts; and the 'Copernican Revolution' of the eighteenth century occurred in the field of chemistry – the most descriptive and least philosophical of sciences.

Jefferson clearly exhibits this encyclopedic tendency, though he had more in common with Linnaeus than with Lavoisier. His *Travel Journals* admittedly read more like pages from the *Journals* of Arthur Young. (By coincidence they were touring France and Italy in the same year, 1787.) They speak much of maize and olives. Jefferson's *Notes on the State of Virginia*, however, contains observations of a rather higher order. Chapter 6 deals with 'the mines and other subterranean riches, its trees, plants, fruits, etc'. Having rejected Voltaire's explanation of the existence of sea shells on the upper slopes of mountains, Jefferson turns to attack Buffon, the famous French naturalist and *encyclopédiste*.[9]

Buffon argued in his *Epoques* that Nature was less active and vigorous in America than on the European continent, and that the

American animal species common to both continents were smaller than their European counterparts. Yet, even if the American mammoth is discounted, there remain, says Jefferson:

> the buffalo, red deer, fallow deer, wolf, roe, glutton, wild cat, monax, bison, hedgehog, marten and water-rat, of the comparative sizes of which we have not sufficient testimony. It does not appear that Messieurs de Buffon and D'Aubenton have measured, weighed or seen those of America.

Later, after he had met Buffon in France, Jefferson arranged for John Sullivan, President of New Hampshire, to send to Paris the horns, bones and skin of a moose, and of any other animals he could obtain. Sullivan carried out his commission conscientiously, and presented Jefferson with a bill for 60 guineas. In January 1786 we find Jefferson writing from Paris to Mr Stuart of Virginia, asking for 'the horns, skeleton and skin of an elk, were it possible to procure them'. Confronted with such incontrovertible evidence, Buffon gave way graciously: 'I should have consulted you before publishing my natural history, and then I should have been sure of the facts.'[10]

Jefferson, like Washington, shared the contemporary interest in meteorology – parallelled in the painter Constable's careful observation of cloud formations and weather conditions. In 1790 we find Jefferson urging his daughter to keep a nature diary, while the Duke of Saxe-Weimar, on a visit to Monticello, found Jefferson noting carefully the wind and weather, and watching the changes in the flowers and leaves. And when Jefferson had embarked on his retirement at Monticello 17 years earlier, he began a letter to Madison, his successor in the White House (who was anxiously anticipating war with England) by remarking helpfully: 'The spring is remarkably backward. No oats sown, not much tobacco-seed, and little done in the gardens. Wheat has suffered considerably. No vegetation visible yet but the red maple, weeping willow and lilac.' One is reminded of Washington's entry in his diary on the day of the inauguration of his successor, John Adams: 'Much such a day as yesterday in all respects. Mercury at 41.'[11]

Although the daily routine at Mount Vernon and Monticello seems to have been much the same, Jefferson's home bears witness to the inventive genius of its owner. The seven-day clock in the entrance hall, the revolving door and dumb waiter in the dining-room, a swivel chair, a coffee urn, even a pair of spectacles – all were designed by Jefferson. During his stay in Europe, he was always on the look-out for a new invention or a new process. Writing from Paris in 1786, he describes a two-month trip to England, where the most striking thing he saw was 'the application of the principle of the steam-engine to grist mills'. He is less impressed by the new steam pumps of Paris, finding them nothing more in principle than 'the fire-engine you have seen described in the books of hydraulics'.[12]

His discussion with Buffon on the relative humidity of the American climate leads him to inquire in London for a hygrometer, and we soon find him making daily hygrometric observations, in addition to the thermometric and barometric records that he always kept. But he is surprised to find Buffon disparaging 'the present ardour of chemical inquiry'. Buffon, we learn, 'affected to consider chemistry but as cookery, and to place the toils of the laboratory on a footing with those of the kitchen'. Jefferson, by contrast, reckoned chemistry 'among the most useful of sciences, and big with future discoveries for the utility and safety of the human race'. He shares Lavoisier's interest in ballooning, and Jefferson's letters in the summer of 1785 describe the ill-fated attempt by Pilâtre de Rozière to cross the channel by balloon. He goes to see an early version of the screw propeller which worked in the air instead of in the water. Jefferson characteristically comments: 'The screw, I think, would be more effective if placed below the surface of the water.'[13]

Jefferson's lively interest in every useful mechanical art was not just a foreshadowing of the modern American taste for gadgets: it was typical of the educated man of the eighteenth century. The Age of Reason was also the Age of Invention; and the 28 volumes of the *Encyclopédie* contained 11 volumes of plates, many of them depicting the new industrial and agricultural techniques. He did not himself edit an encyclopedia, but he did propose an Anglo-Saxon dictionary 'in which the Anglo-Saxon roots should be arranged alphabetically, and the derivatives from each root, Saxon and English, entered under it in their proper order and connection'. He also spent much of his life collecting vocabularies of the various Indian tribes.[14]

The *Encyclopédie* was, of course, more than an alphabetical compendium of knowledge: it embodied a political philosophy. That philosophy is echoed in Jefferson's almost Voltairean boast: 'I have sworn upon the altar of God, eternal hostility against every form of tyranny over the mind of man.' Yet when Jefferson arrived in France in August 1784, he was obviously not expecting to be caught up in another revolution. He described his diplomatic duties as being confined to 'the receipt of our whale-oils, salted fish and salted meats, on favourable terms; the admission of our rice on equal terms with that of Piedmont, Egypt and the Levant; a mitigation of the monopolies of our tobacco by the Farmers-general, and a free admission of our productions into their islands'. Jefferson soon learned from the Comte de Vergennes that Louis XVI's government dared not break the tobacco monopoly of the Farmers-general, however much it might desire the continuance of friendly relations with the United States.[15]

By the summer of 1785, Jefferson was already sending back letters that painted a gloomy picture of the social and political condition of France. In August of that year he wrote to Mrs Trist of Philadelphia that 'of twenty millions of people supposed to be in France, I am of opinion there are nineteen millions more wretched, more accursed in every circumstance of human existence than the most conspicuously wretched individual in the whole United States'. In his autobiography, Jefferson lists the grievances that he believes had caused the Revolution. The catalogue of ills runs to a dozen lines and ranges from 'the oppressions of the tithes, the tailles, the corvées, the gabelles, the farms and the barriers' to 'the atrocities of the rack' and 'the luxury, indolence and immorality of the clergy'. As early as October 1785 he was suggesting that one 'means of lessening the inequality of property' would be to 'exempt all from taxation below a certain point, and to tax the higher portions or property in geometrical progression as they rise'.[16]

Jefferson's proposal of a graduated income tax may be regarded as evidence either of statesmanlike vision or of blindness to the political realities of eighteenth-century France. But the description he gives in his autobiography of the plight of the Paris worker in the freezing winter of 1788–9 is both vivid and perceptive:

All out-door labour was suspended, and the poor, without the wages of labour were, of course, without either bread or fuel. The government found its necessities aggravated by that of procuring great quantities of fire-wood, and of keeping great fires at all the cross-streets, around which the people gathered in crowds, to avoid perishing with cold. Bread, too, was to be bought and distributed daily, gratis, until a relaxation of the season should enable the people to work...

The bread shortage had been foreseen by the French ministry, and Jefferson had been asked to inform American merchants that a premium would be paid on all imports of grain and flour from the United States.[17]

It was against the background of high bread prices that the States-General had first met on 5 May 1789. Jefferson records that he went 'daily from Paris to Versailles, and attended their debates, generally till the hour of adjournment'. Lafayette, as a Frenchman who had fought under Washington and as a nobleman whose sympathies were with the Third Estate, was rightly regarded as the key figure. On 6 May Jefferson wrote to him, urging him to disregard the instructions he had received from the nobles of the Auvergne, who had elected him to the States-General:

> My Dear Friend, As it becomes more and more possible that the Noblesse will go wrong, I become uneasy for you. Your principles are decidedly with the tiers état and your instructions against them...It appears to me the moment to take at once that honest and manly stand with them which your principles dictate...[18]

Less than a month later Jefferson was offering to Lafayette a draft of a 'Charter of Rights' which he proposed that Louis might be persuaded to promulgate at a *séance royale* of the States-General. This remarkable document contained ten articles, the first of which began: 'The States-General shall assemble, uncalled, on the first day of November, annually, and shall remain together so long as they shall see cause...' The States-General was thus to fill the role of an English Parliament, and 'laws shall be made by the States-General only, with the consent of the King'. Article 4 guaranteed freedom from arbitrary arrest, and Article 6 freedom of the press. A promise to honour the king's debts was written into the document, and, as a step towards national solvency, 'all pecuniary privileges and exemptions enjoyed by any description of persons are abolished'.[19]

How did Jefferson find himself in a position to offer advice to Lafayette and his fellow 'Patriots'? Jefferson explains it, modestly if ungrammatically, in his autobiography: 'Being from a country which had successfully passed through a similar reformation, they were disposed to my acquaintance, and had some confidence in me.' Lafayette, who was evidently much influenced by his own experience in America, seems genuinely to have sought Jefferson's advice. A draft of Lafayette's 'Declaration of Rights' was sent by Jefferson to James Madison as early as January 1789 – nearly four months before the States-General met. On 6 July, eight days before the storming of the Bastille, Lafayette ended a letter to Jefferson by asking: 'Will you send me your Bill of Rights with your notes? I hope to see you tomorrow. Where do you dine?' Three days later the Frenchman wrote again: 'Tomorrow I present my bill of rights about the middle of the sitting. Be pleased to consider it again, and make your observations.'[20]

It is difficult to find specific evidence of Jefferson's influence on the version of the Declaration of Rights that Lafayette presented to the Assembly on 11 July, but it is beyond doubt that Jefferson's comments were invited, and it seems likely that some at least of his suggested emendations were incorporated in the final text. Jefferson himself would have been too discreet to advertise his contribution. Thus, on 20 July, when the chairman of the committee appointed to draft a constitution wrote to Jefferson inviting him to attend meetings of the committee and assist them in their deliberations, Jefferson excused himself 'on the obvious considerations that my mission was to the King as Chief Magistrate of the nation, and that my duties were limited to the concerns of my own country...' Yet when, on 25 August, Lafayette asked whether he might, 'for liberty's sake', bring eight members of the National Assembly to dinner with him, Jefferson assured him they would be welcome. At the end of a long discussion after dinner, the Patriots agreed to give the king a suspensive veto, and that there should be a single legislature chosen by the people. 'This Concordat,' comments Jefferson, 'decided the fate of the Constitution.'[21]

But the course of the French Revolution was not altogether decided over a glass of Jefferson's madeira. On 12 July his carriage had passed through the Place Louis XV when some 300 troops confronted a menacing mass of people, drawn on to the streets by the news of Necker's dismissal, who had now 'posted themselves on and behind large piles of stone'. The carriage was allowed through, but 'the moment I had passed,' records Jefferson, 'the people attacked the cavalry with stones.' The cavalry retreated, and Jefferson thus seems to have witnessed the first instance of the successful mob violence that was to be directed next day against the St Lazare prison, and two days later against the Bastille itself.[22]

After the bloody events of 1789 were over, Jefferson apparently thought that the Revolution had reached its climax. In September he wrote to Tom Paine: 'Tranquillity is well established in Paris, and tolerably so throughout the whole kingdom; and I think there is no possibility now of anything hindering their final establishment of a good constitution, which will in its principles and merit be about a middle term between that of England and the United States.' A fortnight later he was on his way home. So Jefferson did not stay long enough in Paris to see the worst excesses of the Revolution, missing even the march of the women to Versailles. 'I hope you will never see such another 5th or 6th of October,' he writes to Lafayette. But he also reminds him that 'we are not to expect to be translated from despotism to liberty in a feather-bed.' In the same letter, dated 2 April 1790, Jefferson admits that the last news he has heard from Paris was as long ago as 8 January. News did not cross the Atlantic any more quickly than it had done during the War of Independence. Yet not all Jefferson's subsequent comments on the course of the Revolution can be explained in terms of the enchantment lent by distance. Though receipt of news might be irregular, the information (when it came) was detailed enough.[23]

William Short, the American *chargé d'affaires* in Paris, took pains to send him full reports. In a long letter to Jefferson on 5 September 1790, Short instanced, as proof of the remarkable freedom of the Paris press, a pamphlet in which the author 'tells the people that the only remedy to their present evils is to seize and kill the queen, imprison the dauphin, and hang seven or eight hundred members of the assembly with Mirabeau at their head'. Yet as late as January 1793 – before the execution of Louis XVI, but after the news of the August Days, the September Massacres and the declaration of the Republic had reached Philadelphia – Jefferson wrote to Short in defence of the Jacobins. The abolition of the monarchy was, according to Jefferson, 'of absolute necessity'. He continued:

> In the struggle which was necessary, many guilty persons fell without the forms of trial, and with them some innocent. These I deplore as much as anybody, and shall deplore some of them to the day of my death. But I deplore them as I should have done had they fallen in battle. It was necessary to use the arm of the people, a machine not quite so blind as balls and bombs, but blind to a certain degree...

Jefferson continued, somewhat more surprisingly:

> The liberty of the whole earth was depending on the issue of the contest, and was ever such a prize won with so little innocent blood? My own affections have been deeply wounded by some of the martyrs of this cause, but rather than it should have failed I would have seen half the earth desolated; were there but an Adam and an Eve left in every country, and left free, it would be better than it now is.[24]

These startling words were written before the Terror; but they almost foreshadow Robespierre's justification for the extremities of his own Republic of Virtue. Jefferson's seemingly eccentric judgment is an effective reminder that the Reign of Terror was more a product of the Age of Reason than a reaction against it. Jefferson wrote (and Robespierre ruled) in the context of total war. In May 1794, before the Terror ended, Jefferson could write to Tench Coxe, the American political economist: 'Your letters give a comfortable view of French affairs, and later events seem to confirm it.' He went on to express the hope that the defeat of 'the invading tyrants' would 'kindle the wrath of the people of Europe against those who have dared to embroil them in such wickedness, and to bring at length kings, nobles and priests to the scaffolds which they have been so long deluging with human blood.'[25]

It is true that in 1815 Jefferson would complain in a letter to Lafayette of 'the unprincipled and bloody tyranny of Robespierre and the equally unprincipled and maniac tyranny of Bonaparte.' But that was much later when the events of the 1790s could be seen in a different perspective. And it was Napoleon rather than Robespierre whom Jefferson regarded as the real betrayer of the Revolution. After the final defeat of Napoleon, Jefferson could still console himself with the hope that the French 'will finally establish for themselves a government of rational and well-tempered liberty. So much science cannot be lost; so much light shed over them can never fail to produce to them some good, in the end...' The Founding Father of the American Republic, who saw the French Revolution as an extension to Europe of what he called 'the appeal to the rights of man', could still (in his autobiography of 1821) speak of that Revolution as being 'in the first chapter of its history'. That Jefferson could support French republicanism through so many vicissitudes is a striking illustration of his faith in the ideals of the Enlightenment.[26]

The 17 years of retirement left to Jefferson, after the conclusion of his second term as President of the United States in 1809, allowed him to demonstrate his continued commitment to those ideals. As early as his *Notes on Virginia* (1784) he had sketched a scheme for public education in that state, and 30 years later he proposed a system in which elementary and secondary schools in the state should be integrated with his projected University of Virginia. The founding of the university, which opened its doors the year before his death, is perhaps his most enduring monument. The design of the university buildings was regulated by Jefferson, down to the last window-pane;

and he watched the progress of construction through a telescope positioned on the terrace at Monticello. His vigilance even extended to the diet of the students: 'Their drink at all times water, a young stomach needing no stimulating drinks, and the habit of using them being dangerous.'[27]

In a letter to his cousin John Garland Jefferson in 1790, Jefferson had written: 'All that is necessary for a [law] student is access to a library, and directions in what order the books are to be read.' The eighteenth century saw some notable library collections. Diderot's library was bought by Catherine the Great of Russia; Jefferson's library of 6500 volumes was bought by Congress for $24,000 after the first Library of Congress had been destroyed in the British bombardment of 1814. He did not find it altogether easy to part with his collection. As he wrote to Samuel H. Smith, chairman of the Library Committee of Congress: 'I should be willing indeed, to retain a few of the books, to amuse the time I have yet to pass.... Those I should like to retain would be chiefly classical and mathematical. Some few in other branches, and particularly one of the five encyclopedias in the catalogue.'[28]

When Jefferson died on 4 July 1826, on the fiftieth anniversary of the Declaration of American Independence, he had outlived most of the French *encyclopédistes* by almost half a century. Yet to the very end he continued to embody the ideals of the European Enlightenment, and so helped to perpetuate them long after the excesses of the French Revolution had discredited those ideals in France itself.

4 Reluctant *Philosophe:* John Adams and Republican Government

John Adams was the first United States ambassador to be accredited to the Court of St James. In an historic audience with George III on 1 June 1785, Adams explained that he wished to recommend his country 'more and more to Your Majesty's royal benevolence'. The King graciously replied: 'I must say that I not only receive with pleasure the assurance of the friendly dispositions of the United States, but that I am very glad the choice has fallen on you to be their minister.' This was perhaps to exceed the normal hyperbole of diplomatic courtesy, for it was John Adams whose determined resistance to the British crown led Jefferson to dub him 'the Colossus of Independence'. When in less formal vein, George III asked the new ambassador whether he had just come from France, Adams answered simply, 'Yes, Your Majesty.' He could hardly have admitted that when the French foreign minister, Vergennes, congratulated him on his appointment to the London post, Adams had obligingly dismissed the honour as 'a species of degradation in the eyes of Europe, after having been accredited to the King of France'.[1]

Adams was not suited by temperament or upbringing to be a courtier. As one of his compatriots admitted, he lacked the skills of *'dressing, powdering* and *bowing* well'. His father had been a deacon in Puritan Massachusetts, and John himself attended Harvard at a time when there were fines for 'neglecting to repeat the Sabbath sermon' and for profaning the Sabbath by 'walking on the common, or in the streets or field ... or by any diversion before sunset.' There was more than a hint of the Puritan in his own cast of mind. Thus, writing to his wife Abigail from Paris in June 1778, Adams not only asserted that 'luxury wherever she goes, effaces the image of the Divinity', but went on to claim that, if he had the power, he would 'forever banish and exclude from America all gold, silver, precious stones, alabaster, marble, silk, velvet and lace'. This did not deter Abigail from later writing to ask her husband to send her five yards of 'scarlet broadcloth of the best kind and three yards of satin of the same colour which I want for my own use'. But when George Washington, in the interests of wartime economy, banished wine from his table and served rum and water instead, Adams commented: 'If necessity should reduce us to a simplicity of dress and diet becoming republicans, it would be a happy and glorious necessity.'[2]

Republicanism rather than Puritanism probably accounts for Adams's austere views. As a young schoolmaster newly graduated from Harvard, he recorded in his diary: 'I am resolved to rise with the sun and to study the Scriptures on Thursday, Friday, Saturday and Sunday mornings, and to study some Latin author the other three mornings. Noons and nights I intend to read English authors.' His proposed division of time is instructive. Adams was 21 when in 1756 he began studying law with James Putnam, while continuing as Worcester's schoolmaster. Putnam allowed him to browse in his library. When the double burden of study and teaching hurt his health, Adams followed a diet of 'bread and milk, vegetables and water'. The post of schoolmaster was relinquished, and the young graduate returned to his home town of Braintree, where Jeremiah Gridley ('father' of the Boston bar) took him under his wing, advising him not to marry until he had mastered Coke's *Institutes of the Laws of England*. Adams also sought the support of James Otis, whom he would later describe as the greatest man he had ever met – apart from George Washington.[3]

In the famous dispute about writs of assistance, which centred on whether crown officials had the right to search on mere suspicion, Adams's two mentors in legal matters were on opposite sides: Otis appeared for the merchants and Gridley for the Crown. Attending the court hearing, Adams realized that the parties in dispute were none other than England and America. As he would write 30 years later: 'Then and there, the child Independence was born.' Otis based his arguments not on precedent, but on principle, as he stated unequivocally in his opening words: 'This writ is against the fundamental principles of laws.' That was in 1761. Four years later, at the height of American agitation over the Stamp Act, Adams himself appealed to the doctrine of natural rights in his *Dissertation on the Canon and the Feudal Law*, where he wrote of '*Rights* that cannot be repealed or restrained by human law – *Rights* derived from the great Legislator of the Universe.' But characteristically his appeal was not solely to Providence. He urged his readers to 'read the histories of ancient ages; contemplate the great examples of Greece and Rome' and to remember that 'British liberties are not the grants of princes or parliaments'. Thus did Adams prepare to do battle with George III.[4]

As a Boston barrister, Adams was called on to defend Jonathan Hancock, whose ship *Liberty* had been confiscated for landing madeira without paying duty – an executive act which Adams castigated as 'a repeal of Magna Carta as far as America is concerned'. The case was dropped. And when the Boston Port Act closed the city's harbour in June 1774, Adams was elected one of five Massachusetts delegates to the newly summoned Continental Congress. On arrival in Philadelphia, he and his cousin Sam were swiftly elected to the Committee on Colonial Rights and Grievances. It was John who drew the distinction between regulatory and revenue-raising tariffs, who (under the pseudonym 'Novanglus') wrote articles for the *Boston Gazette* basing the colonists' claim squarely on their royal charters, and who first proposed calling state conventions to draw up new constitutions. His own preferred system was one of Governor, Council and House of Representatives, with subordinate officers of state appointed by the Governor 'by and with the advice and consent of the Council'. He claimed that under such a constitution 'human nature would appear in its proper glory, asserting its own real dignity, pulling down tyrannies at a single exertion, and erecting such new fabrics as it thinks best calculated to promote its happiness'.[5]

Adams's phrases would be echoed in both the Declaration of Independence and the Federal Constitution. For the moment he was credited with having written Tom Paine's *Common Sense*. Joseph Ward, for one, hailed it as 'a glorious performance', telling Adams: 'I think I see strong marks of *your pen* in it.' Although John admitted to Abigail that he himself 'could not have written anything in so manly and striking a style', he criticized Paine's 'crude, ignorant notion of a government by one assembly.' He went into print himself when the North Carolina delegates asked for help in framing a state constitution. His advice was published as *Thoughts on Government*. Although dated January 1776, before he could have read Bentham's *Fragment on Government* published that year, Adams claimed in Benthamite terms that the best form of government is that which 'communicates ease, comfort, security, or, in one word, happiness, to the greatest number of persons, and in the greatest degree'.[6]

On 10 May 1776 Congress passed the resolution, proposed jointly by Adams and Arthur Lee, authorizing the individual states to adopt such new constitutions 'as shall in the opinion of the representatives of the people, best conduce to the happiness and safety of their constituents in particular, and America in general.' A month later Adams could write: 'We are in the very midst of a revolution, the most complete, unexpected and remarkable of any in the history of nations.' And when the Declaration of Independence was at last signed, Adams expressed the hope that its anniversary would in future be celebrated not only 'by a solemn act of devotion to God Almighty', but also 'with pomp and parade, with shows, games, sports, guns, bells, bonfires and illuminations'.[7]

Although appointed a member of the committee charged with drawing up the Declaration of Independence, he and Franklin left the work of drafting to Jefferson. Adams did make half a dozen changes in the wording, but he could spare little time from his other committee work, serving simultaneously on a committee to consider possible alliances with foreign powers, and as chairman of the Board of War and Ordnance. (Adams was in effect Secretary for War.) His committee on treaties produced a plan which was largely his work, and was used as the basis for treaty negotiations with France. Meanwhile Adams chose a Frenchman to design a gold medal commemorating the British evacuation of Boston. By late March 1777 he was writing to James Warren: 'All Europe wish us well, excepting only Portugal and Russia'.[8]

While advising his son John Quincy to read Thucydides in Greek – 'the most perfect of all human languages' – Adams confesses to Abigail that he sometimes thinks of writing a Thucydidean history of the last few years. He also tells her that he was wearying of Congressional service: 'Let the cymbals of popularity tinkle still. Let the butterflies of fame glitter with their wings. I shall envy neither their music or their colours.' He and Sam took leave of absence from Congress that October, but before the year was out, Adams heard that he had been elected minister to France in place of the disgraced Silas Deane. James Lovell wrote from Congress: 'Dr Franklin's age alarms us. We want one man of inflexible integrity on that embassy...'. Adams agreed to go, taking John Quincy with him. As father and son made their first landfall at La Rochelle, they heard that France had declared war on England four days before.[9]

When Adams finally left Europe ten years later, he had collected so many books that it took John Quincy three days to unpack them. Among these purchases were the works of the French *philosophes*, including the 1775 edition of Voltaire's works in 40 volumes. But now, in 1778, Adams met the *philosophes* in the flesh before he had read many of their writings. Thus in April he met Turgot, Condorcet and the Duc de Rochefoucauld, and saw (with some distaste) Voltaire embrace Franklin at the *Académie des Sciences* – where he also heard

D'Alembert deliver several eulogies. He also made the acquaintance of the Marquis de Chastellux and the Abbés Raynal and Mably. Raynal had already written on America, while Chastellux and Mably would both do so in the 1780s. At Turgot's dinner-table Adams met Marmontel, Condillac and Mme Helvétius, and found that Franklin's unicameral constitution for Pennsylvania was much admired. Adams had his own views. Writing to Benjamin Rush early in 1790 to congratulate him on Pennsylvania's new bicameral constitution, he commented: 'Poor France I fear will bleed for too exactly copying your old one.' He added: 'When I see such miserable crudities approved by such men as Rochefoucauld and Condorcet, I am disposed to think very humbly of human understanding.'[10]

Those words were written a week before Edmund Burke launched his invective against the French Revolution, but, unlike Burke, Adams did not dismiss the *philosophes*' ideas entirely. He had read Rousseau, collecting no fewer than four copies of the *Social Contract*, though most of his annotations on Rousseau are in his copy of *Discourse on Inequality*. We nevertheless know that Adams studied the *Social Contract* in the 1760s, and that he also read *La Nouvelle Héloïse*. No wonder one historian has called him 'a *philosophe* in spite of himself'. And as Adams caught his first glimpse of the French coast, he recorded in his diary: 'Europe, the great theatre of arts, sciences, commerce, war! Am I at last permitted to visit thy territories?'[11]

John and John Quincy stepped ashore at Bordeaux. At a dinner of welcome, the toasts were introduced by 13 shots in honour of the 13 newly independent states, while the host's gardens were adorned with a large illuminated inscription: 'God save the Congress, Liberty and Adams.' Well might the conquering hero comment in a letter to Patrick Henry that the *philosophes* of France 'do us rather more honour than we deserve'. Though hailed as *le fameux Adams*, John was probably right in thinking that he had been mistaken for his cousin Sam. On arrival in Paris, he met the other commissioners, Franklin and Lee, and was invited by Vergennes to present himself at Versailles – in his American coat rather than in court dress. Adams burned much midnight oil on his correspondence 'with Congress, with the court, with our frigates, our agents and with prisoners and a thousand others'. Rather characteristically he concluded that 'the business of the commission would never be done unless I did it'.[12]

His letters from Paris reveal his anxiety that Silas Deane's attempts at self-justification would jeopardize the proposed French treaty. Adams was spared embarrassment when Congress decided to appoint

Franklin sole minister plenipotentiary at Versailles. Adams took his leave of Vergennes in an interview conducted in French, and prepared for the voyage home. When father and son at length sailed on 18 June 1779, they found that their fellow passengers included Chevalier de la Luzerne (the new minister plenipotentiary to the United States) and his secretary Barbé Marbois. During the voyage, Luzerne read aloud from Blackstone's *Commentaries on the Laws of England*, while John Quincy corrected his pronunciation.[13]

Back in Massachusetts, Adams busied himself with drafting the state constitution. His proposals were Lockean in tone. The preamble gave thanks to the Almighty for providing the opportunity to enter into 'an original, explicit and solemn compact with each other, deliberately and peaceably, without fraud, violence or surprise'. The accompanying Declaration of Rights followed the Virginian model, and the constitution itself enshrined Montesquieu's separation of powers. The legislature, unsurprisingly, had two chambers, and the Governor was given an absolute veto. The constitution, which contained many features of the future Federal Constitution, was adopted with few amendments to Adams's draft. The veto was made subject to a two-thirds majority of the legislature, and Adams's 'all men are born equally free and independent' was changed to 'all men are born free and equal' – a decidedly more dubious proposition. He could nevertheless be pleased with his work, and when he returned to France, he carried copies of the new Massachusetts constitution with him.[14]

Adams was sent back to Europe at the beginning of 1780 to conclude a commercial treaty with Britain. His instructions made clear that American independence was a prior condition of any treaty. Vergennes, who did not welcome his return, received Adams affably, but did all he could to delay official publication of his commission. When Vergennes objected to Congress's proposal to redeem the American debt at a heavy discount, Adams reminded the French minister that France had profited from American independence. Vergennes resented the lecture, writing frostily: 'I think that all further discussion between us on this subject will be needless.' Franklin's reaction was to smooth the Frenchman's ruffled feathers, while Adams chose this moment to demand French naval help: 'The state of things in America has become alarming, and this merely for want of a few French men-of-war upon that coast.' Vergennes was soon able to tell him that a French fleet had been despatched to American waters, thus showing that 'the King is far from abandoning the cause of America'.[15]

Perhaps wisely, Congress now moved Adams to Amsterdam to deputize for Henry Laurens, who had been captured at sea by the British. Holland was hesitating whether to join the League of Armed Neutrality, and Adams bent all his efforts to forging a Dutch alliance. He had already written 26 letters in reply to Hendrik Calkoen, a leading Amsterdam lawyer, who was so impressed with Adams's answers that he read them to his Amsterdam literary society. Adams was admirably persistent. He wrote articles for the *Gazette de Leyden*, the *Politique Hollandais* and Amsterdam's *French Gazette*; he compiled a catalogue of leading Dutchmen 'with their reputed political characters'; and in an address to the Dutch States General, he reminded them of their own earlier struggle to create an independent republic: 'Every Dutchman instructed in the subject must pronounce the American Revolution just and necessary, or pass a censure upon the greatest actions of his immortal ancestors.'[16]

In the summer of 1781 Adams was recalled briefly to Paris, to hear the peace terms proposed by the courts of Russia and Austria. Returning to Amsterdam, he wrote to Vergennes that it would be unwise to accept the mediation of the imperial courts until they had recognized American independence, adding pompously: 'The dignity of North America does not consist in diplomatic ceremonials or any of the subtleties of etiquette; it consists solely in reason, justice, truth, the rights of mankind and the interests of the nations.' Vergennes's reaction is not recorded, but we know that Congress (perhaps prompted by Luzerne) revoked Adams's commission to negotiate a commercial treaty with England, and appointed him instead one of five commissioners to negotiate a general peace.[17]

Still in Amsterdam, Adams fell seriously ill and was in a coma for five days. He blamed his illness on the 'immense quantities of dead water' that surrounded the city. He was out of action for two months. On recovering, he wrote rhapsodically about an imminent European Revolution that sounds remarkably like the 'Atlantic Revolution' of modern historians. In response to a newly published pamphlet attacking the Stadtholder and demanding democracy, Adams asks: 'Who and what has given rise to the assuming power of the people....?' His answer: the American Revolution. And to Abigail he wrote confidently:

The Emperor of Germany is adopting, as fast as he can, American ideals of toleration and religious liberty, and it will become the fashionable system of all Europe very soon. Light spreads from the dayspring in the west, and may it shine more and more until the perfect day.

Meanwhile the students of the University of Franeker in Harlingen, convinced that Holland's recognition of American independence was 'one of the most important events known to history,' invited Adams to celebrate the event with 'a display of fireworks embellished with decorations suitable to American independence.'[18]

Adams's diplomatic success in Holland, culminating in the signing of the Dutch Treaty in September 1782, freed him to resume his duties as peace commissioner in Paris. He did not like his new instructions, which required the commissioners 'ultimately to govern yourselves by the advice and opinion of the French ministry'. Luckily the commissioners ignored their instructions and, at Adams's insistence, not only safeguarded the unlimited right of the Americans to fish off Newfoundland, but also did a secret deal with Britain over the boundary of Florida. Vergennes was not amused at being excluded from the negotiations, though he admitted surprise at the considerable concessions the Americans had wrung from the British. Adams now had his eyes on London, where he coveted the post of ambassador.

By the end of 1782 Abigail was in any case preparing to join her husband in Europe. She had been robbed of news for almost a year, when three consecutive packets of letters went astray. No wonder she wrote plaintively: 'Who shall give me back time? Who shall compensate to me those years I cannot recall?' And in response to one of her husband's letters, she wrote: 'I want you to say more things to me than you do; but you write so wise, like a minister of state.' It would be another eighteen months before she finally set sail with their daughter, Nabby – and on almost the same tide that took Jefferson to replace Jay at Versailles. In Paris Adams got on well with Jefferson, who gave him a copy of his newly published *Notes on Virginia*. And after Adams left for London, as the new United States ambassador, Jefferson complained: 'My afternoons hang heavily upon me.' When Jefferson himself visited London, he and Adams took time off to be tourists. They inspected stately homes, armed with Thomas Whatley's *Observations on Modern Gardening*. At Stratford-upon-Avon they cut a chip off an old wooden chair on which Shakespeare was supposed to have sat, and at Worcester Adams upbraided some local farmers for not knowing their Civil War battlefields or recognizing 'the ground where liberty was fought for'. But when Jefferson was presented at court, George III turned his back on him. There were limits to the courtesy that diplomatic protocol required.[19]

It was in London that Adams wrote his influential *Defence of the Constitutions*. It was written in some haste. The first volume was begun in October 1786 and published in 1787; two more volumes followed within the year. The *Defence* was prompted by Turgot's criticisms of the American state constitutions which he had expressed in a letter to Richard Price, written in 1778 but not published until 1784. Turgot argued that the states' new constitutions were 'an unreasonable imitation of the usages of England'. He thought the Americans should have seized the chance of 'collecting all authority into one centre, that of the nation'. By contrast Adams argued that the only stable constitution was a 'mixed government' where popular assembly, senate and chief executive shared both legislative and executive roles. He was chiefly concerned, not with Montesquieu's separation of powers, but with the *division* of powers – the overlapping of legislative and executive functions soon to be embodied in the Federal Constitution. Adams's first volume arrived in America just before the Constitutional Convention began its deliberations, thus ensuring maximum impact on the forthcoming debates.[20]

As he made clear in the preface, Adams had the experience of ancient republics very much in mind: 'We shall learn to prize the checks and balances of a free government, and even those of the modern aristocracies, if we recollect the miseries of Greece which arose from their ignorance of them.' The United States was much larger than ancient Greece or modern Switzerland and therefore less likely to be held together by 'simple' governments. Large countries 'are not to be bound long with silken threads: lions, young or old, will not be bound by cobwebs.' European ignorance of the United States had multiplied misunderstandings. Adams had watched anxiously 'the facility with which philosophers of greatest name have undertaken to write of American affairs without knowing anything of them, and have echoed and re-echoed each other's visions'. There was nothing Utopian in Adams's constitutional model. Indeed he was not ashamed of borrowing from the British, whom he describes as having 'blended together the feudal institutions with those of the Greeks and Romans'.[21]

Adams's aim in the *Defence* is to show that 'simple' republics have never lasted, and have always transmuted themselves into aristocracies or dictatorships. His anthology of historical examples is very much a 'scissors and paste' production. Three-quarters of the first volume (on ancient and modern republics) is made up of verbatim extracts from other authors, and he is not always scrupulous in his use of quotation marks. His account of San Marino, the first republic examined, leans heavily on Addison's *Remarks on the Several Parts of Italy* (1705), while two-thirds of the pages on Swiss republics are filled with long excerpts from Archdeacon William Coxe's *Sketches of the Natural, Civil and Political State of Swisserland* (1779). Adams's method is to interpolate his own comments, or adapt the chosen extract to his purposes. Thus his description of Uri (William Tell's canton) begins by following Coxe verbatim, but where the Archdeacon wrote 'those who know the true value of liberty and independence,' Adams substitutes 'the Americans'. Similarly the chapter on Poland comes mainly from Coxe's *Travels into Poland, Russia, Sweden and Denmark* (1784). After copying 16 pages of Coxe's summary of Polish history from the time of Casimir the Great, Adams adds grimly: 'We are now arrived at the consummation of all panegyrics upon a sovereignty in a single assembly – the partition.'[22]

Adams was unashamed of his plagiarism. Machiavelli, he claimed, borrowed from Aristotle without attribution, while 'Montesquieu borrowed the best part of his book from Machiavel, without acknowledging the quotation.' In listing his own authorities Adams admits helpfully: 'I have made free use of their expressions as well as reflections, without noticing them; if you would see how much, you must read.' This method was inevitable, given the speed at which Adams worked. His family had to make the best of it. Abigail told John Quincy that the book on which his father was working in the library, from early morning to late evening, was devoted to 'a subject in which America is greatly interested, and upon which her future happiness depends'. That Christmas of 1786, Adams packed Abigail and John Quincy off to Bath, while he continued working on the *Defence*. He claimed that he found his 'state of philosophic solitude...very tolerable'. But Abigail felt she needed to warn him to wear his flannel underwear, and not to let his library fire die down. Adams got copies of the first volume from the printers in January – complete with misprints to compound the author's own errors. He sent copies to Lafayette and Jefferson in Paris, to friends in America, and to each of his sons; and 30 copies went to a Boston bookseller for sale in the United States.[23]

Adams had made clear that his aim was not simply to answer Turgot: 'I wish to assemble together the opinions and reasonings of philosophers, politicians and historians...whose writings were in the contemplation of those who framed the American constitutions.' There was room in his anthology for Polybius and Plato, Machiavelli and Montesquieu, Beccaria and Delolme; but his principal authorities were English – Bacon, Sidney, Harrington, Milton and the now forgotten Marchamont Nedham. Adams's apparent admiration of British institutions is partly explained by his surprising insistence that England is a republic 'and has been ever so considered by foreigners, and by the most learned and Enlightened Englishmen.' He was not thinking of Cromwell's Commonwealth, or Milton's favoured single assembly, which would have ensured that 'the liberties of England would have been at this hour the liberties of Poland, or the island would have been a province of France'.[24]

Adams's second volume, dated 'Grosvenor Square, April 19, 1787', has no chapter divisions into 'letters' on the pattern of the first. The entire volume is devoted to a 'cluster of governments' in medieval Italy, which Adams thinks deserve the attention of Americans, and will 'farther illustrate and confirm the principles we have endeavoured to maintain.' He allots some 120 pages to Machiavelli's history of Florence, interspersed with comments of his own. He then turns to Guicciardini's *Storia d' Italia*, which Adams himself painfully translated from the Italian even though an English translation already existed. Guicciardini's account begins in 1492, the same year (Adams reminds us) that 'Christopher Columbus, of plebeian birth, but of noble genius … laid the first foundation of the constitutions of the United States of America'. The examination of the Italian republics continues in Volume III, but after pursuing the history of Pistoia for 124 pages, Adams abruptly stops the account at 1425, remarking, 'The rest of this history you will consult at your leisure.' Shorter sections follow on Padua, Mantua and Montepulciano and the remainder of the work is devoted to Marchamont Nedham.[25]

The expense incurred in researching into Italian history was later put by Adams at 800 dollars – apart from the pain of teaching himself Italian in the process. In August 1787 he wrote to Jefferson: 'It has cost me a good deal of trouble to search into Italian rubbish and ruins,' though he added: 'Enough of pure gold and marble has been found to reward the pains.' Was the effort of devoting almost 300 pages to demolishing Marchamont Nedham equally rewarding? Nedham's *The Excellency of a Free State* had first appeared under the Commonwealth. It had been reprinted in 1767, when Thomas Brand Hollis (who would carry the key of the Bastille to Mount Vernon) sent a copy, requesting 'his friend Mr Adams to accept benevolently this book, to be deposited among his republican tracts.' In his *Thoughts on Government* (1776) Adams had mentioned Nedham as one of those English writers whose works 'will convince any candid mind that there is no good government but what is republican'. Now in the *Defence*, Adams painstakingly repudiates Nedham's arguments – chiefly, it seems, because he mistakenly believes that they had influenced Turgot. Adams uses Nedham's text to focus on the danger to the rights of minorities in popular assemblies. Accountability, he insists, is the safeguard, and a single representative assembly is accountable to no one, except its electorate.[26]

Adams's voice was that of the Enlightenment, tempered by a politician's grasp of priorities. He brought his final volume to an end with these words:

> The vegetable and animal kingdoms, and those heavenly bodies whose existence and movements we are as yet only permitted faintly to perceive, do not appear to be governed by laws more uniform or certain than those which regulate the moral and political world. A prospect into futurity in America is like contemplating the heavens through the telescopes of Herschel: objects, stupendous in their magnitudes and motions, strike us from all quarters and fill us with amazement.

Yet, as if to underline the practical purpose of Adams's hastily written encyclopedia of republicanism, the draft text of the new Federal Constitution is added as an appendix.[27]

Perhaps even here Adams had one eye on Europe, for only the first volume of the *Defence of the Constitutions* reached America in time to influence the Convention debates. Further editions of that volume were published in Philadelphia (1787) and Boston (1788). Joel Barlow, writing to Adams in June 1787, claimed that no book 'was ever received with more gratitude or read with greater avidity'. And when the complete three-volume work reached Benjamin Rush, he wrote enthusiastically that the work would be 'the almanac of my boys upon the greatest subject of political happiness'. A French edition of the complete work appeared in two volumes in 1792, but the first volume had reached France in 1787, when the Gallo-American Society decided to have it translated and published in the newspapers.[28]

The French Constitution of 1791 and Condorcet's ill-fated version of 1793, would nevertheless follow Turgot rather than Adams. Later, when President of the United States, Adams noted that Condorcet could have done little harm as a writer, but that 'as a legislator he contributed to destroy all the good he aimed at'. Yet in his *L'Influence de la Révolution d'Amerique sur l'Europe* (1786) Condorcet described the Americans as 'the only people among whom the teachings of Machiavellianism are not erected into political doctrines, and whose leaders do not profess the impossibility of so perfecting the social order as to harmonize prosperity and justice'. Adams and Condorcet might disagree over whether (in the Frenchman's words) 'the legislative power may reside, without danger, in a single assembly'. But they both helped to popularize the image of Revolutionary America as the political embodiment of the Enlightenment.[29]

Transatlantic Citizens

Thomas Cooper in Old Age in South Carolina
Silhouette done from life by William H. Brown and first published
in his Portrait Gallery of Distinguished American Citizens, 1845

5 Bridging the Atlantic: Paine's Three Revolutions

Tom Paine died in 1809, not in his native Norfolk but on the other side of the Atlantic – in New York State. The Quakers refused his request to be buried in their cemetery, and he was interred instead on his own farm at New Rochelle. The small group of mourners was led by a Frenchwoman, Mme Bonneville, and two of her three sons. Standing at one end of the grave, she told the youngest, Benjamin, to stand at the other. 'O! Mr Paine!' she exclaimed. 'My son stands here as testimony of the gratitude of America, and I for France.' The graveside scene is as symbolic of the interaction between the French and American Revolutions as the fact that the key of the Bastille hangs in the hallway of George Washington's home at Mount Vernon. When in 1790 Lafayette entrusted Paine with the key to deliver to Washington, Paine wrote in a covering letter: 'The key is the symbol of the first ripe fruits of American principles translated into Europe.... That the principles of America opened the Bastille is not to be doubted and therefore the key comes to its right place.'[1]

Paine was proud of the part he had personally played in establishing the United States of America, through his *Common Sense* (1776) and his less well-known *Crisis* pamphlets written during the War of Independence. With the publication of *Common Sense*, he sprang to international fame at the age of 39. He would later claim that 'its success was beyond anything since the invention of printing.' The *Connecticut Gazette* likened it to a 'landflood that sweeps all before it', and added: 'The doctrine of independence hath been in times past greatly disgustful... it is now become our delightful theme and commands our purest affections.' This was the importance of *Common Sense*. It presented independence as the only rational option. And in spite of his uncomplimentary reference to William the Conqueror – 'a French bastard landing with an armed banditti' – Paine was insistent that America's roots were European, not British: 'Europe and not England is the parent country of America.'[2]

Behind the rhetoric there were nevertheless some practical proposals. There should be annual assemblies – 'their business wholly domestic and subject to the authority of a continental congress.' The prime business of this 'congress' would be to 'frame a Continental

Charter of the United Colonies, answering to what is called the Magna Charta of England'. *Common Sense* was not only an early assertion of the importance of a *union* of the thirteen states, but also proposed a proclamation on the lines of the Declaration of Independence, drawn up later that year:

> Were a manifesto to be published, and despatched to foreign courts, setting forth the miseries we have endured, and the peaceable methods we have ineffectually used for redress ... at the same time assuring all such courts of our peaceable dispositions towards them, and of our desire of entering into trade with them; such a memorial would produce more good effects to this continent, than if a ship were freighted with petitions to Britain.[3]

How had *Common Sense* come to be written? Paine had arrived in America at the end of November 1774. By January 1775 he was writing for the newly established *Pennsylvania Magazine* at Philadelphia, and soon became its editor. His first polemical piece to be written on American soil – within a few weeks of his arrival – was entitled 'African Slavery in America'. Paine was uncompromising: 'Certainly one may, with as much reason and decency, plead for murder, robbery, lewdness and barbarity as for this practice.' He asked Americans to consider how they can 'complain so loudly of attempts to enslave them while they hold so many hundred thousands in slavery'. A month later the first anti-slavery society in America was founded in Philadelphia, with Paine as one of its members. And in October of that year Benjamin Franklin, who had met Paine in England and had recommended him to friends in Philadelphia, suggested that he should write a history of events leading to the outbreak of war. *Common Sense* was the result.[4]

In his account of events, from January 1776 to the British surrender at Yorktown in 1781, Paine was to claim that there was 'no instance in the world' where a people was 'so instantly and effectually pervaded by a truth in politics, as in the case of independence, and who supported their opinion undiminished through such a succession of good and ill fortune, till they crowned it with success'. And it was that 'succession of good and ill fortune' which his *Crisis* pamphlets would chart. The first issue of the *American Crisis* appeared on 19 December 1776 in the *Pennsylvania Journal*. Paine had been serving with the revolutionary army since August, and had taken part in Washington's retreat across New Jersey. The first *Crisis* was written on a drum-head by the light of a camp fire during that march. It opened with the famously resonant words:

These are the times that try men's souls. The summer-soldier and sunshine patriot will, in this crisis, shrink from the service of his country; but he that stands to it *now*, deserves the thanks of man and woman. Tyranny, like hell, is not easily conquered: yet we have this consolation with us, that the harder the conflict, the more glorious the triumph.[5]

Paine's initial purpose was to play down the set-back suffered at the hands of Sir William Howe's army, and to foster the fighting spirit of the colonists: 'Wisdom is not the purchase of a day, and it is no wonder we should err at first setting off.' What was needed was continued courageous resistance:

By perseverance and fortitude we have the prospect of a glorious issue; by cowardice and submission, the sad choice of a variety of evils – a ravaged country – a depopulated city – habitations without safety – and slavery without hope – our homes turned into barracks and bawdy-houses for Hessians – and a future race to provide for, whose fathers we shall doubt of.

The piece was signed 'COMMON SENSE'. Washington was sufficiently impressed with it to order it to be read at the head of every regiment. Its effect on morale was perhaps reflected in the victory over the Hessians at Trenton on 26 December.[6]

The second *Crisis* appeared on 13 January 1777, and was chiefly directed at Lord Howe's proclamation requiring 'all such persons as are assembled together under the name of general or provincial congresses, committees, conventions or other associations ... to desist and cease from all such treasonable actings and doings.' In pointing out the absurdity of such a proclamation in the wake of British defeats at Trenton and Princeton, Paine predicts that ' "the United States of America" will sound as pompously in the world, or in history, as "The Kingdom of Great Britain" '. This seems to have been the first use in print of the term 'United States of America', though it would soon appear on continental banknotes. Paine also correctly predicts the course the war will take. Howe has already missed his chance of conquering America: 'If you could not effect it in the summer, when our army was less than yours, nor in the winter, when we had none, how are you to do it? In point of generalship you have been outwitted; and in point of fortitude outdone.' Then there comes a more ominous warning: Howe should not neglect the risks at home. From what Paine knows of the disposition of the British people, 'it is easier for us to effect a revolution there, than you a conquest here'. And if this seems far-fetched, we need only recall John Wesley's anxious letters to Lord North and Lord Dartmouth in June 1775.[7]

The third *Crisis*, 'written this fourth year of the Union, which God preserve', was composed while waiting for the British to come out of winter quarters. The British army, Paine observes, is 'like a wounded, disabled whale'. It wants 'only time and room to die in; and though, in the agony of their exit, it may be unsafe to live within the flapping of their tail, yet every hour shortens their date and lessens their power of mischief.' In the previous *Crisis*, he had (he explains) tried to show 'the impossibility of the enemy's making any conquest of America'. He now sees the need to 'go over some of the leading principles in support of independence'. By seizing her freedom, America would 'exchange Britain for Europe – shake hands with the world – live at peace with mankind – and trade to any market where we best can buy and sell'. War and desolation are become 'the trades of the Old World' whereas in America 'the present happy union of the states bids fair for extirpating the future use of arms from one quarter of the world'. This, the longest of the *Crisis* pamphlets, concludes with a proposal to tax the Tories and with the assertion that 'the only road to peace, honour and commerce is INDEPENDENCE'.[8]

Another dozen *Crisis* pamphlets were to follow – two of them after the final conclusion of peace in 1783. When Philadelphia fell to the British at the end of September 1777, Paine accompanied Congress first to Lancaster and then to York, Pennsylvania. The following month he was carrying messages from Congress to Washington's army. During the winter of 1777–8 Paine divided his time between the army at Valley Forge and Congress, but in March he was ready to recommend embalming Howe for posterity: 'In a balmage, sir, of humble tar, you will be as secure as Pharaoh, and in a hieroglyphic of feathers you will rival in finery all the mummies of Egypt.' Meanwhile George III's recent speech at the opening of Parliament is 'like a soliloquy on ill luck', and the capture of Burgoyne's army at Saratoga (Paine correctly predicts) 'will sink [the King's] consequence as much in Europe as in America'.[9]

When, a decade later, the Marquis de Chastellux published his *Travels in North America* in an English edition, the translator inserted his own tribute to Paine, whom he thought the Marquis had underestimated. The anonymous translator, who claimed to have been in America during the War of Independence, wrote of Paine:

His productions were instantly published in every town, of every state (for every town has a newspaper) on grey, brown, yellow or black, but seldom on white paper, a very rare commodity; the people took fresh courage and, 'have you read *the Crisis*' was the specific against every political apprehension.

Paine's standing in American eyes, after publication of the early issues of *Crisis*, is shown by his appointment in the spring of 1777 as Secretary to the Congressional Committee on Foreign Affairs – a post he held for nearly two years. His resignation early in 1779 was occasioned by public interest in the extent of French intervention in the American War before the conclusion of a formal alliance in 1778. Paine always insisted that the Americans owed the success of their Revolution primarily to France. As he told George Washington in the notoriously bad-tempered letter he addressed to him in August 1796, 'Had it not been for the aid you received from France in men, money and ships, your cold and unmilitary conduct... would in all probability have lost America.'[10]

Paine was well placed to know the value of the military assistance afforded by Louis XVI's government, for, as secretary to the foreign affairs committee, he was privy to the terms on which help was provided. But he made the mistake of publishing the facts of the transaction in the Philadelphia newspapers, and so had to resign in January 1779. By November he had become Clerk to the Pennsylvania Assembly, and the following year he was urging Congress to appeal to Louis XVI for further support. Congress agreed to ask the French court for 25 million *livres* and to send John Laurens as their emissary. Laurens invited Paine to go with him. Later Paine was able to record the success of the mission:

> The aid obtained from France was six million *livres* as a present, and ten millions as a loan borrowed in Holland on the security of France. We sailed from France in the French *Resolve* frigate... bringing with us two millions and a half in silver and convoying a ship and a brig laden with clothing and military stores. The money was transported in sixteen ox-teams to the national bank at Philadelphia, which enabled the army to move to Yorktown...[11]

No wonder Paine felt justified in claiming in his *Letter Addressed to the Abbé Raynal* (1782) that 'perhaps no two events ever united so intimately and forcibly to combat and expel prejudice as the revolution of America and the alliance with France.' Paine, the enemy of kings, saw nothing incongruous in attending a celebration given by La Luzerne, French plenipotentiary in Philadelphia, in honour of the birth of the Dauphin. La Luzerne had earlier commissioned Paine to write articles on the advantages to America of the French alliance; and when the *Letter to Raynal* appeared, the French minister paid him a bonus of 50 guineas. Paine's *Letter* was published in five French versions, and an American wrote from France: 'I have lately travelled much and find him everywhere. His *Letter to Raynal* has sealed his fame'[12]

The Versailles Treaty of 1783, which formally ended the War of Independence, seems temporarily to have left Paine as a rebel without a cause. However he did produce the last two of his *Crisis* pamphlets – No. 14 (undated) headed *The Last Crisis* and the misleadingly titled *Supernumerary Crisis* (dated December 1783). No. 14 begins: 'The times that tried men's souls are over – and the greatest and completest revolution the world ever knew, gloriously and happily accomplished.' But there was now a need to strengthen 'that happy union which has been our salvation, and without which we should have been a ruined people'. It is, he explains, 'the flag of the United States which renders our ships and commerce safe on the seas, or in a foreign port.'[13]

Paine showed no sign of sailing back to Europe. By now he had bought a small house and meadow at Bordentown near New York, perhaps with French money. He would later tell a correspondent: 'I had rather see my horse, Button, eating the grass of Bordentown...than see all the pomp and show of Europe.' But in the summer of 1784, New York State presented him with a farm in the township of New Rochelle. Its French name was prophetic. Soon after Paine's move to New Rochelle, Franklin returned to Philadelphia, after his ten years in Paris. His return seems to have revived Paine's scientific interests. Franklin did not show much enthusiasm for Paine's packet of 'smokeless candles', but he was impressed with the design for a prefabricated bridge. The bridge, Paine explained, was to have a single arch capable of spanning 'three, four or five hundred feet, and probably more', and would be built in 13 sections 'in commemoration of the thirteen United States'. He had based the design on the construction of a spider's web, as he assumed that 'when nature enabled that insect to make a web, she taught it the best method of putting it together'.[14]

Apart from the prefabricated nature of its construction, the novelty of Paine's bridge is that it was based on a small segment of a large circle, rather than a large segment of a small one. Wilkinson's iron bridge at Coalbrookdale, built in 1779 with a span of 100 feet, is almost a half-circle. Paine was attempting a span at least three times as long, for which a half-circle would be impracticable. His design was improved upon by Rowland Burdon, who built the bridge across the Wear at Sunderland. It was cast by Samuel Walker & Co. of Rotherham, who had cast Paine's bridge, and some parts of Paine's bridge were used in the construction. Its span of 236 feet exceeded that of any single arch then known. Robert Stephenson, the nineteenth-century engineer, would call it 'a structure which, as regards the proportions and small quantity of material employed, will probably remain unrivalled'. Or as Paine is supposed to have told Mme Bonneville: 'Nothing in the world is so fine as my bridge – except a woman.'[15]

With his iron bridge Paine steps briefly into the Industrial Revolution, and (in an apt piece of symbolism) it was the bridge that took him from America to France. In the summer of 1787 he presented a wrought-iron model of the bridge to the *Académie des Sciences*, which after some delay reported on it favourably. Armed with this endorsement, Paine set off for London to obtain similar approval from the Royal Society. Jefferson (now American envoy in Paris) and Lafayette promised him that they would try to persuade the French government to use his design for a bridge to be built over the Seine. They did not succeed, but Paine's bridge brought the three men together and laid the basis for a lasting friendship. While in England in the summer of 1788, seeking a suitable foundry, Paine obtained a patent. The notes accompanying his application answer a number of objections. Will the iron rust? No, since 'it is to be varnished over with a coat of melted glass.' Will wooden piles support the weight? Yes, because the piles will be encased in concrete and pinned together. And the iron arch, Paine explains, has other uses such as vaulted ceilings, and therefore presents 'a new and important manufacture to the iron works of the nation'. Above all the bridge is portable, 'as the bars and parts of which it is composed need not be longer or larger than it is convenient to be towed in vessel, boat or wagon'. This means that it can be made in England and 'sent to any part of the world to be erected'.[16]

On the day before the Bastille fell, Paine was writing to Jefferson to report progress on the manufacture of the bridge. The news of the march of the women to Versailles in October brought him hurrying back to Paris, yet the following spring he was again on his way to London 'expressly for the purpose of erecting an iron bridge'. He arranged for an actual bridge, with a span of 110 feet, to be built in a field at Paddington, and he was still in London in November when Burke published his *Reflections on the Revolution in France*. As Paine remarks: 'I therefore ceased my work on the bridge to employ myself on the more necessary work, *Rights of Man*, in answer to Mr Burke.' Paine would later call *Rights of Man* 'my political bridge'. What was happening in France, he claimed, was a carrying over into Europe of the principles of the American Revolution. As he wrote in the preface to the French edition: 'The cause of the French people is that of all Europe, or rather of the whole world.'[17]

Rights of Man appeared in two parts, separated by a gap of eleven months. The first part contains quotations from Lafayette's address to the National Assembly three days before the Bastille fell, and gives prominence to the Declaration of the Rights of Man and Citizen – the text of which is printed as an appendix. The National Assembly, Paine argues, is an embodiment of the 'social compact', which must be seen not as a contract between government and governed, but as one where 'the individuals themselves ... entered into a compact with each other to produce a government.' He thus looks to Rousseau rather than to Locke, and asks provocatively: 'The genealogy of Christ is traced to Adam. Why not the Rights of Man to the creation of Man?' The first part of the *Rights of Man* had been dedicated to George Washington. The second was dedicated to Lafayette. Paine had started to write it in Paris in the summer of 1791, and he was at work on it when Lafayette burst into his bedroom with the news that the royal family had fled. Later that day Paine narrowly escaped being strung up on a lamppost for not wearing his tricolour cockade. He soon removed any doubts as to his loyalties. In June he published an open letter to the editors of the newly established *Le Républicain*, offering his services, though he admitted that 'from my ignorance of the French language, my works must necessarily undergo a translation.'[18]

The second part of *Rights of Man*, published in February 1792, describes what a republic is. It is 'not any *particular* form of government', Paine explains. 'Republican government is no other than government established and conducted for the interest of the public.' The only true republic is the United States of America, where 'the poor are not oppressed, the rich are not privileged'. He predicts that 'the present age will hereafter merit to be called the Age of Reason', adding: 'From a small spark kindled in America, a flame has arisen, not to be extinguished.'[19]

Paine would record that *Rights of Man* had 'the greatest run of any work ever published in the English language', and he later estimated that between 400 000 and 500 000 copies were printed in various versions and translations. The cheapness of many of the editions ensured a wide market. By the summer of 1792 Paine's revolutionary ideas were finding their way into petitions to Parliament, and on 26 August (just after the fall of the monarchy in France) the Assembly conferred honorary citizenship on 17 foreigners 'who, by their writings and by their courage have served the cause of liberty and prepared the freedom of the people.' Among them were George Washington and Tom Paine.[20]

In the elections for the forthcoming Convention, Paine was chosen by no fewer than four *départements*. He decided to sit for Calais, whose electors sent him the irresistible summons: 'Come, friend of the people, to swell the number of patriots in an assembly which will decide the destiny of a great people, perhaps of the human race. The happy period you have predicted for the nations has arrived...'. One night in mid-September, having had his baggage searched by a customs officer at his Dover hotel, Paine sailed for France. He was accompanied by John Frost of the Society for Constitutional Information, and by Achille Audibert, emissary of the electors of Calais. As Paine boarded the ferry 'he was hissed a great deal', and was mocked about his former trade of corset-maker. Rather than wait for the wind, the packet-boat was towed out of harbour. An observer noted: 'I believe, had we remained much longer, they would have pelted him with stones from the beach.' This contrasted with their rapturous reception at Calais. The guards saluted 'Citizen Paine'. The guard commander embraced him and presented him with a cockade. A salute was fired from the battery. The streets were lined with people shouting '*Vive* Thomas Paine!' At the town hall there was another embrace, this time from the mayor, who addressed him in French. Audibert translated, and Paine, entering into the spirit of the occasion, placed his hand on his heart and vowed to devote his life to their cause.[21]

Arriving in Paris, Paine seems to have voted in the Convention in favour of the abolition of the monarchy. Soon afterwards Nicolas Bonneville published his *Letter of Thomas Paine to the People of France*, in which Paine expressed his gratitude at being elected, and likened the war against the European monarchies to 'the late revolutionary war in America'. It is important now, he thinks, to remove the 'contradictions' in the constitution of 1791, and to make it 'conformable to the Declaration of Rights'. In October the Convention appointed Paine to a committee of nine to devise a new constitution.

Condorcet, whom Paine already knew, did most of the drafting, taking as his starting-point the Pennsylvania constitution of 1776.[22]

The Girondins were opposed to putting the King on trial, but when it was revealed that Louis had corresponded with France's enemies, the trial could not be postponed. On 20 November Paine sent to the President of the Convention a paper setting out his reasons for bringing Louis to trial. The introductory paragraph illustrates Paine's flair for publicity, as it concludes: 'I should be happy if the convention would have the goodness to hear this business read this morning, as I purpose sending a copy of it to London, to be printed in the English journals.' A secretary read the paper on his behalf. Its principal theme is contained in the sentence: 'If Louis is innocent, let us put him to prove his innocence; if he is guilty, let the national will determine if he should be pardoned or punished.' He should be arraigned 'not only on the part of France, but for having conspired against all Europe.'[23]

When, however, Louis was brought to trial in November – a week before Paine himself was put on trial *in absentia* in London – the arch-enemy of hereditary monarchy pleaded for the King's life. In an address to the Convention on 15 January, he left his hearers in no doubt that he thought the King was guilty. But Louis had done one thing that entitled him to clemency: he had enabled the Americans to 'shake off the unjust and tyrannical yoke of Britain.' Let banishment to America be his fate, Paine urged. 'Let then these United States be the safeguard and asylum of Louis Capet.' When the vote was taken, there was a majority of one in favour of death. Despite Paine's protests, the Convention voted by 380 votes to 310 that Louis should be executed within 24 hours. That vote marked the end of the Girondins' ascendancy in the Convention, and the end of Paine's influence on its debates. Yet on the day that war was declared against England and Holland, Paine was one of four deputies chosen to write an address to the British people. In January 1793, before the King's execution, Paine had moved to a small house at St Denis, on the outskirts of Paris. Among its attractions, he tells us, was a garden 'well laid out and stocked with excellent fruit trees'; it was 'the only place where I saw the wild cucumber'.[24]

Paine did not try to write any other political tracts, since, he explained, 'no good could be done by writing and no printer dared to print'. But he did write the first part of his attack on Christianity, *The Age of Reason*, which was to earn him more enemies than the *Rights of Man*. He also watched the progress of the Terror, punctuated by knocks on the street door at St Denis. First a guard 'with muskets and fixed bayonets' came to arrest two of his companions, who had luckily escaped to Switzerland two days before. Then, Paine's record continues, 'the guard came about a month after, in the night, and took away the landlord, Georgeit; and the scene in the house finished with the arrestation of myself.'[25]

He was committed to the Luxembourg prison in December 1793 and lodged in a room on the ground floor. His portrayal of life in the Luxembourg at the height of the Terror is grimly laconic: 'Scarcely a night passed in which ten, twenty, thirty, forty, fifty or more were not taken out of prison, carried before a pretended tribunal in the morning and guillotined before night.' Only Robespierre's fall, it seems, prevented Paine from being guillotined himself. Now that the risk had passed, he could not understand why the American government did not secure his release. Gouverneur Morris made no move, and when James Monroe succeeded him, Paine was still left to languish in prison. He heard to his dismay that he was no longer regarded as an American citizen. Monroe wrote to reassure him: 'By being with us through the revolution, you are of our country as absolutely as if you had been born there; and you are no more of England than every native American is... To the welfare of Thomas Paine the Americans are not, nor can they be indifferent.' Yet it was not until 4 November that Paine was finally released.[26]

Monroe tried to make amends by inviting Paine to be a guest in his house, where he remained for 18 months. This was a longer stay than Monroe had bargained for. As he remarked wryly, Paine seemed likely to be his guest 'till his death or departure for America, however remote the one or the other event may be'. Paine's chances of returning to America were not improved by the publication of his bitter *Letter to George Washington*. It incorporates a number of letters written in 1795 and 1796, beginning with complaints of Washington's neglect of him during his imprisonment, and denouncing the Jay treaty between England and America as 'a satire upon the Declaration of Independence'. The *Letter* ends:

> And as to you, sir, treacherous in private friendship (for so you have been to me and that in the day of danger) and a hypocrite in public life, the world will be puzzled to decide whether you are an APOSTATE or an IMPOSTOR – whether you have abandoned good principles, or whether you ever had any.[27]

Could Paine ever return to America now? William Cobbett circulated in Philadelphia an essay in which he likened Paine to

Judas – though it was Cobbett who eventually brought Paine's bones back to England. For the moment the principal casualty of the Jay Treaty was Monroe, who was recalled. Paine offered to accompany him home to defend his record – a piece of embarrassing generosity that Monroe declined. Paine set off to find his own passage back to America, but, on hearing that Monroe's ship had been searched at sea by the British, he decided to return to Paris. He would wait for a revolution in England.

By now he was guest of the Bonnevilles who had offered to put him up for a week or two: he stayed for five years. One day he received a visit from General Bonaparte, who allegedly told Paine that he always slept with a copy of *Rights of Man* under his pillow, and that a statue of gold ought to be erected to him 'in every city in the universe.' He invited Paine to visit him soon to discuss the scheme he had put forward for the invasion of England by gunboat. Paine's proposals were published in two articles in Bonneville's *le Bien informé*, but in the event the Directory despatched Bonaparte to Egypt instead. Paine did not comment publicly on Bonaparte's *coup d'état* of *18 Brumaire*, nor on the death of Washington. Nor did he stay in France long enough to see the proclamation of the Empire. When in January 1801 Jefferson succeeded Adams as President, Paine asked that he should be allowed to serve the new administration in Paris, or alternatively travel home in an American warship.[28]

Jefferson offered him a passage in the sloop *Maryland*, but Paine decided to wait for the ship bringing the new ambassador, Robert Livingston, to France. It was not until late autumn that Paine at last landed at Baltimore. Livingston jokingly advised him to make his will, leaving 'the mechanics, the iron bridge, the wheels and so forth to America, and your religion to France'. But Jefferson received Paine in Washington and took his arm in public; and on Independence Day 1803, Paine was guest of honour at a banquet in New York. Most of his fellow Americans, however, could not forgive him for his *Age of Reason* or for his *Letter to George Washington*. One drunken American tried to kill him by discharging a musket at him, as he sat by a window on his farm at New Rochelle. The hero of 1776, whose writings had inspired the victory at Trenton, was now refused a seat in the Trenton stage-coach, and denied a vote in the mid-term Congressional elections on the grounds that he was not an American citizen.[29]

The Bonneville family, who followed him to America, still befriended him, but he did feel forsaken, and told one visitor that he regretted returning to America. Posterity has dealt with him more kindly. He may not have built his iron bridge across either the Seine or the Delaware, but his literary and political career spanned the Atlantic, and formed a bridge between the American and French Revolutions. As he wrote while still in France: 'An army of principles will penetrate where an army of soldiers cannot; it will succeed where diplomatic management would fail; it is neither the Rhine, nor the Channel, nor the Ocean that can arrest its progress; it will march on the horizon of the world, and it will conquer.'[30]

6 Burke's Grasshoppers: Dr Price as 'Apostle of Liberty'

On a Sunday in May 1791, Joseph Priestley preached a funeral sermon in the Unitarian meeting-house at Hackney. It was a pulpit normally occupied by Dr Richard Price, but once a year Price asked Priestley to preach a sermon for him, and it so happened that the date appointed in 1791 fell a few days after Price's death. In his tribute to Price, Priestley reminded his hearers that the French National Assembly – what he called 'the most august assembly in the world' – had styled Price 'the apostle of liberty'. Then, with typical British practicality, Priestley turned to Price's warning to his own countrymen of 'the danger arising from the increasing weight of the *national debt*'. The debt, Priestley added, had for a long time alarmed only Price himself, but all could now see that it 'must work either our reformation or our ruin'. Yet (claimed Priestley) Price's political pamphlets were even more influential than his exhortations on financial matters: 'In the writings of Dr Price, citizens may ever see their rights, and magistrates their duty.'[1]

Richard Price is best remembered for provoking Edmund Burke into issuing his famous indictment of the French Revolution. The full title of Burke's work, published in 1790, was: *Reflections on the Revolution in France, and on the Proceedings in certain Societies in London relative to that Event*. Burke's particular target was the London Revolution Society, whose congratulatory address to the French National Assembly had been warmly acknowledged by the French. Of course, Burke knew that the 'Revolution' of the society's title referred to the Glorious Revolution, not the Revolution of 1789. As he wrote in the opening pages of the *Reflections*:

> I find, upon inquiry, that on the anniversary of the Revolution in 1688, a club of dissenters, but of what denomination I know not, have long had the custom of hearing a sermon in one of their churches; and that afterwards they spend the day cheerfully, as other clubs do, at the tavern.

Pretending to address his pamphlet to a Frenchman, and through him to the National Assembly in Paris, Burke warns the Assembly against according any official status to the proceedings of so private a club.[2]

The address does indeed read more as an international manifesto than as a private communication:

> The Society for commemorating the Revolution in Great Britain, disdaining national partialities, and rejoicing in every triumph of liberty and justice over arbitrary power, offer to the National Assembly of France their congratulations on the Revolution in that country, and on the prospect it gives to the two first kingdoms in the world, of a common participation in the blessings of civil and religious liberty.

The address goes on to express 'particular satisfaction' at the 'glorious example' which the French have given to encourage other nations 'to assert the unalienable rights of mankind', and thus to bring about 'a general reformation in the governments of Europe and to make the world free and happy'.[3]

It was Price who had proposed the sending of the congratulatory address to mark the publication of a sermon he had delivered to the London Revolution Society on 4 November 1789, at the dissenting meeting-house in Old Jewry. He had taken his text from Psalm 122: 'Our feet shall stand within thy gates, O Jerusalem . . .' and his theme was 'Love of Our Country'. After commending the 'three chief blessings of human nature' as truth, virtue and liberty, Price urged that 'our first concern, as lovers of our country, must be to enlighten it'. He proposed to greet George III's recovery from illness with the wish that the King will henceforth 'consider yourself as more properly the *Servant* than the *Sovereign* of your people'. The bulk of the sermon is devoted to imperfections remaining in the British constitution after the expulsion of James II. The remarks about Louis XVI's France occupy only the last two-and-a-half pages of a 51-page address – though (when printed) the text of the French Declaration of Rights was attached as an appendix. Price speaks approvingly of 30 million Frenchmen 'demanding liberty with an irresistible voice; their king led in triumph, and an arbitrary monarch surrendering himself to his subjects'. He expresses gratitude that 'after sharing in the benefits of one Revolution, I have been spared to be a witness to two other Revolutions, both glorious'. And he calls on the 'oppressors of the world' to recognize that a new age has dawned: 'Restore to mankind their rights; and consent to the correction of abuses before they and you are destroyed together.'[4]

Richard Price had been ordained to the Presbyterian ministry at the age of 21. By 1789, now aged 66, he was Unitarian pastor of the Gravel-pit Meeting House at Hackney, where Priestley would not only preach the funeral sermon, but also succeed Price as minister. Burke condemns pulpit-politics: 'No sound ought to be heard in the church but the healing voice of Christian charity. The cause of civil liberty and civil government gains as little as that of religion by this confusion of duties.' What alarms Burke about Price is his claim that English liberties date from 1688. In his sermon Price had argued that the 1688 Revolution had given the people three fundamental rights: freedom of conscience in religious matters, the right to resist the abuse of power and finally 'the right to choose our governors; to cashier them for misconduct; and to frame a government for ourselves.' Burke dismisses these claims as 'this new, and hitherto unheard-of bill of rights.'[5]

Price's arguments, Burke suggests, have more to do with the execution of Charles I and the storming of the Bastille than with the 1688 Revolution, whose principles (if they are to be found anywhere) are embodied in the Declaration of Right. That Act, Burke reminds us, was entitled 'An Act for declaring the rights and liberties of the subject and for *settling* the *succession* of the crown.' (Burke's italics.) Neither the invitation to William and Mary, nor the Act of Settlement in 1701 providing for their failure to produce an heir, infringed (in Burke's eyes) the principle of hereditary succession. He would once have ignored Price's arguments, but now, Burke tells his imaginary French friend:

> We ought not, on either side of the water, to suffer ourselves to be imposed upon by the counterfeit wares which some persons by a double fraud export to you in illicit bottoms, as raw commodities of British growth, though wholly alien to our soil, in order afterwards to smuggle them back again into this country, manufactured after the newest Paris fashion of an improved liberty.[6]

Thus Burke makes clear his true preoccupation. Despite the literary device of addressing his remarks to a Frenchman, it is not the revolution in Paris that concerns him, but the risk of revolution in England. In Burke's words: 'Whenever our neighbour's house is on fire, it cannot be amiss for the engines to play a little on our own.' Yet in an equally memorable metaphor, Burke summarily dismisses Price and his flock:

> Because half a dozen grasshoppers under a fern make the field ring with their importunate chink, whilst thousands of great cattle reposed

beneath the shadow of the British oak, chew the cud and are silent, pray do not imagine that those who make the noise are the only inhabitants of the field; that, of course, they are many in number; or that, after all, they are other than the little, shrivelled, meagre, hopping, though loud and troublesome insects of the hour.

That famous passage occurs half-way through Part I of the *Reflections*. It makes one wonder why so much rhetorical fire-power should be brought to bear on grasshoppers. What was there about Richard Price that made it so important to assert his insignificance? Why, despite protestations to the contrary, does Burke take him so seriously?[7]

Price was admittedly not just a dissenting minister, but (like Priestley) a Fellow of the Royal Society. He owed his election to his work on mathematical probability. He had written a number of pamphlets on actuarial topics, and had declined an invitation to edit the works of Sir Isaac Newton. He had also declined a more interesting invitation. On 6 October 1778, the American Continental Congress resolved to instruct its three commissioners, Benjamin Franklin, John Adams and Arthur Lee, to inform Dr Price that 'it is the desire of Congress to consider him as a citizen of the United States and to receive his assistance in regulating their finances'. The resolution included an assurance that, if Price felt he could bring his family to live in America and could render such assistance, Congress would make 'generous provision ... for requiting his services'. That was more than ten years before Price preached his Old Jewry sermon. His importance in the eyes of the French revolutionaries lay in the fact that he was already a hero of the American Revolution.[8]

Price's first pamphlet in support of the American colonists was *Observations on the Nature of Civil Liberty, the Principles of Government and the Justice of the War with America*, published in February 1776. It went through a dozen London editions in a year, and was republished in Philadelphia, Boston, New York and Charleston. In his preface to the fifth edition in May 1776, Price claimed political kinship with John Locke: 'The principles on which I have argued form the foundation of every state as far as it is free; and are the same with those taught by Mr Locke.' In Part I of the *Observations*, Price defines government as the 'creature of the people'. He continues: 'It is conducted under their direction and has in view nothing but their happiness.' By contrast, Price scornfully suggests, the theory of Divine Right 'represents mankind as vassals formed to descend like cattle from one set of owners to another'.[9]

It is in this first part of his *Observations* that Price conjures up a vision of a United States of Europe. He pictures 'a general confederacy' presided over by a senate made up of 'representatives from all the different states'. This senate would have the power of 'managing all the common concerns of the united states, and of judging and deciding between them, as a common arbiter or umpire in all disputes', while having the assistance of 'the common force of all states to support its decisions'. There are obvious similarities to the American Articles of Confederation, drawn up in 1777, though not ratified until 1781.[10]

In Part II of the *Observations*, Price turns to consider the War of Independence. Upon what, he asks, is Britain's claim to superior power based:

> Is it our wealth? This never confers real dignity. On the contrary, its effect is always to debase, intoxicate and corrupt. Is it the number of our people? The colonies will soon be equal to us in numbers. Is it our knowledge and virtue? They are probably equally knowing and more virtuous.

And if Britain's claim was based on the fact that she was the mother country or 'parent state', then we were unnaturally possessive parents. Price also ridicules claims based on territorial ownership: 'If sailing along a coast can give a right to a country, then might the people of Japan become, as soon as they please, the proprietors of Britain.'[11]

Price asserts the inviolability of the colonial charters, which 'if any power on earth may change without their consent, that power may likewise, if it thinks proper, deliver them over to the Grand Seignior'. But constitutional propriety apart, the attempt to coerce the colonies will be counter-productive. The outcome, Price warns, will be the destruction of Britain's profitable transatlantic trade, the ruin of her navy and the collapse of her system of paper money. In Price's view, 'a kingdom on an edge so perilous should think of nothing but a retreat.' Since Englishmen are unwilling to enlist, and 'the attempt to procure armies of Russians, Indians and Canadians having miscarried', the British forces will be outnumbered by 'determined men fighting on their own ground, within sight of their houses and families'. In such a situation, the author reminds us, 'a handful is a match for millions'.[12]

The navy, 'could it sail at land as it does at sea', might achieve something. As it is, all that the navy can do is to blockade the American ports, thus (Price thinks) doing the colonists 'unspeakable good by preserving them from the evils of luxury and the temptations of wealth'. In all the necessities of life, America was self-sufficient, and Britons would do well to live less luxuriously too. It was a time for national repentance:

> From one end of North America to the other they are fasting and praying. But what are we doing? We are ridiculing them as fanatics and scoffing at religion. We are running wild after pleasure and forgetting everything serious and decent at masquerades. We are trafficking for boroughs, perjuring ourselves at elections, and selling ourselves for places. Which side then is Providence likely to favour?

And he bluntly asks: 'Instead of contending for a controlling power over the governments of America, should you not think more of watching and reforming your own?'[13]

The *Observations* sold over 60,000 copies in six months, and was translated into German, French and Dutch. Although it urged the British Government to disengage itself from a potentially disastrous war, it also implicitly recognized the inevitability of American independence: 'In 50 or 60 years they will be double our number and form a mighty empire, consisting of a variety of states all equal or superior to ourselves.' There was a rash of pamphlets in reply – most of them hostile and many of them by writers in the pay of the government. A more weighty critic was John Wesley, who recorded in his *Journal*: 'I began an answer to that dangerous tract, Dr Price's *Observations upon Liberty*, which, if practised, would overturn all government and bring in universal anarchy.' So vigorous was the critical response, that Price wrote *Additional Observations*. It appeared early in 1777 and was addressed to the Lord Mayor, Aldermen and Commons of the City of London, who had honoured him by presenting him with a gold snuff-box and granting him freedom of their city.[14]

While deploring the notion that he could be considered 'an advocate for a pure democracy', Price nevertheless re-emphasizes the contractual nature of government. Magistrates are to him mere employees of the state and are 'no less properly servants of the public than the labourers who work upon its roads or the soldiers who fight its battles'; similarly a king is 'only the first executive officer'. Although he pledges support for the British constitution, Price makes clear how far it falls short of his ideal – and he repeats his earlier assertion that the American war will make the British political system even more rickety. He concludes with a plea for reconciliation, while recognizing that it may already be too late: 'America may have formed an alliance with France. And the die may be cast.'[15]

France did not formally ally with the Americans until the following year. By then Price had republished his first two American tracts in a single pamphlet, together with a 'General Introduction and Supplement'. He had been stung by Burke's critical (though anonymous) reference in his famous *Letter to the Sheriffs of Bristol*; and Price was similarly incensed by the Archbishop of York's disparaging reference in a published sermon to 'some loose opinions which have lately been current on two very important subjects, religious and civil liberty'. In responding to the Archbishop, Price predicts the future glory of the colonies:

> A great people likely to be formed, in spite of all our efforts, into free communities under governments which have no religious tests and establishments! A new era in future annals and a new opening in human affairs beginning among the descendants of Englishmen in a new world. A rising empire extended over an immense continent without bishops, without nobles and without kings.[16]

By the time Price produced his *third* pamphlet on America, Britain's defeat had been enshrined in the 1783 Treaty of Paris. In March 1784 he published *Observations on the Importance of the American Revolution and the Means of Making it a Benefit to the World*. It was originally written for American readers, and was dedicated to 'the Free and United States of America', but he soon published an English edition (1785) to forestall pirating. While professing to see 'the hand of Providence in the late war working for the general good', he also speaks in the authentic accents of the Age of Reason. He lists the major discoveries of what he calls 'the present age of increased light' and likens the success of the American Revolution to Newton's formulation of the laws of universal gravitation. He goes even further in claiming that 'next to the introduction of Christianity among mankind, the American revolution may prove the most important step in the progressive course of human development'.[17]

The author nevertheless has some advice to proffer. In a section entitled 'Of the means of Promoting Human Improvement and Happiness in the United States', he starts with recommendations for reducing the national debt; but these proposals imply a period of peace. The existing Articles of Confederation, which had loosely held the states together during the war, are insufficient to preserve the union in peacetime: 'Without all doubt the powers of Congress must be enlarged.' He does not want a standing army, but he thinks Congress should have power to call out quotas from the state militias 'to force at once the compliance of any state which may show an inclination to break the union by resisting its decisions'. And in order to ensure that the burdens of keeping the peace are shared equally, he proposes a periodic census. Both provisions would be embodied in the Federal Constitution.[18]

Price's next objective is to ensure religious toleration. Governments, he argues, 'go miserably out of their proper province whenever they take upon them the care of truth'. Their role should rather be to encourage their citizens to 'search for truth wherever they can find it', and to protect them in their quest from 'the attacks of malevolence and bigotry'. But toleration does not imply the devaluing of religious belief: 'Atheism is so repugnant to every principle of common sense that it is not possible it should ever gain much ground or become very prevalent.' What he condemns are hierarchical religious establishments, and he contrasts the state of established religion in England with the clause in the Massachusetts constitution which accords 'every denomination of Christians' the equal protection of the laws. Price would have preferred to extend the protection to 'all men of all religions', and the Bill of Rights annexed to the Federal Constitution did in the event guarantee that Congress would make 'no law respecting an establishment of religion, or prohibiting the free exercise thereof'.[19]

After commending what he calls 'a wise and liberal plan of education' to buttress the liberties he is seeking to defend, Price exposes the shortcomings of traditional schemes of schooling, which had led to 'a contraction, not an enlargement of the intellectual faculties'. And in accents that echo those of Rousseau, and herald those of Wordsworth, Price claims that, were he offered the choice between 'the plain sense of a common and untutored man, or the deep erudition of the proud scholars and professors in most universities', he would unhesitatingly choose the former. Price concludes with a swift recapitulation of the practical difficulties facing the infant American republic. Besides the need to redeem the national debt and enlarge the powers of Congress, there is also a need to ensure the equal distribution of property, to abolish hereditary titles and to avoid undue dependence on foreign trade. In words resembling President Washington's famous Farewell Address, Price asks: 'Thus singularly happy, why should they seek connections with Europe and expose themselves to the dangers of being involved in its quarrels?' He urges Americans to avoid dependence on luxury goods and instead to show the 'disdain for tinsel in which true dignity consists'. He does not expect that the Americans will quickly abolish slavery or the slave trade, but 'till they have done this, it will not appear they deserve the liberty for which they have been contending'.[20]

In this third pamphlet on transatlantic politics, Price shows he is aware of the significance of events in America for the reform movement in France. Whatever the impact of the American example, France's participation in the American war had irredeemably unbalanced French finances, as Turgot, Louis XVI's Controller-General from 1774 to 1776, had predicted. And it is a letter from Turgot, written to Price in March 1778, which is published as an appendix to Price's *Observations on the Importance of the American Revolution*. Turgot criticizes the new constitutions of the 13 colonies, which he thinks are too closely modelled on the British pattern of King, Lords and Commons, while the union of the states is too loose. It is, he adds disparagingly, 'only a copy of the Dutch republic'.[21]

Turgot is realistic enough to note the diverse interests that have to be reconciled within a federal system, and he points prophetically to the southern negroes 'whose slavery is incompatible with a good political constitution'. Also prophetically, Turgot emphasizes the importance of controlled westward expansion:

> I imagine that the Americans must aggrandise themselves not by war, but by agriculture. If they neglect the immense deserts which are at their backs, and which extend all the way to the western sea, their exiles and their fugitives from the security of the laws will unite with the savages and settle that part of the country.

Fortunately not even life in the Wild West would quite measure up to his prediction that 'bodies of banditti will savage America, as the barbarians of the North savaged the Roman Empire'. Turgot ends his letter on a more encouraging note, with an epitome of the Americans' destiny: 'They are the hope of the world. They may become a model to it.' And in words that pre-empt the sentiments of the well-known inscription on the Statue of Liberty, Turgot predicts: 'The asylum they open to the oppressed of all nations should console the earth.'[22]

The Frenchman asks Price to treat his letter as confidential and not to answer it by post, 'for your letter will certainly be opened at our post-offices, and I shall be found too great a friend of liberty for a minister, even though a discarded minister'. By 1784 Turgot was dead, and Price could explain in a footnote that he regarded publication of the letter as 'a duty which I owe to his memory, as well as to the United States and the world'. Benjamin Franklin, whom Price consulted, approved the idea of publication, though it goaded John Adams, America's first Vice-President, into writing his *Defence of the Constitutions of the United States of America against the attacks of M. Turgot*. (Price would send Adams a copy of his Old Jewry sermon, which the Vice-President acknowledged, applauding 'the zeal and the spirit which dictates this discourse', but admitting misgivings over a French republic 'of thirty million atheists'.)[23]

Price had written to Franklin in December 1780 that there was 'nothing in the conduct of my life that I reflect upon with more satisfaction than the part I have taken in the dispute with America, and the endeavours I have used to serve and warn my country'. And in a later letter acknowledging Franklin's gift of 'a case for an air balloon and a print', and remarking that 'the discovery of air balloons seems to make the present time a new epoch', Price added that he looked upon the American Revolution as 'one of the most important events in the history of the world'. Aptly enough, the first manned balloon flight and the signing of the treaty that ratified American independence both took place in Paris in the same year – 1783.[24]

Two years later, by which time Jefferson had succeeded Franklin in Paris, the future President of the United States wrote to Price commending the first edition of *Observations on the Importance of the American Revolution*. Price had expressed regret that the pamphlet had been so badly received in the South. Jefferson replied reassuringly that Price could expect few readers 'southward of the Chesapeake' to sympathize with his views on slavery, but he should not be discouraged. 'What you have written,' Jefferson insisted, 'will do a great deal of good and could you still trouble yourself with our welfare, no man is more able to give aid to the labouring side.' Indeed Jefferson wondered whether Price could write an address to the young men of William and Mary College. Price declined the invitation, saying that he had stopped writing on politics. He turned down a similar invitation to write an address for 'the United States and Congress', explaining in a letter to Benjamin Rush: 'I am by no means a Franklin who, at 80, preserves so wonderfully his abilities and vigour but a poor weak creature who, at 63, finds himself under the necessity of considering the working time of his life almost over.'[25]

Yet in September 1787, as the Constitutional Convention continued its debates in Philadelphia, Price was writing to Franklin with news of the beginnings of European revolution:

I refer principally to what is now passing in Holland, Brabant and France. This spirit originated in America, and should it appear that it has terminated in a state of society more favourable to peace, virtue, science and liberty... infinite good will be done. Indeed a general fermentation seems to be taking place throughout Europe.

The concept of an 'Atlantic Revolution' was evidently not invented by historians. It was against this background that Price preached his Old Jewry sermon. Burke, in bringing his fire to bear on Dr Price of the London Revolution Society, was attacking a target worthy of his pen. Price may have declined to accept American citizenship, but in April 1781 he and George Washington were voted Doctors of Law at Yale on the same day; and when he published the Old Jewry sermon, Price recorded on the title page that he was not only Fellow of the Royal Society but 'Fellow of the American Philosophical Societies at Philadelphia and Boston'.[26]

Price died in April 1791. Priestley paid tribute to a man whose writings had made 'liberty appear more desirable, and tyranny more detestable', and whose death amid the early triumphs of the French Revolution might be compared to 'the death of a warrior in the moment of victory.' The *Gentleman's Magazine* was no less fulsome:

> Whenever History shall rise above the prejudice which may for a time darken her page, and celebrate the eras when men began to open their eyes to behold their own rights, and when this gave rise to the splendid Revolutions of America and France, the name of Price will be mentioned among those of Franklin, Washington, Fayette and Paine.

Price did not live long enough to enjoy the distinction of French citizenship, soon to be conferred on Priestley and Paine by the French Assembly, but when news of Price's death reached France, the French revolution societies went into mourning.[27]

7 Flammable Gas: Priestley as Propagandist

Joseph Priestley is best known as the discoverer of oxygen. Yet he claimed in a letter written shortly before his death in 1804 that scientific investigation was for him 'never more than of secondary consideration'. He saw his main life's work as the defence of 'rational Christianity' or Unitarianism – dubbed by Coleridge 'One-Goddism'. But it was the third strand in Priestley's career, his political involvement in the American and French Revolutions, and in the constitutional reform movement in England, that earned this Yorkshire weaver's son the nickname of 'Gunpowder Joe'. Priestley's *Essay on the First Principles of Government*, published in 1768, begins by asserting the fundamental axiom of the Enlightenment that knowledge is the key to progress: 'Whatever was the beginning of this world, the end will be glorious and *paradisiacal*, beyond what our imaginations can now conceive.' The role of government, he argues, is to assist 'this progress of the human species towards this glorious state'. His pamphlet is devoted to the examination of the 'fundamental principles' of government, and to a consideration of 'what is most conductive to the happiness of mankind'.[1]

Unitarian in religion, Priestley was evidently Utilitarian in his political philosophy. In words that pre-empt Bentham's description of God as the Great Utilitarian, Priestley wrote:

> To a mind not warped by theological and metaphysical subtleties, the Divine Being appears to be actuated by no other views than the noblest we can conceive, the happiness of his creatures. Virtue and right conduct consist in those affections and actions which terminate in the public good...

Bentham read Priestley's pamphlet while still a young barrister in chambers, and later recorded that 'Priestley was the first (unless it was Beccaria) who taught my lips to pronounce this sacred truth – that the greatest happiness of the greatest number is the foundation of morals and legislation'. Bentham's first work, *Fragment on Government*, appeared anonymously in 1776, and so can scarcely have influenced the drafting of the Declaration of Independence, whereas the English translation of Beccaria's *Crimes and Punishments* was published in 1767, a year before Priestley's *First Principles of Government*. It is probably pointless to speculate on the precise provenance of the 'pursuit of happiness'; but we do know that Priestley's essay was widely read in America. It was later reprinted in Philadelphia, with a chapter on the government of the United States, and it was recommended by Thomas Jefferson himself.[2]

Jefferson and Priestley did not meet until 1797, three years after the Priestleys had settled in Northumberland, Pennsylvania. Jefferson was in Philadelphia for the inauguration of John Adams as President, and came to hear Priestley preach. Three years later, shortly before Jefferson himself became President, they began a correspondence. In a letter dated 18 January 1800, Jefferson thanks Priestley for copies of his pamphlets and others written by Thomas Cooper (the Manchester radical who had also settled in America) and comments: 'The papers of political arithmetic, both in your and Mr Cooper's pamphlet, are the most precious gifts that can be made to us; for we are running navigation-mad, and commerce-mad, and navy-mad, which is the worst of all.' Jefferson went on to ask Priestley's advice about the new university he was proposing to set up in Virginia, to remedy the shortcomings of William and Mary College.[3]

Writing again, just over a week later, Jefferson expresses the hope that he may contrive a meeting between Priestley and Dupont de Nemours, a French physiocrat and political refugee, from whom Jefferson had also sought advice on the establishment of his university: 'How much it would delight me if a visit from you at the same time were to show us two such illustrious foreigners embracing each other in my country as the asylum for whatever is great and good.' A year or so later, Jefferson is writing to convey his good wishes for Priestley's recovery from illness: 'Yours is one of the few lives precious to mankind, and for the continuance of which every thinking man is solicitous.' Jefferson was soon writing to Benjamin Rush and paying tribute to Priestley's *Socrates and Jesus Compared*, which the author had sent him. So Priestley's son does not seem to have been exaggerating when he wrote of his father's last years in America:

> He lived under an administration, the principles and practice of which he perfectly approved of, and with Mr Jefferson, the head of that administration he frequently corresponded, and they had for each other a mutual regard and esteem...[4]

The Priestleys' arrival in America in June 1794 had created a considerable sensation. An editorial in the *American Daily Advertiser* of

New York spoke of the gratification felt by 'every well-wisher to the rights of man, that the United States of America, the land of freedom and independence, has become the asylum of the greatest characters of the present age, who have been persecuted in Europe, merely because they have defended the rights of the enslaved nations'. The Governor called on Priestley the day after they landed, as did the Bishop of New York and many of the wealthier merchants. Addresses of welcome were presented by various delegations, including New York's Democratic Society, the Associated Teachers of the City of New York, the State Medical Society, and the Republican Natives of Great Britain and Ireland resident in New York. The teachers in their address hailed Priestley as a fellow-labourer in 'the arduous and important task of cultivating the human mind', and expressed the wish that he would 'find in this land of virtuous simplicity a happy recess from the intriguing politics and vitiating refinements of the European world'.[5]

The members of the Democratic Society, after expressing their 'ardent gratitude to the Great Parent of the universe' for their 'singular felicity in living in a land where reason has successfully triumphed over the artificial distinctions of European policy and bigotry', go on to 'rejoice that America opens her arms to receive, with fraternal affection, the friend of liberty and happiness'. This pride in the new republic, as an asylum for the friends of liberty, is echoed by the American Philosophical Society in an address signed by its President, David Rittenhouse:

> In this free and happy country, those unalienable rights, which the Author of nature committed to man as a sacred deposit, have been secured: here we have been enabled, under the favour of Divine Providence, to establish a government of laws, and not of men; a government which secures to its citizens equal rights and equal liberty; and which offers an asylum to the good, to the persecuted, and to the oppressed, of other climes.

In acknowledging this address, Priestley sought to dissuade the society from 'supposing that, at my time of life, and with the inconvenience attending a new and uncertain settlement, I can be of much service to it'. But he did also assert his confidence that republican governments 'in which every obstruction is removed to the exertions of all kinds of talents, will be far more favourable to science and the arts, than any monarchical government has ever been'.[6]

Not everyone was impressed with this exchange of compliments between Priestley and the learned societies of New York and

Philadelphia. William Cobbett, who was in Philadelphia at the time, launched a vituperative attack, claiming that Priestley's replies to the addresses of welcome were deliberately misleading, since he sought to 'impose himself on them for a sufferer in the cause of liberty'. Cobbett characterizes Priestley as 'one of those who entertained hopes of bringing about a Revolution in England upon the French plan'. And after describing the excesses of the French revolutionaries, Cobbett remarks: 'From scenes like these the mind turns for relief and consolation to the riot at Birmingham.' Priestley, he continues, is one of those 'system-mongers' for whom 'time, place, climate, nature itself must give way.' He wants 'the same government in every quarter of the globe' on the French model; and 'sooner than not see it established', Cobbett adds unfairly, 'I much question if he would not with pleasure see the massacre of all the human race.' It was Cobbett who dubbed Priestley 'the firebrand philosopher' and 'this apostle of sedition', claiming that Priestley was continuing to challenge established governments and to admire the 'woeful revolution in France'.[7]

No wonder President John Adams, who had met Priestley in England, had to intervene to dissuade Secretary of State Pickering from deporting 'the firebrand philosopher' under the 1798 Aliens Act. Meanwhile Priestley carefully avoided inflammatory statements or any kind of political involvement. He persisted with his works on theology and with attempts to reconcile his discovery of oxygen with the existence of phlogiston – and he even found a new interest in botany. But he declined all new honours: he rejected a professorship of chemistry at the University of Pennsylvania and the presidency of the American Philosophical Society, a post held by both Franklin and Jefferson.

Priestley had met Franklin in London, as he records in his *Memoirs*:

> Being introduced to Dr Price, Mr Canton, Dr Watson (the physician) and Dr Franklin, I was led to attend to the subject of experimental philosophy more than I had done before...I mentioned to Dr Franklin an idea that had occurred to me of writing a history of discoveries in electricity, which had been his favourite study. This I told him might be a useful work, and that I would willingly undertake it, provided I could be furnished with the books necessary for the purpose.

Franklin not only supplied the books, but gave Priestley a detailed account of the famous kite experiment he had carried out 15 years before. Indeed Priestley's *History of Electricity* has alone preserved the full story for posterity, since Franklin never published it himself. Franklin had a hand in Priestley's election as Fellow of the Royal Society in 1766; and it was to Franklin that the Council turned in 1767 'as the best judge present' of the electrical experiments which would earn Priestley the Society's Copley medal. In 1771, when Franklin was on a tour of the industrial towns of northern England, he called on Priestley, who was then living in Leeds as minister of the Mill Hill congregation. And it was Franklin who was largely responsible for persuading Priestley to publish his *Address to Protestant Dissenters*.[8]

The full title of this pamphlet, which appeared anonymously in London in 1774 was: *Address to Protestant Dissenters of All Denominations, on the Approaching Election of Members of Parliament, with Respect to the State of Public Liberty in General and of American Affairs in Particular*. The first part is devoted to urging Dissenters to vote for parliamentary candidates who favour the removal of religious tests. The second part begins:

> My Fellow Citizens,
> As your late representatives have acted as if they were representatives of all *North America*, and in that assumed capacity have engaged in measures which threaten nothing less than the ruin of the whole British empire, it were greatly to be wished that their successors might learn by their example to know themselves better, and keep within their proper province ...

He protested that he had nothing new to say on the subject; nevertheless he thought it worth while trying 'to comprise the merits of the case in a very small compass'.[9]

Priestley based his arguments on the nature and history of the British Constitution, on 'the nature of things and the principles of liberty in general', and on 'the effects which the oppression of America may have on the liberties of this country'. Arguing from the examples of Normandy, Wales and pre-Union Scotland – all of which had separate jurisdictions, though united under one king – he insists on the political autonomy of the colonies: 'It could not but have been understood that when many of our ancestors, the old *Puritans*, quitted the realm of England, they freed themselves from the laws of England. Indeed they could have had no other motive for leaving this country.' If they had transplanted many of the laws of England to their new territories, that was only because it suited them to do so: 'If they had preferred the laws of *Scotland*, those of *Ireland*, or those of any foreign country, they were at liberty to have done it.' Priestley denounces the Stamp Act as 'absolutely an innovation in our constitution', and claims that it 'even introduced a language quite new to us: viz. that of America being subject to England'. This is as absurd as saying that America is subject to Ireland or Hanover, instead of recognizing that all are 'equally subject to one king who is himself subject to the laws'.[10]

It was 'in this great principle', according to Priestley, that 'the very essence of our liberty, and the independent liberty of each part of the common empire consists'. If a country can be taxed without its consent, the people so taxed 'are in a state of as *absolute despotism* as any of which we read in history, or of which we can form an idea; since the same *foreign power* that can take *one penny* from them without their consent may take *the last penny* that they have'. Turning to the question of representation, Priestley responds to the claim that Leeds and Manchester are not represented in Parliament and yet are taxed by it. He points to an important difference:

> Those who tax Leeds, Manchester, etc., always tax themselves at the same time and in the same proportion ... To make the cases parallel, let parliament lay a separate tax on the towns that send no representatives, and exempt from such tax those that do send members. In this case I doubt not but that the unrepresented towns would complain as loudly as the Americans do now ...

If ever there was a justifiable case of resistance to government, Priestley claims, this was it: 'They are willing to be our *fellow subjects* having the same common head; but are not willing to be our *slaves*.'[11]

Priestley is not impressed by the argument that the colonists ought to bear the costs of defending them from the French: 'Have we not also protected Ireland, and the electorate of Hanover, without pretending either to make laws for them or to tax them?' The ministry resembled 'the man who would kill the hen that laid the golden eggs, in order that he might come at all the treasure at once'. Ought there not to be some reprisal for the damage done by the citizens of Boston to the property of the East India Company? Priestley agrees, but argues that 'reasonable people would have contented themselves with demanding *satisfaction*, and would not have punished the innocent with the guilty by *blocking up their port*.' As far as the consequences for England are concerned, if the British government succeeds in subduing the colonists and commanding the wealth of North America, will George III's ministers 'like to be so arbitrary *abroad*, and have their power confined *at home*?' But England may not win, and Priestley reminds his readers of the example of Philip II, 'who imagined that he could easily reduce the Belgic provinces by writing despatches from his closet', but who achieved only 'the independency of those provinces, and the ruin of Spain'.[12]

The *Address* ends with an exhortation to oppose at the next election every candidate who 'has concurred in the late atrocious attempts to establish arbitrary power over so great a part of the British empire'. The final sentence is a solemn warning:

It is only by justice, equity and generosity that nations, as well as individuals, can expect to flourish; and by the violation of them, both single persons and states, in the course of the righteous providence of God, involve themselves in disgrace and ruin.

In this struggle, Priestley has no doubt that God is on the side of the Americans.[13]

Franklin's own *Causes of the American Discontents* had been published in an edited form in the *London Chronicle* of 1768. It was intended to be conciliatory, and was much milder in tone than Priestley's pamphlet, even in the unexpurgated version that was published in America in 1774 as *The Causes of the Present Distractions in America Explained*. And for Tom Paine's powerful polemic, *Common Sense*, readers on both sides of the Atlantic would have to wait until January 1776. For Priestley, 1774 was his *annus mirabilis*. It was not only the year of his American pamphlet and the year of his discovery of oxygen; it was also the year in which he accompanied Lord Shelburne, his new patron, on a tour of the Netherlands, France and Germany. The offer of the post of librarian to Lord Shelburne had been made in 1772 – chiefly at the instigation of Richard Price, though probably with the help of Franklin too. The new appointment (which he held for several years) more than doubled his salary, provided him with a house at Calne near the Shelburne estate, and enabled him to spend the winter at Lord Shelburne's London home. The Earl provided Priestley with £40 a year for apparatus and materials; and it was in his newly equipped laboratory at Calne that the famous oxygen experiment took place on 1 August 1774. Within the month, Priestley set off on his European tour.[14]

While in Paris, Priestley not only dined with Lavoisier, but was entertained by the *philosophes*. As he records in his *Memoirs*:

I was told by some of them that I was the only person they had ever met with, of whose understanding they had any opinion, who

professed to believe Christianity. But on interrogating them on the
subject, I soon found that they had given no proper attention to it,
and did not really know what Christianity was.

Back in London, Priestley's employment with Lord Shelburne provided frequent opportunities for conversations with Franklin. In
Priestley's words: 'My winter's residence in London was the means
of improving my acquaintance with Dr Franklin. I was seldom many
days without seeing him, and being members of the same club we
constantly returned together.' The club was 'The Honest Whigs', a
group of Franklin's friends, who met on Thursday evenings and talked
'pretty formally, sometimes sensibly, and sometimes furiously', and
had supper at nine. In April, Franklin was writing to Priestley on the
combustible properties of marsh gas, and the same month they both
attended the new Unitarian chapel in Essex Street to hear Priestley's
friend, Theophilus Lindsey, preach.[15]

Franklin was to return to America in March 1775; and perhaps the
most eloquent testimony to his friendship with Priestley is that he
spent his last day in London alone with him, 'having given out that he
should leave London the day before'. Priestley records that much of
that day was spent in reading the American newspapers, with their
accounts of events in Boston, and that, as Franklin 'read the addresses
to the inhabitants of Boston from the places in the neighbourhood,
the tears trickled down his cheeks'. Priestley's greatest regret was that
he was unable to persuade Franklin of the truth of Christianity – even
in its Unitarian form. Franklin apparently admitted that he had not
given as much attention as he ought to have done to 'the evidences of
Christianity', and asked for a list of recommended books, promising to
read them and report his reactions. Priestley suggested Hartley's
writings and his own *Institutes of Natural and Revealed Religion*. But
he noted sadly: 'The American war breaking out soon after, I do not
believe that he ever found himself sufficiently at leisure for the
discussion.' The spectacle of the radical Dissenter, Priestley, striving
to convert the free-thinking Franklin to Christianity, is one of the
more improbable scenes in the story of transatlantic relationships in
the age of the American Revolution.[16]

The two men continued to exchange letters. In July 1775, Franklin
wrote that the colonists had 'not yet applied to any foreign power for
assistance, nor offered our commerce for their friendship.' Perhaps
they never would, though he added: 'It is natural to think of it, if we
are pressed.' Within a year Franklin found himself signing the

Declaration of Independence, and, six months after that, he was appointed one of three commissioners to the court of Louis XVI. In France he found little leisure for intellectual pursuits; but in February 1780 he wrote to Priestley from Passy: 'I am glad my little paper on the *Aurora Borealis* pleased. If it should occasion further enquiry and produce a better hypothesis, it will not be wholly useless.' And in June 1782 he wrote: 'I should rejoice much if I could once more recover the leisure to search with you into the works of nature.' Another two years were to elapse before Franklin was able to secure Priestley's election as a member of the *Académie des Sciences*. As he reported to Price in August 1784, he had mentioned Priestley's name as a candidate for the Academy 'upon every vacancy that has happened since my residence here, and the place has never been bestowed more worthily'.[17]

Priestley was honoured in France for his political principles no less than for his scientific discoveries. The founding in June 1791 of the Birmingham Constitutional Society – 'similar to that in Manchester', as Priestley explained it – had been followed on 14 July by a dinner in Birmingham to celebrate the anniversary of the fall of the Bastille. This was the occasion of the riots that destroyed what Priestley called 'the most truly valuable and useful apparatus of philosophical instruments that perhaps any individual, in this or any other country, was ever possessed of'. While Josiah Wedgwood and James Watt helped to replace the lost apparatus, Priestley received messages of sympathy and support not only from the French Academy of Sciences, but also from the Society of the Friends of the Constitution 'sitting at the Jacobins, Paris.' The Jacobin address hailed him as 'the victim of the interest which you have taken in the cause of human nature, triumphant in the greatest revolution which ever occurred'. Detractors had obscured with cloud the glory of the French Revolution, but 'You, Sir, penetrated this cloud, and drew from it some sparks of light, which, since, have not ceased to illuminate the nations.' Thus Priestley's name (the address continued) 'already dear in Europe, to all who cultivate the arts, or who improve their reason, becomes particularly dear to Frenchmen.'[18]

Priestley admitted that he derived 'much satisfaction as it appeared that the friends of liberty, civil and religious, were of opinion that I was a sufferer in that cause'. In August 1792 he had French citizenship conferred on him, in company with Bentham, Paine and Thomas Clarkson. But when several French *départéments* invited him to represent them in the National Convention, he declined. As he later explained: 'I thought myself more usefully employed at home, and that I was but ill qualified for a business which required knowledge which none but a native of the country could possess.' So he stayed on in London, lecturing at the new Dissenters College established at Hackney. He nevertheless decided to exploit the good opinion he enjoyed in France, by publishing a series of *Letters to the Philosophers and Politicians of France, on the subject of Religion*. And it was in a preface to a sermon preached in London in 1794 – a 'Fast Sermon' comparing the present state of Europe with ancient prophecies – that he explained his decision finally to leave England and settle in America.[19]

In the preface, he admits that after the Birmingham riots he considered emigrating immediately, and that he thought first of France 'on account of its nearness to England and the agreeableness of its climate and my having many friends there'. His decision now to settle in America was prompted by the fact that his three sons had already emigrated, and that he had sent them all his property except his 'library, apparatus and household goods.' In going to join them, he hopes that 'Providence may yet, advancing in years as I am, find me some sphere of usefulness along with them.' In the *Memoirs* he says simply, 'I thought my removal would be of more service to the cause of truth than my longer stay in England.' While at sea, he found time to write *Observations on the Cause of the present Prevalence of Infidelity*, which he published as a preface to a new edition of the *Letters to the Philosophers and Politicians of France*. He also published, soon after his arrival in Pennsylvania, his *Third part of Letters to a Philosophical Unbeliever*, in answer to Tom Paine's *Age of Reason*.[20]

In his *Letters to the Right Honourable Edmund Burke* (1791) Priestley had written that the Americans

> sensible of more evils attending their former government than our ancestors at the [1688] Revolution, ventured to do a great deal more, and set a glorious example to France and to the whole world. They formed a completely new government on the principles of *equal liberty* and the *rights of men*, 'without nobles', as Dr Price expressively and happily said, 'without bishops, and without a king'.

Priestley would later say, of his arrival with his wife at New York, that Mrs Priestley never felt herself more at home in her life. But when his wife died in 1796, Priestley did not take American citizenship, expressing the hope that he might one day 'find a grave ... in the land that gave me birth'.[21]

In November 1800 he made up his mind to sail for France, where he had property, as soon as there was 'free and safe communication'.

But illness kept him in America. He had evidently not entirely abandoned the idea as late as June 1801, when he wrote to Theophilus
Lindsey: 'Mr Russell is just sailed for France, after urging me to
accompany him; but I have no thoughts of leaving this quiet asylum
until there be a settled peace.' 1801 was the first year of Jefferson's
presidency, and on the very first day of 1803 Priestley wrote again to
Lindsey:

> I think, however, as well of this country as of any in the world;
> especially since the election of Mr Jefferson.... You will see by his
> message to Congress that, though all the internal taxes are abo-
> lished, a great proportion of the national debt was discharged last
> year, and we have no war except with Tripoli, which does not give us
> much uneasiness.[22]

Priestley shared with Paine the distinction of being burned in effigy
by English mobs, being elected to French citizenship, and being
buried on American soil. But perhaps more surely than Paine, Priestley found in Jefferson's America his true spiritual home. At the end of
a letter written in February 1802, Priestley had added a postscript
declaring that Jefferson was 'everything that the friends of Liberty
could wish'. And a fortnight before his death, Priestley wrote to
another correspondent:

> Tell Mr Jefferson that I think myself happy to have lived under his
> excellent administration; and that I have a prospect of dying in it. It
> is, I am confident, the best on the face of the earth, and yet I hope
> to rise to something more excellent still.

He died on 6 February 1804. We trust that he was not disappointed.[23]

8 Land-agent of Liberty: South Carolina's Thomas Cooper

President John Adams's dismissive description of Thomas Cooper as 'a talented mad-cap' scarcely does justice to a remarkable transatlantic career. Born in the year Voltaire published *Candide*, Cooper was the son of a wealthy Manchester industrialist. He read law at Oxford, though without taking a degree. On the strength of attending a clinical course at the Middlesex hospital, and observing veterinary dissections at Clerkenwell, he became assistant to a Manchester physician. His own interest in industrial chemistry, and his support for religious toleration, brought him the friendship of Joseph Priestley; and at Priestley's suggestion he crossed the Atlantic to reconnoitre a suitable refuge for what Priestley called 'the friends of liberty'.

Cooper had emerged as a friend of liberty himself at the age of 28, with his *Letters on the Slave Trade*. Appearing first in Wheeler's *Manchester Chronicle* in 1787, the 'letters' were published in an amended form later that year. Cooper had decided that too much had been written on the question for it 'to be properly attended to by those who have not leisure to read much'. So he himself would provide a summary of the methods of procuring slaves, the tasks they are required to perform, and the way they are treated by their masters. He describes the rigours of plantation life after the first two years of 'seasoning', and instances the inhumanities of the plantation penal laws. He calculates that only one negro out of 14 survives capture and transportation, and that one third of the survivors die during seasoning. Appealing to Abbé Raynal's statement that nine million slaves had been 'consumed' by Europeans, and allowing for a lapse of ten years since Raynal wrote, Cooper computes the true figure for negro deaths at an astonishing 180 million. We do not have to accept Cooper's arithmetic in order to share his indignation. Why, he asks, have so many negroes died? His answer: 'That the Gentlefolk of Europe, (my friend) may drink sugar to their tea.'[1]

To give practical point to his campaign, Cooper became a committee member of the newly formed Manchester Society for the Abolition of the Slave Trade, and in February 1788 a petition carrying 10 000 Manchester signatures was forwarded to Parliament. His fellow Mancunian, Thomas Walker, later said of Cooper that he was a man whose talents and learning were 'uniformly devoted to the great interests of mankind'. Among those interests was religious toleration. In 1789 the Test and Corporation Acts (which debarred non-Anglicans from holding public office) were under attack. But the supporters of repeal were divided, and Cooper was among those who wanted to broaden the campaign by extending toleration to Unitarians. That famous Unitarian, Joseph Priestley, not only invited Cooper and Walker to dine with him in Birmingham, to discuss the removal of religious disabilities, but also tried (unsuccessfully) to secure Cooper's election as Fellow of the Royal Society. He claimed that Cooper's knowledge of chemistry and philosophy exceeded his own.[2]

The year 1789 also saw Cooper involved in the campaign for parliamentary reform. He attended a meeting of Dr Price's London Revolution Society, and, next to Walker, was the leading spirit of the Manchester Constitutional Society, founded in October 1790. The Society's statement of principles included the assertion that laws can only be enacted by the majority, expressed 'by means of a full, fair and adequate representation'. But when, in July 1791, the Society celebrated Bastille Day with a dinner, it was careful to stipulate that no question of English politics should be raised and that no cockade or badge should be worn. Cooper was soon to meet the wearers of badges and cockades on French soil. He would later claim that the weeks he spent in Paris in the spring of 1792, at the age of 33, were the happiest of his life. He arrived in France with James Watt Junior in March. Watt was there on business, and Cooper, though avowedly only on holiday, had at least one eye on the use in French industry of chemical bleaching processes, which he would introduce into his own calico business. In April, Watt and Cooper were authorized by the Manchester Constitutional Society to make contact with the patriotic societies of France with a view to starting a cross-Channel correspondence. On 13 April they presented the Society's fraternal address to the Jacobin Club of Paris.[3]

The address spoke of the coalition of despotic monarchs that was forming 'to overwhelm the cause of liberty and annihilate the rights of man', and explained that the Manchester patriots wished to express solidarity with the French societies in their revolutionary cause – 'the cause not merely of the French, but of all mankind'. The Manchester Society also wished to initiate correspondence as a step towards 'a general federation among the Patriotic Societies of Europe', and the address ended by encouraging Frenchmen to proceed with their 'philanthropic exertions' against tyrants, for the benefit of mankind. The Jacobin Club's reply made tactful reference to the recent centenary of the English Bill of Rights, and added (less tactfully) that the French had imitated the English example 'with a degree of perfection which doubtless heretofore, you were not permitted to attain'. As a sign of their fraternal feelings, the Jacobin Society reported that the British flag, 'united and entwined with the three-coloured flag of France and the thirteen stripes of the brave Americans, is suspended from the roofs of almost every patriotic society in France'.[4]

In a covering letter, the Vice-President and two secretaries of the Jacobin Club picture themselves 'hastening to commence that sublime alliance which will one day unite all the inhabitants of the globe'. Cooper and Watt returned the compliment by joining in a procession to the Champs de Mars, with Watt carrying a British flag and Cooper a bust of Algernon Sidney. Cooper wrote to Walker that the occasion was 'the first festival truly civic that Europe has seen'. The Jacobin Club had not yet been captured by Robespierre, and Cooper had more in common with another member, the Girodin Brissot, campaigner against the slave trade and founder-member of *Les Amis des Noirs*. A year later Cooper would feel sure enough of his friendship with Brissot to provide a letter of introduction to him for the American, Gilbert Imlay.[5]

Cooper returned to England in May 1792 to find that he and Watt had been attacked in Parliament by Edmund Burke. In a debate on parliamentary reform, Burke condemned as enemies of the Constitution those societies that had recommended Paine's *Rights of Man*, naming Cooper and Watt as would-be allies of the Jacobins. Cooper's response was to publish the text of the Manchester Address and the French reply, while the Manchester Society published a declaration disclaiming any intention of overthrowing the British Government. They wanted (they said) to restore the constitution to 'its original purity, by removing the corruptions and abuses that deform it'. Cooper's language was less measured. His pamphlet (*A Reply to Mr Burke's Invective against Mr Cooper and Mr Watt*) appeared in Manchester that summer. London editions followed in 1792 and 1793. Burke had called the Jacobins traitors and regicides, but Cooper reports that 'the King of France is alive, and chooses his ministers from among the members of this very Society'. In view of later events, Cooper's description of the early Jacobins raises a grim smile: 'They do nothing but debate political subjects, and now and then direct the publication of a political discourse.' As to the implication that the Manchester delegates were guilty of sedition, Cooper retorts: 'I appeal to the facts, I deny the charge and I challenge the proof.'[6]

Cooper cannot see that there is anything wrong with writing letters: 'Is there any impropriety in the *philosophical* societies of London, Paris or Stockholm corresponding for the improvement of chemistry, or experimental philosophy?' If not, he asks, why should it be improper to correspond on political subjects? Cooper lists 48 French patriotic societies outside Paris, and claims that the letters to and from these societies 'have been regularly printed for public information'. There could be nothing treasonable about such communication, since England and France were not then enemies 'as Britain and America were when Mr Burke corresponded with Dr Franklin and Mr Laurens'. If it is a crime to wish earnestly 'the fraternal Union of all Men, for the Empire of Peace, and the happiness of Mankind', then the Manchester Society and its deputies 'must plead guilty to the charge'. Cooper quotes from Price's famous sermon 'On the Love of Our Country' (which had provoked Burke into writing his *Reflections on the Revolution in France*) and appeals from Burke to the people – 'the only class of the community worth appealing to'. Burke had made a contemptuous reference to 'the Swinish Multitude', and Cooper is not going to let anyone forget it: in the pamphlet's 80-odd pages, he mentions Burke's unhappy phrase no less than 11 times. Cooper quotes Abbé Sieyès on the absurdity of allowing the few to govern the many, and (again echoing Price) he appeals to the example of the American Revolution: 'The American Republics have taught us experimentally that nations *may* flourish and be happy, who have "no Bishops, no Nobles, no Kings".'[7]

As if to confirm Burke's dire predictions, Cooper warns his readers: 'No reflecting man can look back at the last half century, or consider the probabilities of the next, without seeing clearly that the Revolution of Europe is at hand.' He argues that reform is needed to forestall revolution, and echoes the American Declaration of Independence when he writes: 'All government is or ought to be instituted for the happiness of the people who submit to be governed.' Attached as a supplement to his *Reply to Mr Burke*, Cooper printed his *Propositions respecting the Foundation of Civil Government*, first read as a paper at a meeting of the Manchester Philosophical Society in March 1787. It is a statement of political principles, set out (Cooper claimed) 'so plainly as to be generally understood, and so briefly as to be easily remembered'. The content owed much to Priestley, whose *Essay on the First Principles of Government* (1768) Cooper later called 'the first plain, popular, brief and unanswerable book on the principles of civil government'. Cooper reiterates Priestley's 'greatest good of the greatest number' principle (since made famous by Bentham) and re-emphasizes that the right of exercising political power is 'derived solely from the people'.[8]

Burke disdained to take notice of the *Reply*, and Cooper later claimed that the Attorney-General told him that he was safe from prosecution so long as his pamphlet was published in an octavo form, so as to 'confine it probably to that class of readers who may consider it coolly'. When Cooper received from Paris an account of the invasion of the Tuileries, entitled *Narrative of Proceedings relative to the Suspension of the King of France*, he published it in Manchester, with his own explanatory footnotes. He also incorporated Condorcet's *Reflections on the English Revolution of 1688, and that of the 10th of August 1792*, together with the address of the National Assembly explaining why it had suspended the King. Cooper evidently approved of the King's suspension, and not even the September Massacres seem to have dimmed the Manchester Constitutional Society's fraternal feelings for the French. It subscribed to an address of friendly encouragement sent to France by the London Corresponding Society in late September, and joined with several English societies in a warmly worded address read to the National Convention on 7 November. But both the British government and the British people were becoming increasingly hostile to revolutionary antics. In September, 186 Manchester publicans had agreed to deny their premises to the political clubs. In December, Paine was convicted (in his absence) of seditious libel, on 1 February 1793 England declared war on France, and in April Thomas Walker was put on trial for sedition. Cooper helped to secure Walker's acquittal – and the conviction of the chief prosecution witness on a charge of perjury. But the English political climate had become too uncongenial, and in August Cooper set off for America, carrying letters of introduction to John Adams and Thomas Jefferson.[9]

On 24 August Joseph Priestley wrote to Jedidiah Morse, author of *American Geography* (1792), thanking him for his 'excellent treatise' and claiming that it had 'contributed not a little to the spirit of emigration that now prevails in this country'. The chief motive for leaving England, Priestley explains, is the 'increasing spirit of bigotry encouraged by the court' which made it 'very unpleasant and almost unsafe, for the friends of liberty civil or religious to continue here'. He thinks that 'great numbers would go, if they knew how to get to America, or how to live there when they were there'. It was to provide such essential information for would-be political refugees, and to explore the most suitable sites for settlement, that Cooper and two of Priestley's three sons crossed the Atlantic in 1793. The result of their six-month stay was *Some Information Respecting America*, published after their return in 1794, and read that September by the young Coleridge, when formulating his plan to create his pantisocratic community in Pennsylvania, on the banks of the Susquehanna.[10]

In his preface, Cooper explains that he had gone to America 'expressly to determine whether America, or what part of it, was eligible for a person, like myself, with a small fortune and large family to settle in'. He chose America partly because of his 'political prejudice in favour of the government established there', which he goes on to describe in flattering terms:

> There is little fault to find with the government of America, either in principle or in practice: we have very few taxes to pay, and those are of acknowledged necessity, and moderate in amount: we have no animosities about religion...the present irritation of men's minds in Great Britain, and the discordant state of society on political accounts is not known there. The government is the government *of* the people, and *for* the people...

Not only does this passage foreshadow Lincoln's famous phrase in his Gettysburg address, but it shows that Cooper already regards himself as an American.[11]

Cooper's pamphlet takes the form of 'Letters from America to a Friend in England'. It assumes that a settler will invest in land rather than in manufactures, and warns him to avoid New Hampshire, Massachusetts and Connecticut, where 'property is much divided, farms are small and land in general dear'. New Jersey is 'unpleasant to Europeans, particularly in the summer season...Musquetoes and agues are more troublesome in this than in many of the other northern or middle states'. Georgia and the Carolinas are to be avoided not only for the 'parching summers', but also because of 'the prevalence of Negro slavery'. By contrast, he knows of 'very few objections that can be made to the state of Pennsylvania'. Philadelphia is 'the largest and most flourishing city of America', and there is the added attraction of 'numerous projected improvements in roads and canals'. Indeed Cooper quotes in full an advertisement from the Secretary of State's office dated 12 April 1793, listing proposed navigation improvements on the Susquehanna, and no less than 31 road improvement schemes. Lack of good communications is one of Cooper's objections to Kentucky, which Gilbert Imlay had been promoting, following Kentucky's admission to the Union in 1792. Cooper had lighted instead on Loyalsock Creek in Pennsylvania, about 170 miles from Philadelphia and between the east and west branches of the Susquehanna. The land there is agreed to be of 'the best quality to be found in Pennsylvania', and, unlike the Shenandoah Valley, there are no Dutch or German settlers, only English.[12]

The passage to America would cost 25 guineas to £30 each, and would take ten weeks from London. Cooper gives the most detailed advice on the preparations needed. Linen should be made up in ten parcels, each containing 'two or three shirts, two or three pairs of stockings, two or three handkerchiefs, and a towel or two'. This would avoid the necessity of 'running to your trunk every time you want to dress yourself'. The trunk itself should contain glass, crockery, enough clothes for a year, fruit stones and garden seeds. And libraries must not be left behind: settlers are advised to get all their unbound books bound before the voyage. Cooper recommends taking 'lemons, apples or any other fruit that will keep', and making sure that the captain of the ship has 'a filtering stone, or some other machine for the same purpose, for the use of cabin passengers'; if the water still smells offensive, 'powder of charcoal' should be added. There is also advice about suitable laxatives.[13]

Even this does not exhaust Cooper's practical advice to would-be emigrants. He adds appendices containing conversion tables for currency, a list of duties on imported goods, statistics on the volume of exports, and a population census for each state. These tables are supplemented by the text of the United States Constitution and chapter 15 of *A View of the United States of America* by Tench Coxe, offering 'a summary statement of the principal facts which characterize the American people, and the country or territory which has been assigned to them by the dispensations of Providence'. Finally Cooper appends a 13-page reprint of Benjamin Franklin's *Information to Those Who Would Remove to America*, first published in 1782.[14]

Priestley and his wife arrived in America in June 1794, and settled at Northumberland – the nearest town to the proposed settlement. By the end of 1794, 300 000 acres of the Loyalsock lands were being offered for sale in plots of 150, 300 and 400 acres, bearing such names as 'Liberty', 'Equality' or the names of revolutionary heroes:

Brissot, Paine, Price, Washington, Jefferson and Cooper himself. Within 12 months the acreage had risen to 700 000, of which Joseph Priestley Jr bought 20 000 in his own right. His parents stayed at Northumberland. After Mrs Priestley's death in 1796, the Coopers lived under Priestley's roof. Until Priestley's own death eight years later, the two men worked closely together. Priestley dedicated the published version of his 1796 lectures on *Evidences of Revealed Religion* to Vice-President John Adams, whom he had known in England and who attended the lectures. But when Adams became President, Priestley and Cooper found themselves opposed to the new Administration's policies. It is hardly surprising that they objected to the 1798 Alien and Sedition Acts, though they were not to know that Secretary of State Pickering had written to Adams suggesting the deportation of both Englishmen. Priestley did know, however, that Adams had rebuffed an attempt to secure a minor government appointment for Cooper.[15]

For ten weeks in the spring of 1799, Cooper assumed the editorship of the Sunbury and Northumberland *Gazette*. His contributions were later published as *Political Essays*, and form a sustained attack on the Federalists. In the preface to the first edition of the collected essays, Cooper says he hopes they will 'afford some proof that I remain in this country what I was in Europe, a decided opposer of political restrictions on the Liberty of the Press, and a sincere friend to those first principles of republican government, the sovereignty of the people and the responsibility of their servants'. He condemns the Sedition Act (which penalized any speech or writing against the President or Congress) for seeking to indict not only actions but opinions. He also argues for free trade, and insists on the primacy of agriculture. (He thinks that no one should be a legislator who has not read Adam Smith and the principal French writers.) In two essays entitled 'Political Arithmetic', Cooper argues that the existence of navies promotes war, and that essential commerce will continue in any case. America should imitate China, which flourishes without active promotion of foreign trade: 'If they will go to China for tea-cups, they will come to America for bread'. He already sees America as the granary of the world.[16]

The Pennsylvania elections of 1799 found Cooper issuing an address to the electors of Northumberland County in support of Republican candidates for Governor and Chief Justice. He also published a handbill that was to land him in prison. Among more general complaints, Cooper specifically accused President Adams of surrendering an

American citizen (Jonathan Robbins), whom the British claimed as a deserter, 'to the mock trial of a British court-martial'. Cooper describes the President's action as 'a stretch of authority which the monarch of Great Britain would have shrunk from; an interference without precedent, against law and against mercy!' The judge in his summing-up said that there was no doubt that Cooper did publish the libel and that he intended to defame. He described the pamphlet as 'the boldest attempt I have known to poison the minds of the people'. Cooper had pleaded not guilty and conducted his own defence, without calling witnesses – though he tried to subpoena the President, Secretary of State Pickering and several Congressmen. He denied that he was 'in the pay or under the support of any party', and claimed, somewhat grandiloquently: 'I belong here, as in my former country, to the great party of mankind.' A verdict of guilty was inevitable, and Cooper was sentenced to six months imprisonment and a fine of $400.[17]

When Cooper emerged from prison, the Republicans held a mass meeting to congratulate him, describing him as 'the conspicuous victim of the sedition law, the friend of science and the ablest advocate of universal liberty'. In November of that year (1800) the Republicans won the presidential election. With Jefferson in the White House, Cooper's fortunes improved. His first government assignment under the new Administration was (aptly enough) to investigate the rival claims of Pennsylvania and Connecticut settlers in the lands of the Susquehanna Company, founded in 1753 – 40 years before Cooper's own Susquehanna venture. In 1804 he was appointed a district judge in Pennsylvania, where he was confronted by an anti-judiciary campaign taking its stand on the principles of the Declaration of Independence. His resistance involved Cooper in charges of inconsistency. A writer in the *Aurora* quoted some of Cooper's earlier views, and claimed that he had changed his opinions on gaining office: 'He has tasted of the forbidden fruit; he saw that he was naked and has decked himself with fig-leaves. He now *persecutes* those doctrines which he formerly preached'. And the *Argus*, likening his fall from grace to that of Lucifer, reminded its readers that Cooper was once 'as rank a Jacobin as ever wore a red cap'.[18]

Cooper was nevertheless still highly regarded in government circles. Madison was so impressed with his opinion in a case involving the law of admiralty that they began to exchange letters. In August 1810 Cooper was asking Madison's assistance in obtaining recent scientific treatises from France, and that same summer Jefferson commended Cooper to a fellow Virginian as a correspondent in scientific matters:

'He is one of the ablest men in America, and that in several branches of science...The best pieces of political economy which have been written in this country were by Cooper. He is a great chemist and now proposes to resume his mineralogical studies'. This return to scientific studies was forced on Cooper by the loss of his judgeship in 1811, ostensibly for 'arbitrary, unjust and precipitate' judgments, but in reality through the swing of the political pendulum. His new academic career began with the chair of chemistry at Carlisle (later Dickinson) College, Pennsylvania, which he obtained through the support of Benjamin Rush, the college's founder. He combined this post with the editorship of the *Emporium of Arts and Sciences*, where he wrote on such varied subjects as steam engines, the bleaching of paper, manures, roof-covering materials and various aspects of economic theory. His continued correspondence with Madison, whose nephew was one of his students at Carlisle College, mingled advice on the study of law with thoughts on the manufacture of explosives. Meanwhile he embarked on a new edition of the *Institutes* of Justinian.[19]

In 1815 Cooper resigned his professorship in order (as he told Madison) to devote himself to law, but most of the academic posts he now filled were in the applied sciences. He declined the proffered chair of chemistry and law at Jefferson's projected University of Virginia, hoping instead for the chair of chemistry in the Pennsylvania medical school. He was unsuccessful, but his continued insistence on the chemical basis of mental illness put him far ahead of his time. It also increased his unpopularity with the religious establishment, which frustrated a second attempt to appoint him to the University of Virginia, and was to dog his footsteps at South Carolina College, where he became President in 1821. He continued in this post for 12 years, fighting off attempts by the Presbyterian clergy of the state to unseat him, and struggling with campus indiscipline. Students voted to have no dealings with their teachers, refused to co-operate in the investigation of breaches of college regulations or the laws of the state, threatened professors with pistols and broke the President's windows. Towards the end of his time, Cooper was regarded with more affection and respect by the students, but even then he could report to his board of trustees: 'They make noises, and blow horns on a moonlight night. They sometimes burn benches belonging to the college. They refrain from attending lectures on pretence of rain... They are seen (it is said) lounging at taverns.'[20]

So the Manchester radical ends his career in suppressing student rebellion. Was Cooper now entirely an establishment figure? He was certainly no longer a Jacobin. At the time of losing his judgeship, he had written:

> I went over to France in 1792 an enthusiast, and I left it in disquiet. I came here; and seventeen years experience of a democratic government in this country has also served to convince me that it is not quite so perfect in practice as it is beautiful in theory, and that the speculations of my youth do not receive the full sanction of my middle age: nor do I feel that justice and disinterestedness, wisdom and tolerance, are the necessary fruits of universal suffrage as it is exercised in Pennsylvania.

Certainly his uncomplimentary references to the negro population (whom he described as 'an inferior variety of the human species; and not capable of the same improvement as the whites') sound illiberal enough in modern ears. But Cooper saw his own resistance to the Northern abolitionists as a defence of the state constitutions against those who would pervert the Federal Constitution to their own ends.[21]

His *Consolidation, An Account of Parties in the United States* had appeared in six newspaper articles in 1824 as a contribution to the election campaign. Now in 1830 it was republished as a telling defence of states' rights. In his additions to Priestley's *Memoirs* published in 1806, Cooper had written approvingly of the Union: 'There has been no republic ancient or modern until the American. There has been no federal union on broad general principles well understood and digested, until the American union'. In that union, he now reminded readers of *Consolidation*, the powers delegated to Congress by the Constitution are 'specific, limited, enumerated'. Those powers do not emanate 'from any abstract principle of what the public good may require; but from the deliberate concessions and absolute will of the sovereign and independent states'. If Congress is going to appeal to the 'general welfare' clause of the Constitution, then it should proceed on the basis of equal treatment of all the states. Echoing the wording of a famous resolution in the British Parliament, Cooper claims that the power of the President, of Congress and of the Supreme Court ('the most dangerous body in the Union') 'has increased, is increasing and ought to be diminished.'[22]

As if to demonstrate his consistency, Cooper had four years earlier republished his *Propositions Respecting the Foundations of Civil Government*, explaining that he was still (after 40 years) the implacable foe of tyranny, but that the ground had now shifted from the rights of man to the rights of sovereign states. That same year (1826) he published *On the Constitution of the United States*. Here he claims that the Federal Constitution is simply a 'power of attorney'; he denies the assertion of the preamble to the Constitution that it was created by the *people* as opposed to the *states*; and he warns that the 'general welfare' clause is the tool of despotic power, reducing the states to the level of petty municipalities controlled from Washington. And at a meeting held on 2 July 1827 to protest against a proposed tariff increase, Cooper coined a phrase that was to become famous in the South. He spoke of the need to 'calculate the value of the union', and denounced the economic exploitation of the South by the 'master-minds of Massachusetts, the Lords of the spinning-jenny, and Peers of the power loom'. It was thus Cooper who first raised the spectre of secession.[23]

In the preface to the second edition of *Consolidation* in 1830, Cooper condemned the majority in Congress which had 'brought this Union of independent, sovereign states nearly to its close'. In speaking of 'independent sovereign states', Cooper was re-echoing the language of the Declaration of Independence, signed when he was 17. His importance lies in the fact that he bridged the gap between the rationale of the American Revolution and that of the American Civil War. The fact that the North won the debate, by winning the war, should not be allowed to obscure the fact that Cooper and those who placed a 'strict construction' on the text of the Constitution had good constitutional arguments on their side. Cooper retired from the presidency of South Carolina College in 1834, and devoted his last years to editing the Statutes of South Carolina and cataloguing his library of 2500 volumes. When he died in 1839 at the age of 80, his obituary in the Columbia *Telescope* paid tribute to a mind which 'coursed the whole field of learning with untiring rapidity' and 'incessantly sought for knowledge'. The tribute continued: 'He did not hesitate to follow his reasoning wherever it led, and what he thought he said. Authority had little weight with him. He always endeavoured to apply the touchstone of reason to every proposition, and to judge of it by that test alone.' It was an epitaph worthy of Voltaire himself.[24].

Frenchmen in America

JEAN PIERRE BRISSOT

9 Slaves, Quakers and 'Free Americans': Brissot's America and the French Revolution

It was Jean-Pierre Brissot who in July 1789, as a representative of the revolutionary commune of Paris, handed the key of the Bastille to Lafayette, thus starting the key on its journey to George Washington's home at Mount Vernon, Virginia. The incident is all the more piquant because Brissot, as a 30-year-old lawyer with journalistic aspirations, had himself been briefly imprisoned in the Bastille five years before, for allegedly libelling Marie Antoinette. He would later acquire fame as leader of the dominant group of deputies from the Gironde – the Girondins – in both the Legislative Assembly and the National Convention. And he would pay the penalty of opposing Robespierre without matching his ruthlessness.

As one of history's failures, Brissot has been somewhat neglected by historians. Yet he was an articulate agent in the transatlantic traffic in revolutionary ideas, and was one of the principal interpreters of the American Revolution to his contemporaries. His six-month stay in the United States, in the latter part of 1788, led to the publication three years later of his *New Travels in the United States of America*. Its appearance in 1791, when the French were themselves embarking on a new constitution, gave the book an added topicality. As Brissot remarked at the end of the preface: 'Great proposals are opening before us. Let us hasten, then, to make known that people whose happy experience ought to be our guide.'[1]

The *Travels* take the form of 'letters', the first six of which were written by Etienne Clavière, one of Brissot's sponsors. Clavière was a Genevan banker and a future finance minister in the Girondin ministry of Jean-Marie Roland. Clavière gave Brissot his financial support mainly, it seems, for commercial reasons, though the image of a free America provided the inspiration. Thus, in his first letter, Clavière writes: 'The present state of independent America will, perhaps, give us a glance at the highest perfection of human life we are permitted to hope for.' He nevertheless urges Brissot to concentrate on physical resources rather than on 'the details which interest the painter, the poet or the lover of an English garden'. Brissot is also enjoined to 'study the history of emigrants', and Clavière's third letter proposes a 'Plan of a Colony to be established in America'. In outlining his plan, Clavière asks whether those who propose such a colony should be condemned 'as having formed an Eutopia'. He does not think so. On the contrary, he believes that circumstances now favour such an enterprise which 'before the American Revolution, might have been judged impracticable'. Brissot's preface similarly stresses the importance of that Revolution: 'The object of these travels, was not to study antiques, or to search for unknown plants, but to study men who had just acquired their liberty.'[2]

The preface is dated April 1791. Brissot had first talked of crossing the Atlantic at least five years earlier. From 1786 onwards he had tried unsuccessfully to persuade the French ministry to subsidize his visit to America, suggesting optimistically that he be appointed 'historiographer of the French navy'. Disappointed in this hope, Brissot instead wrote a spirited attack on the picture of North America given by the Marquis de Chastellux in his *Travels in North America*, published in 1787. Before succeeding to his title, the Marquis had been a major-general in Rochambeau's army, and had taken part in the siege of Yorktown. His *Travels* was based on observations made during his military service in America between 1780 and 1782.[3]

Brissot complains that the Marquis's account is misleading on Quakers, on negroes, on the American people and on mankind in general. All four categories feature in the full title of his *Letter to M. the Marquis de Chastellux*, and Brissot announces that he has rushed out his reply in order to counteract the dangerous effects of such errors being propagated by so illustrious an author as Chastellux. The need for an immediate response allows no time for 'general censure' of the *Travels*, Brissot explains, and he tells the Marquis acidly that he will 'leave to journalists the task of appreciating your style'. He dismisses derisively the Marquis's frequent comments on the comforts of wayside inns and the quality of his suppers. Instead of menus, the earnest Brissot would have preferred 'details on the number of criminals, on the nature of the most frequent crimes, on manners, on how these differ in town, country and forest, on the state of the national finances etc.' He quotes Chastellux on the Quakers – verbatim for half a dozen pages – asking him whether he can fairly form an estimate on the strength of attending a single Quaker meeting. And does not the

Marquis's cast of mind – academic, military and aristocratic – in any case make him 'a suspect witness and a biased judge?' The Marquis's criticism of the Quakers is opposed by quotations from Crèvecoeur's complimentary description of Quaker women in his *Letters of an American Farmer* and his conclusions on visiting the Quaker botanist, John Bartram: 'What reader indulging in pleasant day-dreams, has not wanted to become like them good, simple, the child of nature?' Brissot upbraids Chastellux for setting out to 'destroy this enchantment', which (he adds revealingly) even if only an illusion, is a *useful* illusion 'consoling the virtuous and inspiring remorse in the vicious'.[4]

Chastellux, Brissot thinks, is equally misleading on the negroes – and indeed contradictory. The Marquis adopts simultaneously 'the tone of a philosopher and that of a *colon*; the tone of a defender of the negroes and that of their enemy'. His mistake is to accord them pity, when he should offer justice and protection. Brissot challenges the designation of negroes as being below the lowest class of whites. 'Differences which separate individuals,' he writes, 'are tricks of fate, results of varying circumstances: but the negro is born as sensitive as the White, the Peruvian as the European.' Chastellux might claim that slaves in Virginia live in better conditions than in the West Indies, but in Virginia they are 'ill-housed, ill-clothed, overwhelmed with labour'. What the negro needs, Brissot argues, is political freedom. They should enjoy the protection of the same laws as ourselves 'since they are our brothers, our fellow-men'. And amid appeals to Rousseau and Algernon Sidney, he asks Chastellux what he was fighting for in America if it was not the principle that 'all men are born free, equal, independent'.[5]

Brissot's *Letter to Chastellux*, with its representation of the American Republic as a beacon of political enlightenment, foreshadows both his founding of transatlantic societies and the political slant given to his own *Travels in North America*. His pamphlet against Chastellux was published in the late summer of 1786. That same autumn Brissot drew up a memorandum, probably for Clavière, in which he repeated his intention to travel to America. His proposal is to 'traverse the country for a year, and indeed to see the principal towns such as Boston, New-York, Philadelphia, Charlestown'. He explains that he could not afford to undertake the tour at his own expense, and suggests that the French government should give him a free passage and an honorarium, or alternatively that 'some friends of liberty will join in making up the sum the author needs'. If such a group of supporters could be found to subsidize this project 'and all projects favourable to liberty and the progress of enlightenment', it might agree to call itself the *Société Américaine*. Although the hoped-for funds to take Brissot to America did not materialize in 1786, that year saw the founding of the Gallo-American Society. The other founder-members were Clavière, Crèvecoeur and a Lyons barrister, Nicolas Bergasse (who shared Brissot's interest in Mesmerism). Clavière, as a citizen of Geneva, argued against defining the Society's objects exclusively in transatlantic terms, and at the second meeting it was resolved that papers could be presented that were concerned with the well-being not merely of Americans and Frenchmen, but of 'mankind in general'. Brissot insisted that membership must be open to men of all religions, and suggested inviting Abbé Jean-Baptiste de Montmignon to expound to the Society his newly published scheme of pronunciation, which was claimed to be equally applicable to French and English.[6]

Louis XVI's summoning of the Assembly of Notables was hailed as a hopeful opportunity, but for the moment the Gallo-American Society would opt for *une obscurité prudente*, and rely on its founder-members to propose suitably qualified candidates for membership. The prospectus of the Society affirmed that 'France has, by its arms, helped to establish the independence of free America', and expressed the belief that 'a commercial treaty based on the interests of the two nations' would cement transatlantic friendship. In approving the draft text, it was agreed that United States citizens should be described as 'free Americans', and the Society undertook to 'make every effort, both orally and in its writings, to spread this usage'. Meanwhile the Society would take note of what is done in America and 'publicize it', and more generally employ 'the Society's influence to secure useful institutions'. In January 1787 Brissot reported to members that the Duc d'Orléans had agreed to naturalize American trees in French forests. Seeds would be needed, and so Brissot presented a list of trees 'with their Latin, French and English names and a note of the countries where they flourish'.[7]

The constitution of the Gallo-American Society provided for 12 members resident in Paris, 24 resident in the provinces, a similar number in the United States and 'an infinite number' elsewhere. There would also be 'corresponding members' who were required to inform the Society of relevant events in their own district, since, it was explained in language worthy of the *Encyclopédie*, 'it is only by observation of individual facts, multiplied in various places, that a sound theory of man and society can be established.' Thus one corresponding

member is charged not only with translating 'works of political arithmetic by the celebrated Dr Price', but with encouraging the inhabitants of Normandy to cultivate the potato. It is agreed to send a copy
of the prospectus to both Lafayette and Jefferson, and to print it as an
appendix to *De la France et des Etats Unis*, which Clavière and Brissot
are about to publish. A proposed seal for the Society is presented,
showing two women (personifying France and America) holding
hands with the legend *le bien des deux Mondes, Société Gallo-
Américaine, 1787*. The receipt of a copy of John Adams's *Defence of
the American Constitutions* is reported, and Brissot proposes publishing extracts in the newspapers (with translations) in order to 'make
the principles of the American constitutions known in Europe'.[8]

Crèvecoeur's return to America in order to resume his post of
French consul in New York, after a two-year leave of absence, came
as a blow to Brissot and the Society. Although it would facilitate the
Society's work on the other side of the Atlantic, the Paris society
would lose one of its founder-members. It was decided not to hold
meetings during the summer, though Brissot was insistent that the
work must go on, in order to 'prepare for the revolution which will
regenerate political ideas'. Meanwhile he declined an invitation to
join the Villefranche Academy, explaining that 'if I am to be an
academician, it will only ever be at Boston, Philadelphia or London,
because there my ideas will not be fettered in any way, and I can be
myself.' He was to find himself in London sooner than he expected.
He had been there twice before, in 1782 and 1783, before he was
imprisoned in the Bastille. Now, compromised by his Orleanist links,
he again found himself in disfavour at court, and in the summer of
1787 he sought refuge in England. It was the year of Thomas Cooper's
Letters on the Slave Trade, and Brissot's acquaintance with the British
anti-slavery agitation dates from this visit. It would kindle his
enthusiasm for another great cause.[9]

But first, while still in England, Brissot wrote his *Plan of a Society
for Promoting the Emigration from Europa in the United-States*. Written
in not entirely flawless English, the memorandum spoke of a large
number of sober, industrious and healthy Europeans who would be
happy to emigrate 'if they could find some means to execute it with
safety and advantage'. Brissot's proposal was that a society 'be possessed in the United-States of large tracts of lands, they should be
glad to sell and clear'. The society would need a headquarters in
Europe, centrally situated, close to a seaport and 'in a free government' where its operations 'should not be liable to be enquired into'.

A pamphlet should be circulated throughout Europe, in English, German and French, setting out 'the advantages physical, political, commercial etc' of the United States and 'the happiness to be enjoyed by emigrants'. The society should advance money to suitably qualified emigrants who required help with the initial financial outlay. On the emigrants' arrival in America the society should have proper contracts drawn up for the sale of land, and 'after having supplied them with all necessaries, should despatch them to the country where they are to settle'. The proposals closely foreshadow the scheme promoted in the mid-1790s by the Priestleys on the banks of the Susquehanna, through the agency of Thomas Cooper.[10]

Safely back in Paris in February 1788, Brissot founded a different society – *Les Amis des Noirs* – for which he nevertheless sought transatlantic endorsement. Jefferson declined to join, declaring his support for the campaign against the slave trade, but pleading that, accredited as he was to the French court, it was his duty 'not to show too publicly my desire to see [slavery] abolished'. Lafayette (according to Brissot) declared that he did regard himself a member of the society, and promised to enlist other influential members. Meanwhile Yzarn de Valady, an officer in the *Gardes Françaises*, and one of 11 founder-members of *Les Amis des Noirs*, asked Brissot for a letter of introduction to Lafayette so that he could present himself 'in the livery of an American and of a friend of liberty'.[11]

Brissot was himself obtaining letters of introduction in readiness for his voyage to America. In April 1788 the Comte de Montmorin, minister of foreign affairs, wrote to the French plenipotentiary in the United States, the Comte de Moustier, telling him of Brissot's coming visit:

> I have given him the necessary passport for this voyage. M. the Marquis de La Fayette, who is interested in everything concerning him, has asked that I give him at the same time a letter of introduction to you. He will therefore have the honour to present this. Please, Monsieur, be kind enough to give a favourable welcome to this individual... and to assist him with your protection if he finds himself in need of it.

Moustier, who had not liked Brissot when he met him in London, endorsed the letter with a somewhat tart description of his fellow countryman. Brissot (he wrote) was 'a self-styled philosopher' whose pamphlet against Chastellux was 'full of invective'; he presumed to criticize and instruct the French government and to exalt the English nation. Moustier concluded: 'Such a man cannot without inconvenience be received by the minister of the King.'[12]

This time, however, Brissot did get to America. His financial backers, apart from Clavière, were Theophile Cazenove and Pierre Stadinski. In a contract drawn up between them, Brissot undertook to obtain information regarding the size of the Congressional debt and the debts of individual states, together with details of the various government bonds on offer and the method of paying interest. The commercial object was evidently to find the most profitable way of buying into the American national debt, but Brissot doubtless saw the contract as a convenient way of obtaining funding for his own transatlantic plans. He set sail in May 1788, armed with a letter of recommendation from Lafayette to George Washington. The bearer of the letter, Lafayette explained, 'intends to occupy himself with a history of America, and you will accordingly make him very happy if you will permit him to glance at your papers, a favour which he seems to me to deserve, for he is a great lover of America, writes well and represents things in their true light.' On the way out, Brissot's vessel met a ship returning to Europe. He entrusted it with a letter to Clavière, which was passed on to Brissot's wife. Well might she write in return that the letter 'caused me such surprise that I could scarcely recognize your handwriting. I read it and re-read it in order to convince myself that it was not a dream'.[13]

A letter from his wife, written in mid-August and addressed *c/o Monsieur Saint-John de Crèvecoeur, consul de France*, announced the calling of the States-General for May 1789. The news does not seem to have altered Mme Brissot's intention to join her husband. Her letter asks what one will need for the sea voyage, what luxuries can be obtained in America and what one must bring, and whether they inoculate as well as in France. The last question is explained by her reminder that 'it is this autumn that I am counting on having the children inoculated'. The eldest child, Sylvain, 'loves talking about the voyage to America'. Meanwhile, she tells her husband, he should beware of *les misses américaines* and not allow himself to pass for anything other than a married man. And in a postscript intended for her brother, François Dupont, who had already settled in Pennsylvania, she adds: 'We impatiently wait for details about America, particularly about acquiring a small property in the event that I cannot leave until the spring.' Mme Brissot never reached Pennsylvania. By the spring of 1789 François Dupont had bought a half-share in a plot in America for £25, but Brissot was back in France.[14]

He had immediately published a 'Plan of Conduct' for the use of those who would sit in the States-General. His proposals explicitly reflect his faith in American political principles and practice. A constitution could be drawn up only by democratically elected representatives of the people, in a specially commissioned constitutional convention. Brissot explains where he got the idea: 'We owe its discovery to the Free Americans, and the convention which has just formed the plan for a federal system has infinitely perfected it.' He goes on to suggest that the American procedure 'can perhaps be very easily adapted to the circumstances in which France finds herself'. Brissot failed to get himself elected to the States-General, and therefore did not appear in either the National Assembly or the Constituent Assembly. In October 1791 he would eventually take his seat in the Legislative Assembly, as one of the representatives for Paris, and then in the National Convention, representing Eure-et-Loire. But for the intervening two years he devoted himself to serving in the Paris Commune, editing his own newspaper *Le Patriote française* and preparing his *Travels* for the press.[15]

The preface to the *Travels* was written to point out the aptness of the book, now that France was experiencing a revolution of her own. But the main text was written before the fall of the Bastille. Brissot's comments on what he finds in America centre very much on what any disciple of the French Enlightenment would have had an eye for. And he is often as concerned with the influence of France on America, as with the impact of America on France. Thus he notes that one of Harvard's professors gives lectures based on the work of French chemists, while the university library of 13 000 volumes prompts him to exclaim: 'The heart of a Frenchman palpitates on finding the works of Racine, of Montesquieu and the Encyclopaedia where, 150 years ago, arose the smoke of the savage calumet.' And when he stops at Henderson's Tavern, only 20 miles from the Susquehanna, he reports: 'The town here is called Havre de Grace, a name given it by a Frenchman who laid the foundation of the town.' More predictably, Brissot is pleased to find that at most public dinners he attends, a toast is drunk to Lafayette.[16]

Brissot does not meet Jefferson, who is still in Paris, but he does find John Adams returned from his diplomatic assignments in Europe and now 'occupied in the cultivation of his farm, and forgetting what he was when he trampled on the pride of his king'. Brissot presumably intends a compliment when he describes John's cousin, Sam, as having 'the excess of republican virtues', and he reports having supper at

Governor John Hancock's home 'with a hatter, who appeared to be in great familiarity with him'. When Washington receives him at Mount Vernon, Brissot finds that 'everything has an air of simplicity', – which appeals to the Frenchman's republican tastes. He admires Washington's new barn, based on a plan sent to him by Arthur Young, and is impressed to hear that the General has 'planted this year eleven hundred bushels of potatoes'. They discuss slavery and the possibility of forming an American abolitionist society, but Washington 'did not think the moment favourable'.[17]

A chapter devoted to the octogenarian Benjamin Franklin – beginning with the exclamation: 'Thanks to God he still exists!' – gives a summary of Franklin's life 'to rectify some of those false anecdotes which circulate in Europe'. Brissot cherishes a copy of one of Franklin's early newspapers, a relic which he intends to use 'to teach men to blush at the prejudice which makes them despise the useful and important profession of the editors of daily papers'. And he applauds the fact that Franklin, who rose from printer to ambassador, has in retirement returned to his first trade – by installing a printing-press and type-foundry in his house. It is no surprise to find the founder of the Gallo-American Society taking an interest in the newly invented 'Franklin stove', designed for economical fuel consumption, or in the steam-boat with an engine that 'gives motion to three large oars of considerable force, which were to give sixty strokes per minute'. Characteristically Brissot concludes that if the design could be adapted to the needs of transatlantic travel (as one of its inventors proposed) it would 'introduce into commerce as great a change as the discovery of the Cape of Good Hope'.[18]

Although recording that Massachusetts (like Pennsylvania) has 'a society formed for the encouragement of manufacture and industry', and commending Boston for having its streets 'well illuminated at night', most of Brissot's descriptions are derived from what he found in Pennsylvania. He marvels at Philadelphia's philanthropic institutions, such as 'the *Dispensary*, which distributes medicines *gratis* to the sick who are not in a situation to purchase them', and the Hospital for Lunatics which Franklin had helped to found. Brissot records that most of the inmates are 'victims of religious melancholy or of disappointed love', and admires Dr Rush's invention of 'a kind of swing chair for their exercise'. Continuing his tour of the city, Brissot visits the 'Bettering-House or House of Correction' designed for the confinement of 'vagabonds, disorderly persons, and girls of scandalous lives'. He is pleased that every room is constructed with 'windows

placed opposite, which introduce plenty of light, that great consolation to a man confined, of which tyrants for this reason are cruelly
sparing'. (Was he thinking of his own days in the Bastille?) He exults
to find that 'blacks are here mingled with the whites, and lodged in
the same apartments'. This is, he writes, 'a balm to my soul'. He thinks
that the abolitionist cause has been given a stimulus by the War of
Independence, despite the obstructionism of the Southern states, and
remarks that 'we may regard the general and irrevocable proscription
of the slave trade in the Unites States as very near at hand.' Within
20 years 'the sentiments of humanity and the calculations of reason
will prevail.' It was not a bad guess.[19]

Unsurprisingly the founder of *Les Amis des Noirs* devotes another
three dozen pages to the consideration of slavery itself – apart from
such occasional comments as the observation that General Washington 'makes it a practice to have all his slaves inoculated'. Health and
hygiene indeed attract some notice. Thus Brissot praises the clean-
liness of American packet-boats, which are well ventilated so that 'you
do not breathe that nauseous air which infects the packets of the
English Channel', and he is glad to find that the Philadelphia meat-
market is so arranged that 'the spectator is not tormented with the
sight of little streams of blood, which infect the air and foul
the streets.' To achieve comparable standards in France would require
'four Judges and a dozen soldiers', while in America by contrast 'the
law has no need of muskets; education and morals have done everything.' Perhaps it was education that also explained why so few
Pennsylvanians ended up in gaol. At Philadelphia, Brissot reports,
90 per cent of prisoners come from outside the state, and are mostly
Frenchmen or Irishmen.[20]

Brissot recalls that Voltaire used to express a wish to end his days in
Philadelphia – 'the City of Brothers'. He wonders what the sage would
have said if he could have realized his dream and 'been a witness of
the peace which reigns in this town'. Brissot decides, somewhat mis-
chievously, that Voltaire would quickly have returned to Europe:

> The gravity of the Quakers would have appeared to him a gloomy
> pedantry: he would have yawned in their assemblies, and been
> mortified to see his epigrams pass without applause; he would
> have sighed for the sparkling wit of his amiable fops of Paris.

For his part, Brissot contrasts the 'religious decency' of the Philadelphians with the 'light and wanton airs of those Europeans who go to a
church as to a theatre', noting that nobody is barred from office for

his religious faith. He attends a Quaker funeral, and eagerly looks forward to the possibility of 'a nation of Deists', asking: 'What difference would there be between a society of Deists, and one of Quakers, assembling to hear a discourse on the immortality of the soul, and to pray to God in simple language!'[21]

Forty-five pages of the *Travels* are devoted to praising the Quakers – not surprisingly, perhaps, as Brissot was one of the first Frenchmen to wear his hair unpowdered, 'Quaker-fashion'. There is indeed an un-Voltairean puritanism about Brissot. Thus he credits the Quakers with ensuring that 'Philadelphia has hitherto been preserved from the danger of theatres.' And at dinner with the President of Congress, our puritan philosopher sees that two of the female guests 'had their bosoms very naked.' He adds: 'I was scandalised at this indecency among republicans.' Montesquieu's belief in the moral benefits of certain climates is matched in Brissot by the alleged moral effect of different political systems. Predictably, we are told that Maryland 'would soon become extremely flourishing if slavery were banished from it'.[22]

Brissot describes Connecticut as 'the Paradise of the United States', and refers to Crèvecoeur's description to substantiate his claim. But it is the Ohio valley that captures our author's attention. He is interested in the Quaker settlements in the Carolinas and 'near the Ohio', though he does not visit the Ohio himself, and relies instead on the French naturalist, Saugrain:

> The immense valley washed by the Ohio, appears to him the most fertile he has ever seen...The crops of Indian corn are prodigious; the cattle acquire an extraordinary size, and keep fat the whole year in the open fields...A man in that country works scarcely two hours in a day, for the support of himself and family...

No wonder Southey thought there would be time for ploughing *and* poetry. The merits of Pennsylvania, as presented in the *Travels*, are perhaps more prosaic. The state of Penn and Franklin offers 'not the pleasures of Arcadia of the poets, or those of the great towns of Europe; but it promises you independence, plenty and happiness – in return for patience, industry and labour'.[23]

This, in Brissot's view, is the road to well-being: 'The time will doubtless come, when we shall be convinced that physical health, as well as political happiness, may be greatly promoted by equality and independence of opinion among all members of society.' Brissot backs up his claim by offering the reader 'A Comparative Table of the

Probabilities of Life in New England and in Europe', purporting to show that men live longer in the United States 'than in the most salubrious countries of Europe'. Brissot's idyllic picture evidently embarrassed his English translator, who explains in a footnote that he has abridged the highly-coloured description of the way of life of the first planter, in order to 'save the credit' of the author. We are nevertheless left with Brissot's portrayal of 'the man, detached from society, with his axe in his hand, felling the venerable oak that had been respected by the savage, and supplying its place with the humble spire of corn'.[24]

Recording his arrival at Boston on 30 July 1788, Brissot had pictured himself fleeing from despotism, and coming 'at last to enjoy the spectacle of liberty, among a people, where nature, education and habit had engraved the equality of rights, which everywhere else is treated as a chimera'. And in 1790 – by which time the principles of America were thought to have been transplanted to France – Brissot added a postscript to the long section in the *Travels* devoted to the Quakers. Here he urges the French revolutionary government to offer the Quakers asylum in France because 'the spirit of that society agrees with the spirit of French liberty' and because 'we are all striving for the same object, universal fraternity.' In the event, though Brissot did not live to see it, the traffic was reversed: French refugees crossed the Atlantic to settle near the Priestleys' settlement on the Susquehanna. Coleridge later sought to distance himself from both Brissot and the Susquehanna scheme, but in 1795 he bracketed Brissot with Sieyès, Mirabeau, Tom Paine and the seventeenth-century heroes – Sidney, Harrington and Milton. And the severest punishment Coleridge proposed for Burke was that 'he may be appointed under-porter to St Peter, and be obliged to open the gate of heaven to Brissot, Roland, Fayette and Priestley.' Brissot was in good transatlantic company.[25]

10 Hero of Two Worlds: Lafayette, Freemasons and Liberty

The key of the Bastille is displayed at Mount Vernon, Virginia, to symbolize the fact that the American Revolution was a European event. This memento of revolution was handed by the Marquis de Lafayette to Tom Paine at a special ceremony in the gardens of the Louvre in late October 1789 – three months after the Bastille fell. The Frenchman wrote to George Washington acknowledging the personal debt he owed to his experience in the American army during the War of Independence, and calling the gift 'a tribute which I owe as a son to my adoptive father, as aide-de-camp to my general, as Missionary of Liberty to its Patriarch'. The Marquis was always one for the grandiloquent gesture.[1]

In October 1789 he was Commandant of the Paris National Guard and a member of the self-styled National Assembly. He had been one of the first nobles to join the Third Estate and to drop the aristocratic style of Marquis de la Fayette, in future writing his name as one word. As a member of the National Assembly, he had proposed his own draft of a Declaration of Rights – assisted by Jefferson who was in Paris at the time, representing the United States. That July, when the commander of the National Guard was being chosen at the city hall, the first name proposed was Alexandre de Lameth, who had been a late arrival in the American war, crossing the Atlantic in 1782. So he had not been at Yorktown, where his elder brother, Charles, had distinguished himself. Now, at the suggestion that he should command the National Guard, Alexandre is supposed to have replied: 'If it's "Americans" you want, choose the most prominent – Lafayette.' The decision was clinched when Saint-Méry pointed to the bust of Lafayette by Houdon, which graced the city hall. It had been commissioned by the State of Virginia, and placed there with royal permission. Thus did America shape the course of the French Revolution.[2]

Accustomed to fighting alongside Washington's raw Virginian militia, the new commandant of the French National Guard was not daunted by the prospect of training a citizen army. He designed a uniform – royal blue jacket with scarlet and white trimmings – and introduced the tricolour. He wrote to Madame Simiane, 'I rule in Paris.' But he added that he had no wish to be a dictator: 'If the King refuses the Constitution, I will combat him. If he accepts it, I will defend him.' This is the clue to Lafayette's actions as the Revolution unfolds. As commander of the National Guard, he takes centre stage whenever the Paris crowd is on the move. He is a reluctant participant in the March of the Women to Versailles in October, but his guardsmen intervene to protect the royal family when it looks as if the king's bodyguard will be butchered by the demonstrators. And it is his dramatic gesture in drawing Marie Antoinette out on to the balcony, and publicly kissing her hand, that turns the jeers of the crowd into shouts of *Vive la reine*! It is Lafayette who stage-manages the return march to Paris, and it is in his name that the Commune's order to demolish the Bastille is proclaimed with trumpets through the Paris streets. It is at his suggestion that the first anniversary of the fall of the Bastille is celebrated with a Festival of Federation on the Champ de Mars, to be attended by representatives of provincial National Guard contingents in the presence of the King.[3]

The *Fête de Fédération* was the high point of Lafayette's popularity. The following Easter he failed to ensure the King's unimpeded progress to St Cloud to make his communion; and in May 1791 he was at the Tuileries on the eve of the royal family's flight to Varennes. He inspected the sentries before going to bed, which left him open to the charge of connivance. But it was he who signed the order for the King's arrest. The celebrations surrounding the second anniversary of the storming of the Bastille ended with the National Guard opening fire on demonstrators in the Champs de Mars and killing a dozen people. However, when the Assembly finally approved the Constitution and the King accepted it, Lafayette felt that in any case his work was done. He resigned his command of the National Guard and retired to his estate of Chavaniac in the Auvergne, hoping (forlornly as it turned out) to devote himself to agriculture. His grateful guardsmen voted him a sword forged from bolts of the Bastille, while the Commune presented him with a medal and a marble statue of George Washington.

How had Lafayette first met his 'adoptive father'? The Marquis tells us in his memoirs that the idea of serving in America came to him after a dinner at the Comte de Broglie's, when his young heart was 'captured' on hearing the Declaration of Independence read aloud. His memory was faulty, because the dinner took place almost a year before the Declaration was signed. But Lafayette was correct in remembering that the Declaration's sentiments would help to persuade him that the Americans' cause was his own. What he did hear at dinner was Broglie's scheme for exploiting American hostility to Britain, and gradually escalating French involvement until France was forced to declare war. A dummy French company formed by Beaumarchais, in collaboration with the American agent Silas Deane, was already supplying arms to the colonists. Broglie even cherished hopes of himself becoming commander of the rebel army, and evidently saw Lafayette's high birth and youthful enthusiasm as an aid to his plans.

So it was Broglie who encouraged Lafayette to ignore the French government's opposition to his wish to fight in America. (The ministry, Broglie argued, was pretending disapproval in order to placate the British ambassador.) And it was probably Broglie's secretary who suggested that the Marquis might use his great personal wealth to commission a ship of his own. Lafayette told Deane: 'Up to now, sir, you have witnessed only my zeal. Now I am going to turn it to some account. I am buying a ship to transport your officers.' He also impressed Deane by insisting that he would serve without pay and by claiming that his aristocratic status entitled him to the rank of major-general. The Marquis was only 19 when he wrote to Deane's secretary the day before he sailed: 'I hope that I will prove as good a general as I am a good American.' He left behind him an 18-year-old wife, Adrienne, and announced from London to his angry father-in-law, the Duc d'Ayen: 'I have found a unique chance of distinguishing myself and learning my profession. I am now a general officer in the army of the United States of America.'[4]

He was determined to fall in love with America. On the very day after his arrival at Charleston he wrote: 'The customs of this country are simple, honest and altogether worthy of the country where everything re-echoes the beautiful name of liberty.' Two days later he was writing that 'delightful equality ... reigns everywhere here'. Lafayette's party arrived in Philadelphia on 27 July 1777. Four days later Congress approved his commission 'in consideration of his zeal, illustrious family and connections'. On the same day Washington himself arrived in Philadelphia and invited the youngest of major-generals to dine with him and his staff. And three weeks later Lafayette rode at Washington's side as the army marched through Philadelphia.[5]

The young Frenchman quickly fell under Washington's spell. He later wrote to Adrienne: 'We live like two closely-united brothers in mutual intimacy and confidence.' And when in December 1779, his wife bore a son, he was christened George Washington Lafayette. It was perhaps natural for the Marquis, who never knew his own father, to regard Washington as a father-figure. It is less obvious why Washington warmed to him, particularly as Lafayette constantly badgered the General to give him a command – whereas Congress had indicated that the Frenchman's rank was honorary. Perhaps it was Gallic exuberance and youthful zest which broke through Washington's well-known reserve. When Lafayette was wounded at the battle of Brandywine, Washington told Dr John Cochran (his own physician): 'Treat him as though he were my son.' When returned to duty, Lafayette again demonstrated his qualities in a successful skirmish with a troop of Hessians. Washington now wrote to Congress warning that a continued refusal to grant the Marquis a command 'will not only induce him to return home in disgust, but may involve some unfavourable consequences'. Perhaps the General had in mind the young man's emphatic reminder: 'Consider, if you please, that Europe and particularly France is looking upon me.' He got his division.[6]

His subsequent service during the war was not inconsiderable. He shared the privations of the army in that cruel winter at Valley Forge. He was given command of an expedition to Canada, which petered out at Albany where he found only half the men he had been promised – and those 'naked'. In the spring of 1778 he succeeded, through a mixture of luck and quick thinking, in escaping from a British trap on the banks of the Schuylkill. In June, only the inexcusable vacillations of General Lee robbed Lafayette and Hamilton of a victory at Monmouth. The Marquis was with Washington when they arrived at Benedict Arnold's home on the very morning he defected to the enemy, and it was Lafayette who was chosen to lead the expedition to capture Arnold at his Virginian base – though the mission was aborted when the British blockade cut off essential reinforcements. So Lafayette took his troops instead to Baltimore, and had them equipped at his own expense.

The Marquis's greatest military feat was in Virginia in the summer of 1781, when he pinned down Lord Cornwallis's superior force, while skilfully avoiding battle. Cornwallis had boasted that the 'boy cannot escape me'; but in the event, the British withdrew towards the sea, and the Virginians gave Lafayette the credit for liberating their state. (The Marquis, for his part, called his second daughter Virginie.) And when Yorktown was surrounded, Lafayette commanded the American force that stormed one of the two redoubts, while the French attacked the other. It was the Marquis who received Cornwallis's request to discuss surrender terms, and who insisted that the British should not be accorded military honours. When the defeated troops reached Lafayette's part of the parade, his band cheekily struck up 'Yankee Doodle Dandy'. In complimenting the young major-general, Washington wrote: 'Should it ever be said that my attachment to you betrayed me into partiality, you have only to appeal to facts to refute any such charge.'[7]

Lafayette still hoped to attack Canada, but Washington sent him back to France to secure more assistance. The Marquis had been a successful emissary to France in 1779, when he had been given leave to try to obtain men and munitions from Louis XVI's government. His barrage of letters to Maurepas and Vergennes, reinforced by his personal popularity, had then persuaded the ministry to send Rochambeau's expeditionary force of six ships and 6000 men. 'I had the honour,' he wrote, 'of being consulted by all the ministers and, what was far better, embraced by all the ladies.' An anonymous English pamphleteer would scarcely be exaggerating when he wrote of Lafayette:

> It is well known how much his assistance contributed to retrieve American affairs; how much his military and political services supported that revolution, and that by means of the change it wrought in the public opinion in France, it determined the court of Versailles to espouse the cause of the congress. To that single circumstance, therefore, may be referred the establishment of American independence.

Especially, one might add, since the arrival of French troops shamed the states into reviving their own flagging support for the war.[8]

At the end of his 1779 mission Lafayette had taken his leave of Louis XVI in the uniform of an American major-general; now in 1781 the King not only warmly welcomed him back to France, but promoted him *maréchal de camp* over the heads of more senior French officers. The Foreign Minister, Vergennes, told him: 'Your name is held here in veneration.' Franklin, still in Paris, said that Lafayette could plead for military and financial assistance 'with greater weight than I could possibly do'. The Marquis was not optimistic, but he extracted from Vergennes a loan of 6 million *livres* and reinforcements for Rochambeau. Meanwhile Admiral d'Estaing had been putting together a Franco-Spanish expeditionary force, and proposed Lafayette as his army commander.[9]

The Marquis maintained his correspondence with Washington, suggesting in characteristically libertarian vein that they might buy a small property 'where we may try the experiment to free the negroes and use them only as tenants'. Washington, equally characteristically, was non-committal. Congress did not, as Lafayette had hoped, appoint him American envoy at the ratification of the peace treaty in London, and he went instead to Madrid to smooth out Spanish-American relations. Meanwhile he was invested with the royal order of St Louis, and accepted the presidency of the French branch of the association of officers who had fought in the American war – the Society of Cincinnati. In June 1784 he set out again for America, leaving Adrienne behind once more, even though Washington had invited them both to Mount Vernon.[10]

As Lafayette was preparing to leave Paris, Jefferson arrived. The Marquis wrote telling him that his Paris home was at the American minister's disposal: 'I beg you will come and see Madame Lafayette as you would act by your brother's wife.' Landing in New York, Lafayette travelled to Philadelphia, accompanied by a throng of admirers on horseback. He was treated to a 13-gun salute (one for each state), to illuminated towns and to banquets. He was chief guest in Baltimore at a dinner for 300, and in Boston at 'a banquet of five hundred covers'. In August he escaped from the adoring crowds to spend 11 days at Mount Vernon. Honours continued to multiply. Harvard gave him an honorary doctorate, a county was named after him and he was made a freeman of New York. Virginia, Massachusetts and Maryland conferred state citizenship on him, the Maryland legislature going so far as to extend the privilege to all his male heirs. His triumphal tour included many speeches – one to the assembled Indians at Fort Schuyler, who had earlier given him the nickname of *Kayewla* – redoubtable horseman. His last speech before returning to France was delivered to members of a Congressional committee. It contained the grandiloquent but not unprophetic words: 'May this immense temple of liberty which we have just built be forever a lesson to the oppressed and an asylum for the rights of the human species'. In a farewell letter Washington said he did not expect to live long enough to welcome him to America again. Lafayette wrote in reply: 'I shall be back soon.' In the event, 40 years would elapse before he returned as the hero of *two* revolutions.[11]

The development of his ideas during that period is partly reflected in Lafayette's *Statement of his own Conduct and Principles*, published in 1793, while he was a prisoner-of-war in Austria. Not surprisingly the *Statement* is critical of the Jacobins, who had driven him from French soil. The Jacobin Society at war had 'marked its horrid career with blood and destruction, confounding the innocent with the guilty in one promiscuous ruin'. He praises a constitution on the British model – or the French constitution of 1791 – but displays no nostalgia for the court of the *ancien régime*. Instead he points to America where 'the lowest class seemed to live well, and bore an unaffected appearance of decency and independence, and the most wealthy did not pretend to more'. In America, Lafayette had also noticed the absence of hierarchy in the Church, and he claims that 'the sight of a mermaid was never a more terrific omen of a tempest to sailors than the name of a bishop to Americans'. He foreshadows modern historians in finding an anti-clerical thread in events leading to American independence, noting that in 1768 the British government had 'proposed that the Americans should receive bishops'. Well might he conclude: 'These circumstances are very little, if at all known in Europe.' His admiration for republics has been tempered by the French Revolution. He deplores reforms where 'the labour of a century is overturned in the whim of an experiment' and government dwindles into 'what is called republicanism – but what I call mobism'. A republic is certainly superficially attractive – 'a charming illusion, a Paradise in prospect' – but the histories of Greece and Rome 'cannot produce an instance to prove a free republic having outlived the short space of forty years'.[12]

In July 1824, Lafayette returned to the American Republic that he had helped to create. He was accompanied by his secretary Auguste Levasseur (who would keep a journal of the visit), his valet and his own son, George Washington Lafayette. They travelled at the invitation of President Monroe who had offered 'a government vessel to proceed to any port you will indicate, and convey you thence to the adopted country of your early youth, which has always preserved the most grateful recollection of your important services'. Lafayette declined the offer of a frigate, preferring a passage in a packet-boat, and delayed his departure until he could settle all his debts in France – which he eventually did with the help of a loan from the American minister in Paris.[13]

The hero's return to New York took place on 15 August – the 55th anniversary of Napoleon's birth. As it was a Sunday, the French visitors could not make a triumphal entry into the city until next day, when they landed at the Battery. They were received by an escort of Lafayette Guards, all wearing medallions printed with the General's portrait and the words 'Welcome Lafayette'. Lining the shore was a crowd estimated at 200 000. A carriage drawn by four white horses conveyed him to the City Hall, along streets decked with flowers and bunting. After speeches of welcome, the guest of honour reviewed the militia. At 5 pm a state banquet was held, and at 6 pm the balloon *American Eclipse* appeared over the city. During the rest of this initial stay in New York, Lafayette was entertained by all the learned societies of the city, attended a gala performance of *Twelfth Night*, was shown over the steam-frigate *Washington* and watched a parade of the New York Fire Department.[14]

When he left the city, fulfilling a promise to pay an early visit to Boston, he was accompanied by a large escort as far as New Rochelle, where he met war veterans who had not been able to get to New York to see him. As he reported in a letter home: 'Men and women come two hundred miles to shake my hand.' There were frequent echoes of the Revolutionary War. At Fort McHenry, Lafayette was received in Washington's tent, re-erected for the occasion, and the same tent reappeared at Yorktown for the celebrations there. Martial music was often part of the welcome. At Baltimore, the hero was installed in a carpet-draped alcove to listen to the band of the Maryland militia playing 'Lafayette's March'. The noise of welcome sometimes submerged the music, as at Charleston in the spring of 1824, where a troop of Frenchmen, in uniforms copied from the Paris National Guard, escorted Lafayette's carriage – to the accompaniment of shouts of 'Welcome Lafayette!', the ringing of the town's bells and a salute from ships in the harbour.[15]

His final farewell to New York was marked by a fête in the Castle Garden at the Battery. Levasseur describes the scene in the hall of the fort where nearly 6000 people were waiting to welcome them:

> An arch formed the flags of all nations mingled with symmetry and elegance. Over the principal entrance was a triumphal arch of flowers, surmounted by a colossal statue of Washington, resting on two pieces of cannon. In the centre stood the genius of America, having on a shield these words, 'TO THE NATION'S GUEST'.

On Lafayette's entry the band struck up 'See the Conquering Hero Comes'. In front of his chair a large transparency was unveiled depicting the chateau of La Grange with the inscription 'Here is His Home'.[16]

Prominent among those who greeted Lafayette in his perambulations through the Union were the Freemasons. We know that the Marquis had attended a Masonic lodge meeting in France as early as 1775, while still in his teens. The lodge was *La Candeur*, later to be Orleanist in its leanings, and including among its members the Duc de Choiseul, the Comte de Broglie and Alexandre de Lameth. Now, in 1824, Lafayette claimed that his admission to the *American Union* Lodge during the winter of 1777–8 at Valley Forge – with Washington officiating as Master Mason – had been the turning-point in his military career. As he explained to the *Four of Wilmington* at Delaware:

> I could not rid my mind of the suspicion that the General harboured doubts concerning me; this suspicion was confirmed by the fact that I had never been given a command-in-chief. After I had become an American freemason, General Washington seemed to have seen the light. From that moment I never had reason to doubt his entire confidence.[17]

American Freemasons were already active in the 1730s, and in 1755 when their first Masonic Hall was built at Philadelphia, Henry Price noted that 40 lodges had sprung from his first lodge in Boston alone. Washington had been a Mason since the early 1750s, and shortly before his death would write of Freemasons: 'I conceive them to be founded in benevolence, and to be exercised only for the good of mankind.' When laying the corner-stone of the Capitol in the autumn of 1793, the President would wear a Masonic apron, made for him by French nuns at Nantes. Later, the Statue of Liberty would be designed by a Mason, Frédéric Auguste Bartholdi, and Masonic lodges in France and America would be active in raising funds for its construction. When the long-delayed stone-laying ceremony for the statue's pedestal at length took place in 1884, the Grand Master of New York claimed that 'no other organization has ever done more to promote Liberty and to liberate men from their chains of ignorance and tyranny than Freemasonry'.[18]

Too much has sometimes been claimed for the impact of Freemasonry on the French Revolution. As early as 1798, an emigrant French priest claimed that the Revolution was provoked by a Masonic plot. The Duc d'Orléans, focus of opposition to Louis XVI's government, was admittedly Master of the *Grand Orient*. But membership of the lodges was predominantly aristocratic and Catholic, which helps to explain why Louis XVI was himself a Mason. Pope Clement XII condemned the movement for its secrecy, but in January 1781 Marie Antoinette could write: 'Every one belongs to it; consequently what goes on becomes known; where then is the danger?' Some two years before, in November 1778, the Lodge of Nine Sisters had defied the ban imposed by the Archbishop of Paris, by holding Masonic obsequies in Voltaire's honour – a provocative action directed at both crown and altar. The risk of royal reprisal was averted by the replacement of Lalande as Master by Franklin.[19]

Danton, Marat and Robespierre were all at one time Freemasons, and the Jacobins borrowed Masonic symbols for their Republic of Virtue. But Masons were excluded from municipal government; and during the Terror the *Grand Orient* was suppressed. Masonic lodges nevertheless facilitated the spread of Enlightenment ideas, and the Deism of Masonic ceremonies was one thread in the subtle undermining of the Catholic Church – traditional buttress of the French monarchy. And it was a leading Freemason (Abbé Robin) who, describing the American habit of playing music in camp, wrote exuberantly:

> Then, officers, soldiers, American men and women, all join and dance together. It is the Festival of Equality…These people are still in the happy time when distinctions of birth and rank are ignored and can see, with the same eye, the common soldier and the officer.[20]

An American Freemason first, Lafayette became a French Freemason too. When he briefly returned to France after the British surrender at Yorktown, he was affiliated to the *Mother Lodge of Saint John of Scotland and the Social Contract*, and on his return to the United States in 1784, he took with him a Mason's apron which Adrienne had embroidered for Washington. Now, 40 years later, Lafayette found no less than 37 Masonic lodges in America named after him. Within weeks of his arrival, the Masons of New York entertained him to a banquet intended also to celebrate the completion of the Erie Canal. He was soon the guest of the Virginian lodges of Norfolk and Richmond, and in March 1825 there was a Masonic banquet in his honour at Fayetteville. Later the same month the Freemasons of Savannah led the city's procession to Johnson Square, where Lafayette laid the corner-stone of a monument to General Greene, a fellow hero of the Revolutionary War. And when he laid the corner-stone of another monument – at Bunker Hill in June – there were 2000 Freemasons in a crowd of 7000 to watch Lafayette perform the ceremony in his Masonic regalia.[21]

By the time of the Bunker Hill festivities, Lafayette's tour of all 24 states of the Union was nearing its end. It had been a formidable physical feat. On his southern progress alone, between late February and mid-May, he had travelled almost 5000 miles. Much of this was by water: on the Mississipi his steam-boat covered 300 miles in three days, although it nearly foundered in a violent storm in Mexico Bay. A strong carriage was provided for travel over the poor southern roads, but parts of the country had not been settled and had no roads, so the party then had to take to horseback. When the strain of constant celebrations was added to the rigours of travel, it is surprising that Lafayette, now in his late sixties, stood up to it all so well. Adulation is doubtless a great tonic, but after 48 hours of festivities in Augusta, Georgia, Levasseur tells us that the General 'suffered a fatigue which caused us a momentary inquietude'. Yet by the time Miss Quincy saw him in June, she thought he looked younger than he had the previous autumn.[22]

Although, in Jefferson's phrase, Lafayette's education had been 'merely military', the General was invited to a number of colleges. Barely a week after landing in New York in August 1824, he was received by the faculty of Yale, and four days later attended Commencement Day at Harvard. Here someone remarked on how fluently he spoke English. 'And why should I not,' Lafayette replied, 'being an American just returned from a long visit to Europe.' Jefferson's University of Virginia was nearing completion, and the party went with Jefferson and Madison to a university reception, where George was presented with a live rattlesnake to add to the remarkable collection of souvenirs that would be shipped back to France. In a farewell address to the Nation's Guest, at a ceremony in the White House on the day of Lafayette's final departure, President John Quincy Adams spoke of the General's 'consistent and undeviating career of forty years' in which he had devoted himself to 'the improvement of the moral and political condition of man'. He had, said the President, been welcomed by the people of the Union as 'a long absent parent'. Frenchmen would want to claim their hero as the personification of the age, yet Americans too 'shall claim you for our own'. Replying, Lafayette referred with pride to his participation 'in the toils and perils of our unspotted struggle for independence, freedom and equal rights, and in the foundation of the American era of a new social order. He ended by throwing himself into the President's arms, as both cried 'Adieu! Adieu!'.[23]

The descendants of George Washington came to see Lafayette off. He was conveyed by the *Mount Vernon* to the frigate *Brandywine*, which was to take him home. On arrival at Le Havre, the First Lieutenant was meant to make a valedictory speech. But words failed him, and instead he rushed to the stern, seized the American flag and presented it to Lafayette, urging him to fly it from the towers of La Grange on George Washington's birthday and Independence Day. The General accepted the flag as a token of 'the kindness of the American nation towards its adopted and devoted son'. He promised to fly it so as to advertise to visiting Americans that 'at La Grange you are not on foreign soil'. Lafayette had brought back on the *Brandywine* some American soil in which, nine years later, he would be buried. Before then he would appear briefly in a *third* revolution.[24]

In the 1830 Revolution in Paris, Lafayette (aged 73) again commanded the National Guard, and again appeared on a balcony – this time wrapping Louis Philippe in the tricolour. Soon Lafayette was welcoming a deputation of Philadelphians who had come to Paris to present a congratulatory address. Speaking at the *hôtel de ville* he told them: 'I can, with almost the same pleasure, place myself among those presenting the address, or those receiving it.' And at a banquet held that evening, a toast was proposed to 'The emancipation of the American hemisphere, achieved within half a century!' He was elected to the Chamber of Deputies, and one of his few speeches there called for improvements in the 1831 treaty with the United States. It was in this speech that he proclaimed himself a 'Good American' though he added, 'Nobody can say I have been a bad Frenchman.' When he at length died in 1834, the American Congress decreed a month's official mourning in his honour. A joint resolution of both Houses expressed their 'profoundest sensibility' at hearing the news of the death of 'General LAFAYETTE, the friend of the United States, the friend of WASHINGTON and the friend of liberty'. John Quincy Adams was invited to 'deliver an Oration on the Life and Character of General Lafayette, before the two Houses of Congress, at the next session'. And the equestrian statue of the Hero of Two Worlds erected in Paris was paid for by American subscription.[25]

11 Allies in Arms: Ségur, Lauzun and Chastellux

The *Memoirs* of Louis-Philippe, Comte de Ségur, were published in three volumes simultaneously in French and English during 1825 and 1826. This was a few months after the rapturous reception given to Lafayette on his return to America with his son. Ségur called it 'the most splendid triumph enjoyed by any man', and saw it as a demonstration that 'ten million Americans have proved that the services rendered to them, the dangers braved and the efforts made to secure their independence, remain indelibly engraved in their memory'. And Ségur soon records with a certain smugness that 'the three Frenchmen, distinguished by their rank at court, who first offered their military services to the Americans, were the Marquis de Lafayette, the Vicomte de Noailles and myself.' Of this trio of aristocratic young officers, only Lafayette reached America in 1776. Noailles followed in 1780, but it was not until 1782, after the British surrender at Yorktown, that Ségur finally overcame family opposition to his trans-Atlantic ambitions.[1]

Ségur embarked for America with the Duc de Lauzun, the Comte de Loménie, the Prince de Broglie (son of Marshal Broglie) and Baron de Montesquieu (grandson of the author of *De l'esprit des lois*). They were joined by Alexandre de Lameth, destined to be a leading orator in the French Revolution. They crossed the Atlantic in two frigates (the *Gloire* and the *Aigle*). Their passage was slowed by the decision of the commander of the *Aigle* to take his mistress with him – not indeed aboard the *Aigle*, but in a following merchantman which he had under tow. Realizing at last that they were losing too much time, he cut the luckless lady adrift; but the frigates were nevertheless compelled to enter the Delaware without pilots and under the guns of a British squadron. The *Aigle* ran aground, and in the ensuing confusion, the army officers struggled ashore in small boats, setting foot on American soil 'destitute of baggage, of servants, of our trunks, and even of any shirts but those we then wore.'[2]

Given this unpropitious introduction to America, it is not surprising that Ségur's first impression was of a country that 'offered nothing to the view but thick woods and dangerous marshes'. The first town he entered impressed him more favourably, however: 'All the houses in

Dover offered a simple but elegant appearance; they were built of wood, and painted in different colours.' The inhabitants themselves were well dressed 'with boots well cleaned', and the independence of character they exhibited 'seemed to declare that we were in a land of reason, of order and of liberty'. As he was carrying despatches for the Comte de Rochambeau and for General Washington, Ségur could stay barely 24 hours in Philadelphia, but he saw enough to herald 'the great and prosperous destinies of America'.[3]

As he continues his northward journey, he records: 'I experienced two opposite impressions: one produced by the spectacles of a wild and savage nature; and the other by the fertility and variety of industrious cultivation and of a civilized world.' Sometimes he finds himself 'alone amidst vast forests of those magnificent trees yet sacred from the axe', while beyond the woods rose 'populous villages and towns which, with their schools, their temples and their universities, brought back ideas of civilization reaching perfection'. Yet on seeing the Hudson, flowing between mountains covered with pine, ancient oaks and black cypresses, he writes: 'This wild and savage prospect awakened many sad and solemn thoughts, such as might, in the language of the present day, be termed romantic.' The appeal of America to the revolutionary generation of Frenchmen was indeed as much an affair of the heart as of the head.[4]

When he sailed for home on Christmas Eve 1782, Ségur confessed: 'I did not quit North America without experiencing considerable heartache.' And in a letter written at the moment of leaving 'this political Eldorado', Ségur sums up his view of the American republic:

> Here all private interests merge into the general welfare; everyone lives for himself and dresses as he pleases, not as it pleases fashion. People here think, say and do what they like; nothing compels them to submit to the caprices of fortune or of power.

Conscious that his eulogy may seem too fulsome, he concludes: 'I shall, perhaps be told that America will not always preserve such simple virtues and such purity of morals, but were she to retain them no longer than a century, is a century of happiness so inconsiderable a blessing?'[5]

Ségur published his memoirs well after the French Revolution, which doubtless coloured his recollections. Yet nothing in his later life seems quite to have matched the youthful exuberance that his American experience unleashed. During the early days of the French Revolution he wrote articles for the *Moniteur*, the leading revolutionary newspaper.

He survived the Terror by going into hiding, and under Napoleon was successively Grand Master of Ceremonies, Count of the Empire and a member of the Senate – though in 1814 he voted for the restoration of the Bourbons. He died in 1830, but not before welcoming the overthrow of Charles X and the accession of the Orleanist claimant, Louis-Philippe, the only French king to have lived in America.[6]

The Duc de Lauzun, who crossed the Atlantic with Ségur in 1782, had less tenuous Orleanist connections. In 1792 the future Louis-Philippe (then Duc de Chartres) would be placed in Lauzun's care, when serving with Rochambeau's army at Valenciennes. Lauzun's links with the Orléans family date from the time of his final return from America, when he and the Duc d'Orléans were both courting Mme de Coigny. The risk of rivalry was removed when Orléans transferred his affections to Mme Buffon (daughter-in-law of the naturalist) who followed Orléans into temporary exile in London but refused his suggestion that they should emigrate to America. When fighting broke out in Paris on 12 July 1789, Orléans was still in the capital and shut his doors to everyone except the Duc de Lauzun and Mme Buffon. Lauzun, having helped to vote away aristocratic privileges on the night of 4 August, was asked by Orléans to consult Mirabeau on the advisability of going into exile, as Lafayette was insisting that the Duke should do. Mirabeau advised him not to go, and urged him to challenge Lafayette in the National Assembly. When Orléans nevertheless accepted exile, Lauzun was left to defend him in his absence. The imprisonment of the royal family in 1792 spelt danger for Orleanists. Lauzun now commanded the Army of the Rhine, and when the commissioners arrived to administer the affirmation of loyalty to the new republic, he was the first to affirm his acceptance 'without reservation'. The commissioners reported favourably on Lauzun, commending his 'honesty, courage, and unlimited devotion to the cause he has embraced'. This did not, however, prevent his being relieved of his post as commander-in-chief on the Rhine.[7]

By the time Lauzun received a new command in the Alps, with headquarters at Nice, the National Convention was in session with the Duc d'Orléans as one of its members. Lauzun agreed to the Duke's request to take Montpensier (his second son) under his command, though when the Orléans family was proscribed, Lauzun had the unwelcome duty of arresting him. On hearing of the dismissal of Kellerman and three other generals, Lauzun wrote asking whether he should resign, or whether it would be 'more respectful to await my dismissal in silence'. By way of answer, he was posted to La Rochelle to direct operations against the rebels in Poitou and Brittany. Here he again offered to resign, this time in favour of a general who had come up through the ranks, since 'to obey seems so remote from equality that hardly a man regards it as his duty'. When the commissioners drew up a plan to evacuate Anger and Nantes without consulting Lauzun, he refused to implement it. The Committee of Public Safety wrote to him in complimentary terms, promising that 'all will concur in your military projects', but then reversed its decision to recall the commissioners. Instead their position was confirmed in view of their 'usefulness' to the army. This was too much for Lauzun: he resigned, pleading ill health, while assuring his political masters that 'in all places and in any rank, I will willingly dedicate my remaining strength and days to the service of the Republic.'[8]

That was on 10 July 1793. Ten days later he was examined by the Executive Council. On 25 July he was arrested and consigned to the Abbaye prison. At his trial, Lauzun protested that his conscience did not reproach him with anything, that he had done all in his power in most difficult circumstances, and that no one could have done better in his place. He asked for formal confirmation that 'I have served the Republic well and deserved well of my country, and that I may take with me into the retirement which my health requires, this satisfaction which really is worthy of a Republican soldier.' Far from receiving the testimonial he sought, Lauzun was sent to the guillotine at the age of 46, four weeks after the Duc d'Orléans had met the same fate. One of the commissioners with the army wrote that Lauzun was 'really a man of the *ancien régime*, whatever he might do to appear as if he belonged to the new order of things'.[9]

Lauzun's early career certainly supports that view. His amorous pursuit of Princess Czartoriska led (aptly enough) to a scheme for a Franco-Russian alliance. He was at the time a favourite of Marie Antoinette, and seems to have wanted the Russian alliance for her sake. As he wrote: 'I wanted to make Marie Antoinette the monarch of a great Empire, to see her at the age of twenty playing a splendid part which might have made her for ever famous.' (He could not have guessed the notoriety she was destined to enjoy.) The Empress liked the idea of an alliance, but Lauzun could not persuade his queen – though Marie Antoinette continued to go riding with him almost every day, to the point of causing gossip.[10]

By 1777, at the age of 30, Lauzun had debts of over two million livres. Refusing various offers of relief, including a royal pension, he handed over all his assets to the Prince de Gréménée in return for an annual income of 80 000 livres. Lauzun's wife left to live with her grandmother, and from now on communicated with him only on business. Events in America now encouraged the French government to think of taking advantage of England's discomfiture by mounting an assault on India. Lauzun was keen to take part, and was offered the post of second-in-command of the expedition. He was empowered to raise a corps of 4000 troops under his command – the Foreign Marine Volunteers. Within two months he had raised 2000 men. He returned to court only once, for a grand masquerade in the Queen's honour at which Vergennes appeared with a globe on his head, a map of America on his front and a map of England on his back.

Vergennes's fancy dress proved to be prophetic. The expedition to India never sailed, although Lauzun was sent to silence a British fort on the coast of Senegal – an exploit for which he received scant praise. (It was Madame de Coigny's loyal refusal to ostracize the victor of Senegal that led the hero promptly to fall in love with her.) Meanwhile, finding that his patiently assembled marine corps had been dispersed, Lauzun offered to become Inspector-General of Prisoners of War. But when Rochambeau was released from the aborted invasion of England, and diverted instead to America, Lauzun sailed with him on 2 May 1780. The expeditionary force of 5000 included Chastellux, Noailles, the Duc de Castries and Count Fersen – perhaps too many stars for one show. 'In this corps everything breathes jealousy and in subordination', was Lauzun's comment on the voyage. On landing at Newport, Rhode Island, in early July, Lauzun was put in charge of coastal defences; but in the new year, Rochambeau sent him to General Washington so that the American commander-in-chief could converse with a French officer in English. Lauzun stayed several days, while Washington explained his plans, which included the promise of an important post for the Frenchman. However, Maurepas wrote to reveal that there would be no reinforcements, and so in June 1781, when the French army left Newport en route for Yorktown, Lauzun's hussars were the only cavalry taking part in the advance. Although it was Charles de Lameth who was the first Frenchman to leap the ramparts of the British redoubt, it was Lauzun's hussars who defeated Tarleton's English dragoons in a brilliant skirmish that would find its way into cavalry textbooks. And it was Lauzun whom Rochambeau deputed to carry the news of the British surrender back to France.[11]

This time he did receive a hero's welcome, and despite his commitment to the American cause, his devotion to Mme de Coigny made him reluctant to return to America when ordered to do so. As Lauzun himself admits: 'I was strongly tempted to remain [in France] for Mme de Coigny's sake. For her sake I went.' That is how he came to be crossing the Atlantic with Ségur in June 1782. At the end of the war, Lauzun came back to France with the rest of the army, and found that one of the transports provided by Congress was named *Lauzun* – an eloquent tribute. Yet, alone among the 'American' officers, Lauzun received no official recognition in France, while his corps of foreign volunteers was soon disbanded. Perhaps his attachment to Mme de Coigny explains his neglect by the court. Marie Antoinette is supposed to have said: 'I am Queen at Versailles, but Mme de Coigny is Queen in Paris.' It was his heart rather than his head that led him into the rival court of the Duc d'Orléans, but Lauzun's American experience ensured that his sympathy for republican ideas was more than political time-serving.[12]

It was in 1784, the year that Lauzun joined the Orleanists at the Palais Royal, that Francois Jean Chastellux succeeded to the title of Marquis on the death of his brother. The new marquis himself had only four more years to live: he died on 24 October 1788, aged 54, thus happily avoiding the guillotine. Unlike Ségur and Lauzun, whose memoirs were not published until the 1820s, Chastellux did much to popularize the American cause in France during the years before 1789. The newly promoted Marshal Chastellux crossed the Atlantic in 1780 with Rochambeau's corps, at the same time as Lauzun. Apart from his military experience – having fought in all the European campaigns of the Seven Years' War – he had the added advantage of being a good linguist. His knowledge embraced not only German, but Greek, Latin, English and Italian – all good republican languages. He had links with the *philosophes* and wrote for the *Encyclopédie*, though his article was not published. But under Mably's influence, he published *De la félicité publique* (1772), which Voltaire said contained more useful truths than Montesquieu's *De l'esprit des lois*. In 1775, on the strength of his newly published *Eloge d'Helvétius*, he became a member of the French Academy. In his speech of welcome, Buffon complimented Chastellux on being the first academician to be inoculated against smallpox.

On the title page of the English edition of his *Travels in North America* (1787), Chastellux describes himself as 'one of the forty members of the French academy, and major general in the French army, serving under the Count de Rochambeau'. The *Travels* opens with his arrival at Newport, Rhode Island, on 11 July 1780 – barely a week before the British fleet appeared off the town. When, a month later, it became clear that the British objective was not Rhode Island but New York, Chastellux decided he could spend the winter months sightseeing. On 11 November he left Rhode Island in the company of M. de Montesquieu and another aide, together with five servants. Their first stop was at Hartford, which (Chastellux records) 'does not merit any attention either in travelling through it or in speaking of it'. On the road beyond Hartford, Chastellux notes: 'Having fired my pistol at a jay, to my great astonishment the bird fell.' And with the eye of a true *encyclopédiste*, he continues: 'It is quite blue, but it unites all the various shades of that colour so as to surpass the invention of art, and be very difficult of imitation.' He is soon recording that 'the vision of Mr Buffon appeared to me in these ancient deserts', concluding rather too optimistically that 'he is always in the right'. Like other Europeans in America, Chastellux is impressed by the ease with which land can be settled: 'Any man who is able to procure a capital of five or six hundred livres of our money, or about twenty-five pounds sterling, and who has strength and inclination to work, may go into the woods and purchase a portion of one hundred and fifty or two hundred acres of land.'[13]

At West Point, the Marquis liked what he saw of the colonial army: 'The troops were ill clothed, but made a good appearance; as for the officers, they were everything that could be wished.' He is received by a 13-gun salute, fired by guns captured from General Burgoyne. When they reach Lafayette's camp, Chastellux sees his compatriot in conversation with a tall man 'of a noble and mild countenance'. It turns out (predictably) to be Washington himself, who, the Marquis decides after a few glasses of claret and madeira over dinner, is 'the greatest and the best of men'. The Marshal has left us an account of what it was like to dine with Washington:

> The repast was in the English fashion, consisting of eight or ten large dishes of butcher's meat, and poultry, with vegetables of several sorts, followed by a second course of pastry, comprized under the two denominations of pies and puddings. After this the cloth was taken off, and apples and a great quantity of nuts were served, which General Washington usually continues eating for two hours, *toasting*, and conversing all the time.

His estimate of the general's character has a Gibbonian resonance: 'Brave without temerity, laborious without ambition, generous without prodigality, noble without pride, virtuous without severity'. And the discipline of the general's entourage tempts the Marshal to apply to the Americans 'what Pyrrhus said of the Romans: Truly these people have nothing barbarous in their discipline.'[14]

Chastellux does not spend all his time with soldiers. He meets Dr Witherspoon, President of Princeton, and they converse in French – though the Marshal 'easily perceived that he had acquired his knowledge of that language from reading rather than conversation'. From Princeton he went on to Philadelphia, where he paid his respects to the French ambassador, La Luzerne. Before leaving the city, Chastellux has dinner with the Congressional delegates of the Northern states, and calls on Sam Adams, who had missed the dinner. He visits the hall where Congress sits, and with Lafayette, Noailles and other 'Gallo-Americans', attends a session of the state assembly of Pennsylvania. He notices with pleasure that the library of a Philadelphia lawyer contains 'all our best authors on public law and jurisprudence', including Montesquieu. Commenting on the graduation speeches at the University of Pennsylvania, he remarks that, though anti-British in tone, they were 'by no means inferior to those I have heard at Oxford and Cambridge'. He is reminded of Tom Paine's claim in *Common Sense* that the younger generation 'are from their cradle bred to consider [Britain] as their only foe'.[15]

Next day, a party of officers goes to see the battlefield of Brandywine. The *Travels* contains an account of the battle based on what Chastellux had been told by Washington, Lafayette and two other Frenchmen, and by the American generals Wayne and Sullivan, though he admits that 'there is disagreement in some particulars'. A visit to the Delaware forts prompts a long account of the defence of Fort Redbank, followed by the disclaimer: 'Perhaps I have dwelt too long on this event; but I shall not have to apologize to those who will partake of the pleasing satisfaction I experience, in fixing my eyes on the triumphs of America.' It is at Redbank that Duplessis Mauduit conducts them to a Quaker's house. Mauduit tells them: 'I was obliged to knock down his barn, and fell his fruit trees; but he will be glad to see M. de la Fayette, and will receive us well.' This confidence proves to be misplaced. Chastellux finds the Quaker's welcome decidedly cool: 'Except *Dido's* silence, I know nothing more severe'. Unlike other French travellers in America, Chastellux is critical of the Quakers. He thinks it is lack of sympathy with the rebel cause rather than pacifism, that makes them refuse to support the war, and he draws an unfavourable contrast between the Quaker meeting he attends – 'this melancholy, homespun assembly' – and the

Anglican church service, which he describes as 'a sort of opera'. He is glad that Quaker dominance in America is at an end: 'This revolution comes very opportunely, at a time when the public has derived every benefit from them they could expect; the walls of the house are finished, it is time to call in the carpenters and upholsterers.'[16]

The Marquis stays in Philadelphia long enough to attend a meeting of the Academy of Sciences, at which he and Lafayette are elected foreign members. The Academy had been founded by Franklin, whom Chastellux is quick to defend against the charge that he had given his home state 'too democratical a government'. Franklin had 'acted like Solon; he has not given the best possible laws to Pennsylvania, but the best of which the country was susceptible'. (The words recall Franklin's own response to the final form of the Federal Constitution.) La Luzerne, whose guest he was in Philadelphia, impresses Chastellux greatly. He finds him 'noble in his expenses, like the minister of a great monarchy, but as plain in his manners as a republican'. But it is now time to take his leave of La Luzerne and Philadelphia. On 16 December, the *Travels* records, 'I quitted the excellent winter quarters I had with him, and turned my face towards the north, to seek after the traces of General Gates and General Burgoyne, amid heaps of snow.' Passing through towns with German names, like Strasbourg, where he converses with a French-speaking Dutchman, he discovers a widespread view that 'there is no expedition more useful, nor more easy than the conquest of Canada.' General Schuyler, at whose house on the Hudson Chastellux catches up with Noailles and Mauduit, had proposed various plans for attacking Canada – none of which had been adopted. Schuyler now accompanies the Frenchmen as they leave in five sledges to view the battlefield of Saratoga. Having surveyed the British defensive position, Chastellux decides: 'It is very certain that Burgoyne had no other alternative than to let his troops be slaughtered or capitulate.'[17]

Between the journeys described in volume one and those in volume two, Chastellux himself saw action at the siege of Yorktown, for which he would receive a *gratification extraordinaire* and the governorship of Longwy. Volume two is devoted to a journey in the spring of 1782 to Upper Virginia and the Appalachians. Here he records seeing 'a mocking-bird saluting the rising sun', and (more improbably) comes across a cock-fight. He discovers that 'this diversion is much in fashion in Virginia, where the English customs are more prevalent than in the rest of America.' But he notes with 'a secret pleasure' that the stake money is 'chiefly French'. He devotes some ten pages to his visit to

Jefferson at Monticello, which he finds 'rather elegant in the Italian manner, though not without fault'. He decides that 'Mr Jefferson is the first American who has consulted the fine arts to know how he should shelter himself from the weather.' Of Jefferson himself: 'I found his first appearance serious, nay even cold; but before I had been two hours with him we were as intimate as if we had passed our whole lives together.' And the Frenchman is much struck by their 'conformity of sentiments and opinions'. They discuss the poems of Ossian over a bowl of punch, and Chastellux writes of Jefferson that 'it seemed as if from his youth he had placed his mind, as he had done his house, on an elevated situation, from which he might contemplate the universe.' And in less sententious vein, he adds that Jefferson has a score of deer in his park and 'amuses himself by feeding them with Indian corn, of which they are very fond, and which they eat out of his hand'. When Chastellux leaves Monticello to visit a striking natural feature, the Bridge of Rocks, 80 miles away, Jefferson accompanies him for the first 16 miles of the journey.[18]

Though he stops for a moment 'to view the wild but uninteresting prospect of the western mountains, from the summit of the Blue Ridges', the Marshal's reflections centre on natural rights rather than romantic nature. 'The principle on which Reason...may at last rely,' Chastellux asserts, is 'the equality of rights; the general interest which actuates all; private interest connected with the general good; the order of society; as necessary as the symmetry of a beehive.' And although he does admire the 'magnificent but tremendous spectacle' of the 'bridge', he takes his leave of Virginia with some observations on its political system: 'The government may become democratic, as it is at the present moment; but the national character, the spirit of the government itself, will always be aristocratic.' In his eyes, the rebellion of Virginia had been an aristocratic revolt: the indolence of Virginians (deriving, he thinks, from their slave-based economy) 'obliged them to rely on a small number of virtuous and enlightened citizens, who led them further than they would have proceeded without a guide'. And he contrasts the readiness of the New England states to throw off the yoke of monarchy with the states of New York and New Jersey which were 'peopled by necessitous Dutchmen'.[19]

His attitude to slavery is itself aristocratic. He remarks that American slavery is not like that of the Greeks: 'It is not only the slave who is beneath his master, it is the negro who is beneath the white man.' He thinks that 'no act of enfranchisement can efface this unfortunate distinction.' He apologizes for not treating the subject of slavery 'with declamation', but (he explains) he prefers reason to eloquence in those matters 'which can only be effected by time alone'. We can see why Chastellux incurred the censure of the impatient and idealistic Brissot. The perceptiveness of the Marquis is nevertheless illustrated by his noting the lack of episcopally ordained ministers – two years before John Wesley took the dramatic step of ordaining his own ministers for America. Chastellux, having paid tribute to the 'magnificence and hospitality' of the Virginians, turns finally to William and Mary College and the world of scholarship. He explains that he has left learning until last because, after considering other human institutions, the mind 'reposes itself with pleasure on those which tend to the perfection of the understanding and the progress of information'. Again, we hear echoes of the *encyclopédistes*.[20]

Back in his military role, and still commanding the 1st French Division, Chastellux faced the approach of winter and an enforced wait with his troops at Hartford. He decided to take the opportunity to explore the northern parts of Massachusetts and New Hampshire. His companions this time include not only Montesquieu, but the Comte de Vaudreuil. They visit the the battlefields of Concord and Bunker Hill; they see at Portsmouth the *America*, 'the ship given by Congress to the King of France'; and they find New Hampshire in the process of drawing up a new constitution 'founded on the same principles as those of New York and Massachusetts'. Describing a ball in Boston, Chastellux pays tribute to his French colleagues who 'did honour to the French nation, by their noble and easy manner'. But he feels bound to add that 'the contrast was considerable between them and the Americans, who are in general very awkward, particularly in the minuet'. The Americans for their part blend their new sense of national pride with courtesy to their guests by telling the Frenchmen: 'You speak American well.'[21]

On 7 December Chastellux paid an emotional farewell to General Washington, and five days later was back in Philadelphia. His journal ends at this point, and is dated Christmas Eve 1782. An appendix contains a more detailed account of the 'Natural Bridge', a 12-page postscript on birdlife, and a 'Letter from the Marquis de Chastellux to Mr Maddison, Professor of Philosophy in the University of Williamsburgh'. In the letter he refers to 'the progress that the arts and sciences cannot fail of making in America, and the influence they must necessarily have on manners and opinions'. It was not quite his last word on America. In 1787 he published a pamphlet outlining the advantages and disadvantages for Europe of the discovery of America.

It had been written four years earlier for Raynal's prize essay competition on the impact of America on Europe, though (according to Chastellux) it was never submitted. Predictably, the Marquis concludes that the discovery of America was providential, not least because it allowed metropolitan France to rid itself of potential trouble-makers. He died the year after his pamphlet was published, and so was denied the spectacle of the American republic being hailed as their inspiration by the makers of the French Revolution.[22]

Images and Visions

Mary Wollstonecraft Godwin.

12 Armchair Philosophy: Raynal's Bestseller

'It is yet too soon to write the history of the revolution'. So declared Tom Paine from Philadelphia in the summer of 1782. His comment was prompted by Abbé Raynal's premature attempt to produce just such a history. The Frenchman's 180-page pamphlet, *The Revolution of America*, had appeared in 1781 – the year of Yorktown. The English translator seems to have obtained the text by underhand means, before Raynal could publish it. While claiming to deplore the pirating of the pamphlet, Paine is chiefly concerned to expose Raynal's misunderstandings and misrepresentations of America. The title of Paine's riposte is characteristically explicit: *A Letter Addressed to the Abbé Raynal on the Affairs of North America in which the Mistakes in the Abbé's account of the Revolution of America are Corrected and Cleared Up*. Paine's excuse for writing is that 'to be *right* is the first wish of philosophy, and the first principle of history'. So his purpose is simply to put the record straight, and to point out those passages where the Abbé has 'extolled without a reason, and wounded without a cause'.[1]

Paine's chief complaint is that Raynal has 'misconceived and misstated the causes which produced the rupture between England and her colonies'. The Abbé implies that the dispute was over the right to lay a 'slight' tax on the colonies, whereas, Paine argues, it was a larger question of sovereignty: 'Shall we be bound in all cases whatsoever by the British Parliament, or shall we not?' Paine writes patronizingly: 'Though the abbé possesses and displays great powers of genius and is a master of style and language, he seems not to pay equal attention to the office of an historian.' Paine pays tribute to the Franco-American alliance, which he thinks Raynal under-values. This was an alliance 'not formed for the mere purpose of a day, but on just and generous grounds, and with equal and mutual advantages'. It was an alliance 'not of courts only, but of countries'. The abbé is equally misleading, Paine decides, in matters of geography. His account is 'so exceedingly erroneous' that to correct it would take Paine beyond the limits he has set himself. 'I never yet saw,' Paine sternly insists, 'an European description of America that was true; neither can any person gain a just idea of it but by coming to it.' Raynal himself admitted as much.

147

'Heroic country,' he wrote, 'my advanced age permits me not to visit thee.' He was 68.[2]

When writing *The Revolution of America* Raynal is unaware that the French alliance had already ensured Britain's defeat. He is concerned that it is taking so long to win the war, and considers that France has frittered away her strategic advantages. He realizes the inadequacies of Washington's militia, and he claims that French supplies to the revolutionary army are usually intercepted by Howe. He thinks France should have concentrated her efforts on disrupting British commerce, and is scathing about those French admirals who neglected convoy duties because 'such a service had nothing noble in it, and led not to any kind of glory'. He also argues that the French should have sought to 'strengthen and confirm the revolution, by keeping always, on the northern coasts of the new world, a squadron which might protect the colonies'. Even as he wrote, it was just such a French fleet that was forcing the surrender of Lord Cornwallis. Raynal is equally critical of French policy at home. When he asserts that British gains in the Seven Years War will prove a liability, by entailing crippling costs for the British people, he has his eye also on France:

> The gold of the trader, and of the husbandman, with the subsistence of the poor, torn from them in the name of the state, in their fields and their habitations, and prostituted in courts to interest and to vice, goes to swell the pomp of a set of men who flatter and corrupt their master ... It is prodigally squandered in a fatuous show of grandeur ... and in festivities and entertainments ...

Government, Raynal thinks, should be *accountable*. The sovereign should 'render to his subjects a faithful account of the employment of the sums he might exact'. But, the abbé adds sagely, 'this sovereign has not yet appeared.'[3]

America, Raynal argues, provides a more favourable environment for liberty than the corrupted courts of Europe. The very soil of North America breeds freedom for its inhabitants:

> Dispersed throughout an immense continent; free as the wild nature which surrounds them, amidst their rocks, their mountains, the vast plains of their deserts, or the confines of those forests in which all is still in its savage state ... they seem to receive from every natural object a lesson of liberty and independence.

And, in applauding the colonists' success in forcing the British to evacuate Boston – which he calls 'the first step of English America towards the revolution' – Raynal hails it as the triumph of the principles of the Enlightenment: 'These principles, which were indebted for their birth to Europe, and particularly to England, had been transplanted in America by philosophy.'[4]

Many of Raynal's arguments echo those of Paine, Price and Priestley, and the abbé has the grace to pay tribute to *Common Sense*. After commending it for giving 'energy to minds ready to receive it', Raynal provides a résumé of the pamphlet. Encapsulating Paine's arguments in such phrases as 'it is not the affair of a day, it is that of ages' and 'Nature did not create a world to subject it to the inhabitants of an island', Raynal goes on to create images of his own. Referring to the biblical account of the Flood, he writes: 'A single family survived and was commanded by the Supreme Being to re-people the earth. We are this family. Despotism has deluged us all; and we can a second time renew the world.' Paine nevertheless complained that Raynal had borrowed much from *Common Sense* without acknowledgment; and he printed comparable passages in parallel columns to prove his point.[5]

Raynal has no doubt as to the symbolic importance of the new America: 'At the sound of breaking chains, it seems as if our own are about to become lighter'. He accordingly ends his pamphlet with a series of exhortations to the American people. They are urged to guard against 'the affluence of gold, which brings with luxury the corruption of manners' and to 'fear a too unequal distribution of riches'. They should encourage the arts and sciences. Raynal's *Revolution* contained an advertisement from the Academy of Lyons, announcing that the author had provided funds for two essay prizes. The subject for competition in 1782 was purely local, relating 'exclusively to the manufactures and prosperity of the city of Lyons'. But the topic proposed for 1783 reads:

> Has the discovery of America been useful or hurtful to mankind?
> If advantages have resulted from it, what are the means to preserve and increase them?
> If disadvantages, what are the means to remedy them?

The prize was 50 gold *louis*, and the competition was open to 'any person of any nation'.[6]

Despite Paine's strictures, Raynal had considerable stature as an historian. He wrote two histories while still in his thirties, one of the Netherlands and the other of the English Parliament. His real claim to fame, however, is his *Philosophical and Political History of the*

Settlements and Trade in the East and West Indies. *The Revolution of America* is an English translation of Book XVIII of the enlarged 1780 edition of the *History*, first published ten years earlier. The four-volume French edition of 1770 was printed in Amsterdam; but the 1774 edition in seven volumes, published at The Hague, claimed to be the first to appear 'in the form in which it left the author's hand'. The first English edition (Dublin 1776) was quickly followed in the same year by a London edition of five volumes 'revised and corrected with maps adapted to the work.' By now the *History* had been placed on the Index – which perhaps explains why it went through 30 editions by 1789. Its radical tone – and the 1780 edition was noticeably more radical – led to Raynal's banishment from France in 1781, and to the public burning of the book by government decree. The abbé was allowed back to France in 1784, and in 1789 was elected to the Estates-General but declined to sit. The following year he returned to the capital, where he delivered an address to the National Assembly, urging the adoption of a constitutional monarchy on the British model. But with the fall of the monarchy, his property was confiscated, and he died in poverty.[7]

Yet in 1776, his English translator could describe the *History* as 'certainly one of the finest works which have appeared since the revival of letters'. It was something of a collaborative effort. Besides a number of less famous *philosophes*, D'Holbach is known to have contributed sections of the text, while Diderot is credited with having written no less than one-fifth of the 1780 edition. Thus the work is a monument to the Enlightenment, establishing America as a model of liberty even before the Declaration of Independence. The first three volumes of the 1776 London edition cover the Dutch, British and French in the East Indies, Columbus and the Spanish conquest of South America and Mexico, Portuguese colonization 'in the Brasils', and an account of the Caribbean islands and the slave trade. The fourth volume focuses on what Raynal calls 'the American islands', and, with Book XIV, we arrive at the British settlements in North America. The discovery of America, we are told, has hastened the 'advancement' of Europe:

> The mechanical and liberal arts were extended, and were advancing to perfection by the luxury that prevailed. Literature acquired the ornaments of taste, and the sciences gained that degree of solidity which springs from a spirit of calculation and commerce. The circle of politics was extended...

Raynal was writing of the Elizabethan age of exploration, but his words match the Age of Enlightenment.[8]

More prosaically the abbé predicts that, if the British government remained deaf to demands for improved representation, 'The counties of England would rise; the colonies would shake off their allegiance in America; the treasures of both worlds would be lost to an island which nature has made sovereign of the sea.' Among such 'treasures', Raynal counts West Indies cotton, which he regards as unsuitable for export to Europe, 'though it might be usefully employed in making of hats'. More promising crops are ginger, sugar and coffee. Jamaica, Raynal decides, might well become a homeland for the Jews. As they are the money lenders of the planters, he hopes that the Jews may 'one day lawfully possess this or some other rich island of America'. They are, he reminds us, 'our brethren by the ties of humanity, and our fathers by the tenets of religion'.[9]

Raynal is soon offering more general practical advice on the best plan which could be pursued in establishing a new colony. After taking careful note of the prevailing winds, 'the habitations should be built in the wood, and not a tree suffered to be felled about them.' He explains: 'The woods are wholesome; the refreshing shade they afford, and the cool air we breathe in them even in the heat of the day, are a preservative against that excessive perspiration, which is the destruction of all Europeans'. Once the settlers have become acclimatized, they can begin to cut down the woods, though only at some distance from the huts. And even then, 'the slaves should not be sent out to their work till ten o'clock in the morning, when the sun has had time to divide the vapours, and the wind to drive them away.' As early as 1776 Raynal is critical of slavery. When writing of the colonial militia, he points out that one of its principal tasks is 'to keep the negroes in awe'. And he pauses to ask: 'Are then the efforts of men towards independence of such a nature that, when they have shaken off the yoke, they wish to impose it upon others?'[10]

He is equally committed to Enlightenment principles in urging the need to remove restrictions on commerce: 'Men who are inspired with the love of humanity, and are enlightened by that sacred fire, have ever wished to see every obstacle removed that intercepts a direct communication of all the ports of America with all the ports of Europe.' Yet, writing just before the publication of Adam Smith's *Wealth of Nations* (1776), Raynal is pessimistic about the prospects for free trade. He thinks all European countries are pursuing a policy of self-sufficiency. Towards the end of the *History*, Raynal re-echoes this theme: restraints on trade, he claims with a rhetorical flourish, 'have given rise to smugglers and galley slaves, to customs and monopolies, to pirates and excisemen.'[11]

The abbé's immediate concern, however, is that the French should 'prepare for the defence of America'. Only France, he argues, is capable of creating a navy large enough to challenge the British. Aware that so belligerent a proposal may seem to square oddly with enlightened principles, Raynal appeals to his fellow *philosophes*:

> Philosophers of all nations, friends of mankind, forgive a French writer if he urges his countrymen to build ships. His only view is to promote the tranquillity of the earth, by wishing to see that equilibrium established in the dominion of the seas, which now preserves the security of the continent.

So the balance of power is to be seen in maritime and not merely continental terms. Europe, Raynal insists, is waiting impatiently for the creation of a French navy: 'She will never think her liberties secure, till she sees a flag upon the ocean that does not tremble before the British standard.'[12]

In Book XV he examines the reasons for the slowness of French settlement of the American mainland. He concludes that it was lack of vision on the part of French governments, which 'had not even conceived it possible to establish colonies'. In this policy vacuum, 'France therefore suffered the Spaniards and Portuguese to discover new worlds, and to give laws to unknown nations.' In the 1776 edition of the *History*, Raynal still adheres to his original aim – the adoption of a more rational and humane colonial policy. But by the 1780 edition, in a section written by Diderot, colonialism itself is under attack:

> Flee, unhappy Hottentots! Flee! Hide yourselves deep in the forests. The wild beasts who inhabit there are less to be feared than the monsters under whose rule you will fall... Or if you feel the courage for it, take up your hatchets, bend your bows and rain down poisoned arrows on these intruders. May none remain to bring the news back to their fellow- countrymen.[13]

Yet already in 1776, in describing the fortunes of the French Canadians, Raynal is critical of the North American fur trade – what he calls 'that fatal industry exercised in the woods of Canada'. Having considered the fur of deer and ermine, otter and martin, lynx and fox – even the skin of the musk-rat – Raynal comes to the beaver. Here he cannot resist pointing a political moral. After describing the beaver's tree-felling and dam-building skills, Raynal proclaims: 'Such is the system of the republican, intelligent beaver, skilled in architecture, provident and systematical in its plans of police and society, whose gentle and instructive manners we have been describing.' And with a sensitivity as yet uncharacteristic of his age, the abbé reflects: 'Happy if his coat did not tempt merciless and savage man to destroy his buildings and his race.' He then nevertheless describes how to catch the unlucky animal, but at the end of no less than ten pages devoted to the beaver, Raynal decides that the fur trade is bad not only for beavers, but also for the Indians, since it brings them 'guns, powder and shot, tobacco and especially brandy.'[14]

The description of French Canada is punctuated by an account of the Canadian Indians. Echoing earlier writers, Raynal claims that 'no Greek or Roman orator ever spoke perhaps with more strength and sublimity than one of their chiefs.' The abbé considers the Indians a benevolent race, though he admits that 'none of the writers who have described the manners of the savages have reckoned benevolence among their virtues.' He applauds their disregard of titles, and notices their amusement over 'our arts, our manners and all those customs which inspire us with a greater degree of vanity, in proportion as they remove us further from the state of nature'. Conceding that their dances are 'generally an emblem of war', the abbé allows himself to think that 'it might not, however, be improper sometimes to bring back dancing to its first origin...and to adopt the lively and significant images of the rude Canadians.' The theme of the 'liberty of the savage' is resumed in Book XVI. 'All men talk of liberty,' Raynal writes, 'but the savage alone enjoys it.' Yet, at least in the earlier editions, the abbé appears to share Buffon's belief in the physical degeneracy of species on the American continent. This physical inferiority, it seems, applies equally to human beings: 'The men have less strength and less courage; no beard and no hair; they have less appearance of manhood; and are but little susceptible of the lively and powerful sentiment of love, which is the principle of every attachment, the first instinct, the first band of society'. No wonder Paine thought Raynal should have visited America before writing about it.[15]

Still under the influence of Buffon, the abbé can scarcely conceal his surprise that 'no European fruits have degenerated in New England.' Indeed, he adds, 'it is even said that the apple is improved.' The successful cultivation of the American continent inspires one of Raynal's more imaginative flights:

Man appeared, and immediately changed the face of North America. He introduced symmetry, by the assistance of all the instruments of art. The wild beasts were driven away, and flocks and domestic animals supplied their place; while thorns and briars made way for rich harvests...The coasts were covered with towns, and the bays with ships; and thus the new world, like the old, became subject to man.

Yet it does occur to Raynal to wonder, in Rousseauesque vein, if so much civilization is necessarily beneficial. He asks whether 'those untutored nations are more or less happy than our civilized people', and he concludes that, since a sense of independence is 'one of the first instincts in man', anyone who enjoys it (together with sufficient means of subsistence) 'is incomparably happier than the rich man, restrained by laws, master, prejudices and fashions, which incessantly remind him of the loss of liberty'.[16]

From natural liberty to civil liberty. Having commented on the 'blind fanaticism' of New England, Raynal praises the tolerant spirit of Pennsylvania. He condemns the Anabaptists' attachment to 'the chimerical idea of an equality of stations', and in a passage that will read all the more poignantly after the French Revolution, he powerfully expresses the dangers of the quest for equality: 'To preach this system to the people, is not to put them in mind of their rights, it is leading them on to assassination and plunder. It is letting domestic animals loose, and transforming them into wild beasts.' And in a flash of unromantic realism, he reminds us that not even the savages are equal: 'They are only so, while they wander in the woods; and then the man who suffers the produce of his chase to be taken from him, is not the equal of him who deprives him of it.'[17]

Raynal's admiration for Penn, who had 'made toleration the basis of his society', leads him to regard the founder of the Quaker colony as the harbinger of the Enlightenment: 'It is time to observe the dawnings of reason, happiness and humanity rising from among the ruins of a hemisphere, which still reeks with the blood of all its people, civilized as well as savage.' Penn's Quakers would not necessarily have relished the comparison that the Frenchman draws between them and pagan times, when he writes that Pennsylvania's neighbours 'were delighted to see those heroic days of antiquity realized, which European manners and laws had long taught everyone to consider entirely fabulous'. But even the Quakers themselves would have agreed that toleration is good for trade and that religious freedom 'attracted the Swedes, Dutch, French, and particularly some laborious Germans into that country'. Raynal pays tribute to Philadelphia – 'this famous city whose very name recalls every human feeling' – and in particular to the library established by Benjamin Franklin in 1742. And if Europe ever entered another dark age, the abbé feels sure that 'the sacred fire will be kept alive in Philadelphia, and come from thence to enlighten the world.'[18]

By contrast, Virginia and Maryland have a more sectarian ethos – the one Anglican and the other Catholic – but Raynal follows Voltaire in noting that the Carolinas have the advantage that their constitution was 'drawn up by the famous Locke'. Yet Raynal thinks less favourably of John Locke's constitutional ideas than of the Englishman's sensation-based psychology. The abbé writes: 'It is certain that the same man, who had dissipated and destroyed so many errors in his theory concerning the origin of ideas, made but very feeble and uncertain advances in the path of legislation.' The abbé's assessment is a useful corrective to the adulation that the *philosophes* are assumed to have lavished on Locke. The aim of legislation, Raynal declares, should be 'the happiness of society'. And, following Montesquieu's belief that geographical factors shape a people's morals, he adds: 'Climate, that is to say, the sky and the soil, are the first rule of the legislator... The moral system is to be formed on the nature of the climate.'[19]

Raynal does not often observe with a naturalist's eye, but he does report the finding of the sassafras tree in Florida, noting that its root has the virtue of 'promoting perspiration' and has been 'formerly much used in venereal complaints.' He also notices the candleburry myrtle and sugar maple, and gives his famous description of the humming-birds. More often, however, his interest in trees and plants has a strategic thrust: 'Besides timber and masts for ships, America is capable of furnishing likewise sails and rigging, by the cultivation of hemp and flax.' And even viticulture is given a political dimension when he predicts that American wines will one day allow Britain to stop importing French wines. Meanwhile Raynal attributes the good health of Americans to the 'great plenty of everything requisite for food', and to the fact that they are 'not yet polished nor corrupted by residing in great cities'. Indeed it is only in the New World that 'men lead such a rural life as was the original destination of mankind'.[20]

The abbé nevertheless remains insistent on the need for 'a general and public education for children'. No prince or legislator should think of founding a colony 'without previously sending thither some proper persons for the education of youth; that is, some governors rather than teachers; for it is of less moment to teach them what is good, than to guard them from evil'. One hears echoes of Rousseau's *Emile*. More surprisingly, Raynal doubts whether the European powers should support Britain's rebel colonies, but he is certain that America will win her independence: 'Everything tends to this point: the progress of good in the new hemisphere, and the progress of evil in the old.' He now reminds us of his aim, as he draws towards the end of his final volume:

> Let us examine to what extent the conquest of the new world has led and advanced those who have made it. This was the design of a book undertaken with the hopes of being useful: if the end is answered, the author will have discharged his duty to the age he lives in, and to society.

By way of recapitulation, he instances religious toleration as the most important benefit conferred by the new world on the old.[21]

Europe, he thinks, must not miss this favourable psychological moment to open itself to the enlightened spirit of the age: 'The human mind is undeceived with regard to its former superstition. If we do not avail ourselves of the present time to re-establish the empire of reason, it must necessarily be given up to new superstitions.' To reinforce his claim that Europe is ripe for revolution, Raynal conducts a swift survey of European nations. He ridicules the claims of Enlightened Despotism – 'let not, therefore, these pretended masters of the people be allowed even to do good against the general consent' – and thinks that, if Gustavus III succeeds in his reforms, 'Sweden will never have been governed by a more absolute monarch.' By contrast the Dutch Stadtholder has too little power, remaining 'only a captain-general'; while the backwardness of Poland – 'no better than all the European states were ten centuries ago' – is seen as justification for partition, provided the usurping powers lighten the burdens of their new peoples: 'Their subjects will be more faithful, by being more free; and being no longer slaves, will become men.'[22]

Raynal's programme seems to be one of gradual persuasion, rather than violent upheaval – what he calls moderating 'the despotism of the laws by the influence of reason'. Here is a suitable role for the *philosophe*: 'Every writer of genius is born a magistrate of his country; and he ought to enlighten it as much as it is in his power.' The appeal is to public opinion: 'His tribunal is the whole nation; his judge is the public, not the despot who does not hear or the minister who will not attend to him.' The abbé accordingly commends the *encyclopédistes*, especially Buffon whom he calls 'a French Pliny'. And taking up the physiocrats' arguments, he asserts that taxes, whether in the form of the poll tax – 'a sort of slavery, oppressive to the man, without being profitable to the state' – or a tax on commodities, are counterproductive. Only the physiocrats' panacea of a single land tax wins his approval. He is opposed to a government building up a national debt, since it serves to 'mortgage its future expectations for present exigencies', with the result that 'proprietors of land and merchants will all turn annuitants.'[23]

The *History* begins to read like Diderot's *Encyclopédie* in more accessible form – an impression that is reinforced by the author's excursion into a comparison between Renaissance and Gothic art. This provides an opportunity to condemn medieval cathedrals, 'filled with crucifixes' and decorated with 'scaffolds, torture, martyrs and executioners'. One sees why the *History* was placed on the Index. Raynal's denunciation of Italian culture – 'a mixture of Egyptian theology, Grecian philosophy and Hebrew poetry' – leads into a consideration of European languages. French, if not the 'language of the Gods', is at least 'that of reason and truth', though it was the English who were 'the first who ever made use of the expression, *the majesty of the people*'. Spanish, when it has shaken off the stranglehold of the Inquisition and the universities, 'will raise itself to great ideas and to sublime truths', while German, because of its rudeness in appearance and sound, 'has been spoken only by the people, and has been introduced but of late into books'. In the arts, Raynal notes that 'the fine arts are attempting to rise superior to the obstacles of nature even at Petersburgh' while in science, the abbé finds a providential purpose in the invention of gunpowder 'which was to bring America into subjection to Europe'.[24]

So we have returned to America at last! The abbé has used the New World as both a model and a mirror. In his concluding pages, he makes clear that his target has been Europe in general, and France in particular. He reminds us:

> I have informed princes of their duties, and of the rights of the people ... I have sketched all around them the portraits of your misfortunes, and they cannot but have been sensibly affected by them. I have warned them that if they turned their eyes away, those true but dreadful pictures would be engraven on the marble of their tombs, and accuse their ashes while posterity trampled on them.

One can easily understand why Raynal's *History* was in such demand during the years between the Declaration of Independence and the fall of the Bastille.[25]

13 American Farmer: Hector St John de Crèvecoeur

In August 1781 Madame d'Houdetot wrote to her friend Benjamin Franklin, then in Paris, recommending a young American to him: 'He is a Frenchman by birth, but for a long time has been established in your country, under the protection of your laws, to which he is faithful... His name is Crèvecoeur'. The young American was Michel-Guillaume Jean de Crèvecoeur, commonly known as Hector St John de Crèvecoeur. When he himself wrote to Franklin later that August, he signed himself 'St John' – which made Franklin wonder whether this was the same young man. Crèvecoeur deliberately blurred the details of his family history. We know that he was born at Caen in 1735 and that he attended a Jesuit college, where he read the memoirs of Abbé Raynal, whom he came to regard as his favourite author. At the age of 19, Crèvecoeur went to England to continue his studies, and became engaged to an English girl. When his fiancée died, he sailed for Canada as a soldier of fortune, and served with Montcalm's army as scout and cartographer. This period of military service, culminating in the defence of Quebec against Wolfe in 1759, is something that Crèvecoeur never refers to in any of his writings. What is clear is that the young subaltern resigned somewhat hurriedly from his regiment after the Quebec campaign. Whatever the circumstances, Crèvecoeur himself has ensured that they should not be recorded for posterity.[1]

Perhaps it was natural that, having decided to settle in British America, he should conceal the fact that he was on the wrong side in the Seven Years War. He took up surveying, and at New York in 1765 he became naturalized and met his future wife Mehitable Tippet, daughter of a substantial landowner. In 1767 he undertook an exploration of the Ohio River and the Great Lakes. The expedition lasted 161 days, in which he covered over 3000 miles. His observations, together with a certain amount of hearsay evidence from travellers and colonists, were recorded in a *mémoire* he prepared for Marshal de Castries, Minister of Marine. It was this account that

159

made his name known in France. In September 1769 he married Miss Tippet and, three months later, bought 120 acres of uncleared land in Orange county, New York State. This was the beginning of his life as an American farmer. He took to calling himself 'Hector St John', as befitted a loyal American, though his two sons were given unequivocally French names: Guillaume-Alexandre and Philippe-Louis.

It was the War of Independence that eventually drove Crèvecoeur back to France. Suspected of loyalist sympathies by the colonists, he was considered a French agent by the British, who imprisoned him in New York for several months. By the time he reached Paris in 1781, he was a stranger in the country of his birth and an outcast from his adopted country. Yet his career was just beginning. The Countess d'Houdetot and her circle lionized him. As Brissot remarked: 'Proud of having an American savage in her possession, the countess wished to school him and thrust him into society.' Crèvecoeur was thus introduced into the world of the *salons* and of the surviving *philosophes*, notably Buffon. And thanks to the American farmer's prudent foresight in addressing his early *mémoire* on the Ohio to the Minister of Marine, he was well regarded by the French government.[2]

In 1782 *Letters from an American Farmer* was published in London. The author's name was given on the title page as 'J. Hector St John, a farmer in Pennsylvania'. The publishers' advertisement explained that the letters had been 'privately written to gratify the curiosity of a friend', and were published because they contained 'much authentic information, little known on this side of the Atlantic'. The letters, so the advertisement claimed, could not fail to be 'highly interesting to the people of England at a time when everybody's attention is directed towards the affairs of America'. The war had indeed stimulated interest in North America. Andrew Burnaby's *Travels through the Middle Settlements in North America* had appeared in 1775, and Jonathan Carver's best-selling *Travels through the Interior Parts of North America* followed in 1778. These were, as their titles imply, mere travelogues, without the political and philosophical sub-text of Raynal's magisterial history. Crèvecoeur's *Letters* was the first description of America by a settler and a planter. Jefferson's *Notes on the State of Virginia* did not appear until two years later, in the Paris edition of 1784.[3]

But it was not just curiosity about America that the publishers hoped to exploit. The later years of the century saw a great interest in agriculture. The French physiocrats urged governments to regard agriculture as the chief source of national wealth, and the new ideas even reached the Russian gentry, who tried to farm their estates more efficiently – with unfortunate results for their serfs. George Washington corresponded with Arthur Young on agricultural matters, while George III earned the nickname 'Farmer George' by setting up a model farm at Windsor and by writing articles for Young's *Annals of Agriculture*, first published in 1784. Not that Crèvecoeur's *Letters* gives a notably detailed account of colonial agriculture – particularly the plantation agriculture of the southern states. Indeed about one-third of the published text is devoted to a description of the whaling communities of Nantucket and Martha's Vineyard.

The island of Nantucket, 60 miles south of Cape Cod, has an inhospitable soil. Crèvecoeur tells us that it 'furnishes the naturalist with few or no objects worthy observation'. The only town is Sherborn, where there are 'but few gardens and arable fields', though there are 'a good many cherry trees and peach trees planted in their streets'. The inhabitants have 'with unwearied perseverance, by bringing a variety of manure, and by cow-penning, enriched several spots where they raise Indian corn, potatoes, pumpkins, turnips, etc.' But their principal harvest comes perforce from the sea:

> If these people are not famous for tracing the fragrant furrow on the plain, they plough the rougher ocean, they gather from its surface, at an immense distance, and with Herculean labours, the riches it affords; they go to hunt and catch that huge fish which by its strength and velocity one would imagine ought to be beyond the reach of man.

Crèvecoeur comments on the disagreeable smell of whale oil pervading the town, which 'the neatness peculiar to these people can neither remove nor prevent', and he describes in detail how the whales are sighted, hunted and harpooned, and how the whaling industry is organized on shore.[4]

The fourth of the Nantucket letters (Letter VII) ends with these words:

> Thus, had I leisure and abilities to lead you through this continent, I could show you an astonishing prospect very little known in Europe: one diffusive scene of happiness reaching from the sea-shores to the last settlements on the borders of the wilderness... May the citizens of Nantucket dwell long here in uninterrupted peace, undisturbed by the waves of the surrounding element, or the political commotions which sometimes agitate our continent.

This rhapsodic passage reveals that Crèvecoeur's purpose in the *Letters* is not mere reporting of 'certain provincial situations, manners and customs not generally known', as the title page of the first edition proclaimed. Nor is Crèvecoeur 'but a feller of trees, a cultivator of land', as he would have us believe. He may have cleared 'about 370 acres of land, some for the plough, some for the scythe', and may never have possessed 'anything more than what could be earned or produced by the united industry of my family'. And his portrayal of his wife 'by my fireside, while she either spins, knits, darns or suckles our child', foreshadows Robert Southey's romantic vision of American cottage life. But as his dedicatory letter to Abbé Raynal makes clear, Crèvecoeur's life as 'a simple cultivator of the earth' has led him to evolve a political philosophy. That is what makes him an important figure in the transatlantic commerce in ideas during the Revolutionary period.[5]

His philosophical purpose is evident in the five central letters on Nantucket and Martha's Vineyard. He begins this section by describing the American colonies as 'the general asylum of the world'. Had the island of Nantucket been situated off the shores of Europe rather than of America, it would have been peopled by 'a few wretched fishermen' who would have been 'always dreading the weight of taxes, or the servitude of men-of-war'. Instead, the Quaker inhabitants of Nantucket have full and untrammelled scope for their talents:

> I saw neither governors, nor any pageantry of state; neither ostentatious magistrates, nor any individuals clothed with useless dignity: no artificial phantoms subsist here either civil or religious; no gibbets loaded with guilty citizens offer themselves to your view; no soldiers are appointed to bayonet their compatriots into servile compliance.

It is indeed an undemanding form of government – what Crèvecoeur had earlier called 'a system of rational laws founded on perfect freedom'. And, in a passage that reads somewhat strangely after the Boston Tea Party, he remarks that 'a collector from Boston is the only King's officer who appears on these shores to receive the trifling duties which this community owe to those who protect them.' In an equally optimistic passage, Crèvecoeur sees whaling as an effective cure for intolerance. 'Most of these people,' he writes, 'are continually at sea, and have often the most urgent reasons to worship the Parent of Nature in the midst of the storms they encounter.' Consequently Quakers and Presbyterians tolerate one another, and 'those ancient times of religious discords are now gone.'[6]

The Nantucket community provides a striking contrast to Charleston, which is described in Letter IX. The climate of Charleston,

Crèvecoeur tells us, 'renders excesses of all kinds very dangerous, particularly those of the table'. This does not, however, deter the inhabitants: 'Insensible or fearless of danger, they live on, and enjoy a short and merry life: the rays of the sun seem to urge them irresistibly to dissipation and pleasure.' Like Montesquieu, Crèvecoeur takes the moral influence of climate seriously. But all geographical areas have their disadvantages, and even in those mild climates which seem to breathe contentment, 'the poison of slavery, the fury of despotism, and the rage of superstition, are all combined against man'. It is the poison of slavery that most concerns Crèvecoeur at this point, for it is here that he gives the horrific description of a negro suspended in a cage:

> The birds had already picked out his eyes, his cheek bones were bare; his arms had been attacked in several places, and his body seemed covered with a multitude of wounds. From the edges of the hollow sockets and from the lacerations with which he was disfigured, the blood dripped slowly down and tinged the ground beneath.

James, the narrator who speaks for Crèvecoeur throughout the *Letters*, learns at dinner that the slave is being punished for having killed the overseer of the plantation. James quietly observes: 'They told me that the laws of self-preservation rendered such executions necessary; and supported the doctrine of slavery with the arguments generally made use of to justify the practice; with the repetition of which I shall not trouble you at present.' There is no doubt which side the author is on.[7]

What is more doubtful is whether his encounter with the dying slave is an eyewitness account at all. It is more probably an imaginative piece of propaganda, though none the less telling for that. Even his description of the humming-bird in Letter X is not quite what it seems. His account of this 'insect bird' is closely modelled on the description of the humming-bird in Raynal's *Political and Philosophical History*. Crèvecoeur writes: 'Sometimes, from what motives I know not, it will tear and lacerate flowers into a hundred pieces: for, strange to tell, they are the most irascible of the feathered tribe. Where do passions find room in so diminutive a body? They often fight with the fury of lions'. A translation of Raynal's version reads:

> Who could imagine that so diminutive an animal could be so malicious, passionate and quarrelsome? ... These little birds are

all impatience. When they come near a flower, if they find it faded and withered, they tear all the leaves asunder. The precipitation with which they peck it, betrays, it is said, the rage with which they are animated.

Crèvecoeur tells us that it was Raynal who first caused him to reflect 'on the relative state of nations' and who had first 'viewed those provinces of North America in their true light, as the asylum of freedom'. And in the same dedicatory preface to the *Letters*, the American claims his own kinship with the European Enlightenment: 'There is, no doubt, a secret communion among good men throughout the world; a mental affinity connecting them by a similitude of sentiments'. Though much of what Crèvecoeur writes is undoubtedly the fruit of his own American experience, he relied heavily on Raynal's *History*, and thus absorbed the doctrines of the *philosophes* at second hand.[8]

In his famous definition of 'the American, this new man' in the third of his letters, Crèvecoeur goes so far as to describe the Americans as 'the western pilgrims, who are carrying along with them that great mass of arts, sciences, vigour and industry which began long since in the east; they will finish the great circle'. For the *Encyclopédistes* of the European Enlightenment, codification of laws went hand in hand with the classification of plants. And Crèvecoeur describes a visit, not by James our usual narrator, but by 'a Russian gentleman' to Mr John Bartram, the celebrated Pennsylvanian botanist, whom Crèvecoeur calls 'the first botanist in this new hemisphere', though he spells his name 'Bertram'. The botanist (we are told) 'united all the simplicity of rustic manners to the most useful learning', though Bartram describes himself as 'but a ploughman'. Bartram is a Quaker, but over the door of his greenhouse appears a quotation from Alexander Pope:

Slave to no sect, who takes no private road,
But looks through nature, up to nature's God.

That is the language of Deism, and the penultimate paragraph of the twelfth and final letter strikes a similarly deistical note:

O Supreme Being! if among the immense variety of planets, inhabited by thy creative power, thy paternal and omnipotent care deigns to extend to all the individuals they contain...guide our steps through these unknown paths, and bless our future mode of life...[9]

The sense of uncertainty and foreboding in these last pages contrasts with Crèvecoeur's earlier boast that 'we are the most perfect society now existing in the world.' This last letter, entitled 'Distresses of a Frontier Man', describes the agony of a loyalist caught up in the continental conflict. Concealing the Frenchman Michel-Guillaume under the persona of James (the fictitious colonial farmer of English descent) Crèvecoeur articulates the colonist's interior debate:

> Must I then bid farewell to Britain, to that renowned country? Must I renounce a name so ancient and so venerable?... That great nation which now convulses the world; which hardly knows the extent of her Indian kingdoms; which looks towards the universal monarchy of trade, of industry, of riches, of power: why must she strew our poor frontiers with the carcasses of her friends, with the wreck of our insignificant villages in which there is no gold?

James tells us that he has decided to take his family to seek refuge in an Indian village where, 'far removed from the accursed neighbourhood of Europeans, its inhabitants live with more ease, decency and peace than you imagine', and where they find 'in uncontaminated simple manners all that laws can afford'.[10]

Already imagining himself among the Indians, Crèvecoeur (in the guise of James) describes the education of his children in terms that will re-echo in the self-sufficient pantisocratic ideals of Coleridge and Southey:

> If I cannot teach them any of those professions which sometimes embellish and support our society, I will show them how to hew wood, how to construct their own ploughs; and with a few tools how to supply themselves with every necessary implement both in the house and in the field....

And he adds: 'If they do not fear God according to the tenets of any one seminary, they shall learn to worship him upon the broad scale of nature.' Thus Crèvecoeur embraces both the rationalism and the romanticism of Rousseau. And in words that savour of Wordsworth as much as Rousseau, he equates the Supreme Being with 'the great Manitou of the woods and of the plains', adding that 'even in the gloom, the obscurity of those very woods, his justice may be as well understood as in the most sumptuous temples.'[11]

Crèvecoeur himself sought refuge not with the Indians, but in Madame d'Houdetot's France. Within a year of his return to Paris, he was working on a French edition of the *Letters*. It appeared in

December 1784 entitled *Lettres d'un Cultivateur Américain*. The French version, dedicated now to Lafayette, appears as a complete reworking of the English materials. James, the notional author of the *Letters*, is replaced by 'St John', and the original letters are supplemented by a medley of miscellaneous sketches, autobiographical narrative, newspaper accounts and consular reports. The picture of the American landscape and American society that emerges is even more idyllic than their portrayal in the English edition. This is partly because Crèvecoeur's English is natural and unaffected, whereas his refurbished French is the French of high society – the language of the *salons*. 'Twice a week,' he later writes, 'I went with M. de Turgot to see the Duchess de Beauvilliers, his sister; and another twice-a-week I went to the Comte de Buffon's.' There is a shift in sensibility, too: not only is the mood of pastoral romanticism greatly heightened, but the revolutionary war is described from an avowedly anti-British standpoint.[12]

By the time the French edition appeared, Crèvecoeur had been elected to the *Académie des Sciences* and (thanks to Madame d'Houdetot) appointed French Consul in New York. He took up the consular appointment at the end of 1783, and worked hard to preserve the alliance between France and America. His health suffered, and he was accordingly given leave of absence between 1785 and 1787, before finally returning to France in 1790. During his years as consul, he founded a botanical garden at New Haven, Connecticut, published articles on agricultural subjects in American newspapers under the name of 'Agricola', and fostered the first transatlantic shipping-line. He encouraged domestic inventions through an organization called *Le Bureau des Lumières*, whose aim was the political, industrial and moral welfare of the United States and France. He was made an honorary citizen of several American cities, and elected to membership of the American Philosophical Society. The Vermont legislature was even persuaded to name the town of St Johnsburg after him.

While on extended leave in France, he became a founder-member of Brissot's Gallo-American Society. Crèvecoeur had a hand in approving the draft rules of the society and in adopting the design of its seal. When Crèvecoeur announced that he would at last be returning to America, Brissot characterized him as the man 'to whom we chiefly owe the idea and foundation of this society'. In thanking him for 'the assiduity with which he attended its sessions', Brissot proposed that, as soon as the new seal had been engraved, a diploma should be sent to Crèvecoeur expressing the Society's gratitude. Crèvecoeur's resumption of his consular duties marked the effective end of the Gallo-American Society, though Brissot was still using its seal as late as 1792.[13]

The outbreak of the French Revolution, together with continuing ill-health, would bring Crèvecoeur back to France. In 1790 he again obtained leave from his consular duties, this time never to return. He quarrelled with his father, and sought refuge with his daughter in Paris. Her husband, Loius Guillaume Otto, secretary of the French legation to America, was imprisoned for six weeks during the Terror; but he was soon reinstated and, after the advent of Napoleon, was entrusted with the negotiation of the Treaty of Amiens. In 1801, the year before the Amiens treaty, Crèvecoeur published his *Voyage dans la Haute Pensylvanie et dans l'Etat de New-York*. Somewhat loose and fragmentary in construction – a defect implausibly excused by the author's pretence that it is a damaged manuscript salvaged from a ship-wreck – the *Voyage* is the most ambitious of all Crèvecoeur's writings. The frontispiece is a portrait plaque of George Washington, to whom the book is dedicated – though the former President died before it was published. The dedicatory letter describes Washington as being 'as great, as exemplary, while you were perfecting the navigation of the Potomac and Shenandoah rivers and overseeing your vast farm lands, as when you were at the head of armies'.[14]

In spite of the war, this is still the American society of the first half of the *Letters* – an ordered, uncomplicated society, and an unexploited country that rejoices under a mild government. There is admittedly some evidence of industrial development. A list of canals *terminés, commencés ou projetés* is given; and the narrator and his German companion, Gustave Herman, visit Townsend's iron furnace where they see 2000 to 2400 tons of iron, 'three-fourths of which is converted into bars, and the rest into cannon balls, etc'. Townsend is modest about his steel-making process: 'It has not yet reached the degree of perfection that Sweden has; but we are approaching it.' The visitors also hear about a portable threshing-mill, details of which have been sent to George Washington. They then visit Mr Erskine who 'we knew had spent three years in Europe visiting the principal foundries of Scotland, Sweden and Germany'.[15]

When Herman is moved to admire a waterfall, he is as impressed with its industrial potential as with its poetic beauty. The waterfalls nevertheless prompt Crèvecoeur to reflect on the power of nature:

How can one analyze the impressions that result from the sight of these gigantic and threatening objects whose immensity is so disproportionate to the feebleness of our senses? It is only in the quiet of one's study, and not in these places, that it is possible to capture some notion; but even then one would need the brush of Vernet or Thompson or the pen of Rousseau.

When, nearby, he comes across Captain Goldworthy in a primitive cabin, he records the captain's portrayal of his brother-in-law (whose cabin it is) in these words: 'Although he is still wealthy and young, the retreat, the silence, the solitude in the woods hold charms for him that he often prefers to those of society or dissipation.' And as if to emphasize the romanticism of his own reactions, Crèvecoeur devotes no less than one-quarter of his text to the life and culture of the American Indians.[16]

But forests can be threatening as well as romantic. Earlier the travellers had become benighted and lost in a snake-infested forest, victims of what Crèvecoeur calls the terrifying 'effect of darkness on the minds of the majority of men'. They miss the blazed trail, they lose their flint – and with it the means of making a fire. Faced with starvation, they are about to kill and eat their dog when they hear the sound of cow-bells. Finding the herd, they follow the cattle to a clearing and exult in 'the sudden transition from darkness...to light'. For the narrator, it is the 'day of my second birth'. The symbolism seems to confirm, in an almost literal sense, our view of Crèvecoeur as a man of the Enlightenment. Yet by 1801 the ideals of the Enlightenment, in Europe at least, were looking somewhat tarnished. The age of Raynal and Voltaire had given way to the age of Napoleon. The *Voyage* made little impact in France. The French text was translated into German, and fewer than half its chapters were translated into English. Otherwise it was neglected, and when an English translation appeared in 1964, it was the first re-publication of the full text since 1801.[17]

Crèvecoeur's literary fame and influence nevertheless rest securely on his original *Letters* and their French version, the *Lettres*. Published in Dublin and Belfast, Leyden and Maastricht, Leipzig and Berlin, besides London and Paris, the *Letters of an American Farmer* proved to be one of the principal interpreters of America to Europe. Grimm was right to say that Crèvecoeur's *Letters*, 'written without method and without art, but with a high degree of interest and sensibility', had perfectly achieved the author's intention – 'that of making America loved.' One English clergyman felt so alarmed at the encouragement Crèvecoeur had given to the emigration of British citizens that he rushed out a pamphlet in protest. Crèvecoeur does indeed devote nearly 20 pages to the story of a successful Scottish emigrant, 'Andrew the Hebridean', and boasts in the last of his letters that he has 'caused upwards of a hundred and twenty families to remove hither.'[18]

By the time he comes to write his *Voyage*, however, he cautions readers against thinking that the northern states of America offer the prospect of getting rich through agriculture: 'The seasons are too rapid, the winters too long, and labour still too costly.' And in 1782, the year when the *Letters* first appeared, Franklin thought it advisable to write his own pamphlet warning trans-Atlantic fortune-seekers that America was not 'the French *Pays de Cocagne*, where the streets are said to be paved with half-peck loaves, the houses til'd with pancakes, where fowls fly about ready roasted crying, *Come eat me!*' In less satirical vein, Franklin wrote to Crèvecoeur in 1788 that 'the favourable light in which you have so kindly plac'd our country will I am persuaded have the good effect of inducing many worthy European characters to remove and settle among us, the acquisition of whom will be greatly advantageous to us.'[19]

Crèvecoeur also corresponded with Jefferson. In January 1784, shortly before the future President left to take up his diplomatic post in Paris, Crèvecoeur wrote to ask whether it was true that 'in some of the remotest settlements of Virginia or Carolina, brandy has been distilled from potatoes'. He suggests that, on arrival in Paris, Jefferson should ask Franklin to introduce him to the Duc de la Rochefoucauld, whom Crèvecoeur describes as 'a good man and a most able chemist'. Six years later, when he hears of Lafayette's proposal to hold a fête of federation in Paris, to mark the first anniversary of the fall of the Bastille, Crèvecoeur confides to Jefferson his fear 'lest the good Marquis shou'd not be able to maintain peace and good order among so great a concourse of people as will flock there from every part of ye kingdom'. The American farmer's career, oscillating like Lafayette's backwards and forwards across the Atlantic, provides equally convincing evidence of the interaction between France and America in the Revolutionary period. Writing to Franklin in 1781, before the publication of *Letters of an American Farmer*, Crèvecoeur (as Lafayette would later do) described himself as 'a good Frenchman and a good American'. Lafayette may have christened his daughter Virginie and his son George Washington, but Crèvecoeur named his daughter America-Francès.[20]

14 Women and Emigrants: Mary Wollstonecraft and Gilbert Imlay

Mary Wollstonecraft never crossed the Atlantic. Her youngest brother, Charles, emigrated to America, while another brother, James, took French citizenship. Mary herself became a United States citizen through her American lover, 'Captain' Gilbert Imlay, who had fought in the War of Independence although his highest rank was almost certainly only Lieutenant. James Wollstonecraft called Imlay 'a fine, handsome fellow', and Mary wrote him into one of her novels as an engaging though not very intelligent lover, who seduces a married woman and then so neglects her that she is driven to attempt suicide. The unfinished novel (*Maria or the Wrongs of Woman*) has a distinctly autobiographical flavour, though when Imlay and Mary became lovers she was not married, and was on record as saying that, in marriage, women's bodies are 'often legally prostituted'. Before he finally abandoned her to make her own suicide attempt, Imlay apparently promised Mary that they would migrate to America as soon as his business ventures had yielded £1000 – which Mary considered 'sufficient to have procured a farm in America'. Imlay had not only himself speculated in the Kentucky lands, but had played his own part in heightening the general emigration fever through his *Topographical Description of the Western Territory of North America* (1792) and his three-volume novel *The Emigrants* published soon after he and Mary met.[1]

It was the French Revolution that brought them together. They may have met in radical circles in London, where we know that Imlay made the acquaintance of Thomas Cooper, the Manchester anti-slavery campaigner. Mary left London for France in December 1792, to escape an earlier infatuation for the painter Henry Fuseli – a married man with whom Mary had optimistically hoped to live in a *ménage à trois*. She reached Paris in time for the trial of Louis XVI. In a letter home she described how she saw the King's carriage pass her window, 'moving silently along (excepting now and then a few strokes on the drum, which rendered the stillness more awful) through empty streets surrounded by the national guards'. She stayed in Paris for three years. Soon after arriving, she visited Tom Paine, and met at his lodgings Brissot and Roland (the Girondin deputies), Helen Maria Williams (whose writings so impressed the young Wordsworth), and Thomas Cooper.[2]

Before leaving London, Mary had reviewed not only David Ramsay's *History of the American Revolution*, but also the French edition of Brissot's *New Travels in the United States of America*. She commended Brissot's trans-Atlantic quest for 'men who had recovered their freedom', and praised his 'sacred overflowings of an honest heart'. When Gilbert Imlay arrived in Paris in January 1793, he quickly sought out Brissot to whom he had a letter of introduction provided by Cooper. Imlay was keen to promote a scheme for the French to take Louisiana from Spain, and Brissot put him in touch with the French foreign ministry. Imlay presented his *Mémoire sur Louisiana*, which emphasized the strategic position of Louisiana, the opportunity its capture would provide of reducing Spanish influence in America, and the commercial potential of its rapidly growing population. Imlay put the cost of the expedition at 750 000 *livres*, adding confidently: 'With this sum success is certain'. Citizen Gênet, the French Republic's ambassador to the United States, would concert arrangements on the American side, while concealing matters from the US government. Writing in April, Brissot urged the Committee to set things on foot 'within a fortnight'. But by then France and England were at war, and Robespierre's ousting of the Girondins in May finally put paid to these ambitious plans.[3]

It was the war with England, and the National Convention's decree that all resident English nationals should be imprisoned until the peace, that persuaded Mary and her lover to pose as a married couple. Imlay registered Mary as his wife at the US embassy, thus giving her the identity of an American citizen. Mary had earlier refused to marry Imlay, and did not regard herself as married now. In a letter to the American, Ruth Barlow, Mary wrote: 'You perceive that I am acquiring the matrimonial phraseology without having clogged my soul by promising obedience &c &c.' But despite her scruples against marriage, obtaining American citizenship provided the best guarantee against being interned as a traitor to the Revolution. Mary remained in Paris throughout the Terror, losing Brissot and other friends to the guillotine. Yet in a letter to her sister Everina in March 1794, while deploring the revolutionary violence she had witnessed, Mary explained: 'I am certainly glad I came to France, because I never could have had else a just opinion of the most extraordinary event that has ever been recorded'.[4]

Later that year her own history of the Revolution was published in London. Only the first of the three promised volumes was written, and the account of events ends in October 1789, three years before Mary arrived in Paris. She devotes over 500 pages to recording the first three months of the Revolution, interspersing the narrative with extracts from the reported debates of the National Assembly. The preface speaks of sketching 'the rapid changes, the base and nefarious assassinations, which have clouded the vivid prospect that began to spread a ray of joy and gladness over the gloomy horizon of oppression'. But Mary warns the reader to 'guard against the erroneous inferences of sensibility' and to rely instead on reason, while she emphasizes that the Revolution is not the work of a few individuals, but 'the natural consequence of intellectual improvement, gradually proceeding to perfection'.[5]

In spite of Mary's insistence on appealing only to reason, sensibility keeps breaking through, as in her famous description of Versailles after the removal of the royal family to Paris:

How silent is now Versailles – The solitary foot that mounts the sumptuous stair-case, rests on each landing-place, while the eye traverses the void, almost expecting to see the strong images of fancy burst into life. – The train of the Louises, like the posterity of the Banquoes, pass in solemn sadness, pointing at the nothingness of grandeur, fading away on the cold canvas, which covers the nakedness of the spacious walls – whilst the gloominess of the atmosphere gives a deeper shade to the gigantic figures that seem to be sinking into the embraces of death.[6]

Mary's *French Revolution* sold well enough for a second London edition (1796) and a (probably pirated) Dublin edition to follow. Reactions were mixed. The *Monthly Review* praised – apparently without conscious irony – 'the metaphorical cast of her language', while the *British Critic* sought to demonstrate that she had borrowed too freely from the *New Annual Register*. In Britain, opinion was already hardening against the French Revolution, but in America that great annotator, John Adams, future President of the United States, made more marginal comments on the Wollstonecraft *French Revolution* than on any other book in his library. Adams concedes that 'this is a lady of a masculine masterly understanding,' but he adds even more patronizingly that she would have produced a better book 'with a little more experience in public affairs and the reading and reflection which would result from it'. Adams is pleased to note that the author gives due weight to the example of the American Revolution, though where Mary praises the Anglo-Americans for preserving the principles of Magna Carta, he comments sarcastically: 'I thank you Miss W. May we long enjoy your esteem.' He occasionally commends Miss W's perceptions, but when she proceeds to give her views on the King's veto, Adams adds spitefully: 'This ignorant woman knows nothing of the matter. She seems to have half a mind to be an English woman; yet more inclined to be an American. Perhaps her lover gave her lessons.'[7]

Mary Wollstonecraft's *French Revolution* had not been her first published words on the subject. She first sprang to fame in 1790 when she had the temerity to address a 'letter' to Edmund Burke. Her *Vindication of the Rights of Men, in a Letter to the Right Honourable Edmund Burke* was a direct challenge to Burke's *Reflections on the Revolution in France*, published that year. Mary's pamphlet is less concerned with refuting Burke's arguments than with exposing his inconsistencies. The champion of American Independence has, she argues, betrayed his liberal principles by attacking the ideas of 1789. Mary defines the rights of man – in words that anticipate John Stuart Mill's classic statement – as 'such a degree of liberty, civil and religious, as is compatible with the liberty of the other individuals whom he is united with in a social compact'. When Burke condemns the French for wilfully destroying their system of government, Mary asks: 'Why was it a duty to repair an ancient castle, built in barbarous ages of Gothic materials?' And with a rhetorical flourish worthy of Burke himself, she writes:

> Man preys on man; and you mourn for the idle tapestry that decorated a gothic pile, and the dronish bell that summoned the fat priest to prayer. You mourn for the empty pageant of a name, when slavery flaps her wing and the sick heart retires to die in lonely wilds, far from the abodes of man.

Tom Paine's famous charge that Burke 'pities the plumage but forgets the dying bird' had not yet been written.[8]

The anonymous first edition of the *Letter to Burke* quickly sold out, and the second edition appeared before the end of the year with Mary Wollstonecraft's name on the title page. Of the reviews, only the *Analytical* (the journal of her publisher) was complimentary, while the *Gentleman's Magazine* lived up to its title by ridiculing the notion of a woman claiming to be an authority on the rights of man. How had a 31-year-old female schoolteacher dared to challenge the mighty pen of Edmund Burke? Part of the answer lies in her life as a schoolmistress. Following her mother's early death, Mary had gone to live with the family of Fanny Blood, her friend and confidante. Mary persuaded her own sister, Eliza, to forsake her husband – and her newly born child – in order to escape a nervous breakdown. And it was in order to support Eliza that the sisters opened a school, first at Islington and then at Newington Green. Their neighbour at Newington was Dr Richard Price, already famous not only for his actuarial skills, but for his robust defence of American independence. His friendship partly explains Mary's readiness to respond to Burke.[9]

But Mary's literary talents had first been channelled in other directions. In 1785 her friend Fanny Blood married and left for Portugal. Mary abandoned her school and followed her, arriving shortly before Fanny's son was born – whereupon Fanny died in Mary's arms. Fanny's death, following childbirth, foreshadowed Mary's own fate, and the novel she now wrote modelled its heroine (Ann) on Fanny. Its autobiographical nature is advertised by its title: *Mary*. The failure of the Newington Green school in Mary's absence, meant that she must at least partly support herself by her pen. Appealing more to her own views on the education of women than to her experience of schoolgirls, Mary first wrote *Thoughts on the Education of Daughters*, which Johnson published in 1786. Her novel followed in 1788, after Mary had spent several months as tutor to the children of Lord Kingsborough, the Irish peer. Mary was fortunate to have found a sympathetic publisher in Johnson, who would also publish Wordsworth's early poems – though he prudently reneged on his promise to publish Paine's *Rights of Man*. According to Johnson, Mary spent 'many afternoons and most of her evenings' at his rooms, while she told him in a letter that he was 'a *man* before he was a bookseller'. Mary contributed articles to Johnson's *Analytical Review*, though her pieces were unsigned until July 1788. In the first five months of 1789, she wrote over 40 book reviews, and in the second half of that year started reviewing plays and operas. She also reviewed Price's fateful London Revolution Society sermon, *Discourse on the Love of Our Country*, and Francis Oldys's *Life of Paine*. And it was Johnson who published *Vindication of the Rights of Woman* (1792).[10]

This, the most famous of the Wollstonecraft texts, was dedicated to Talleyrand, who would soon himself seek refuge in America. His *Report on Public Instruction* had recently appeared, and he repaid Mary's compliment by calling on her when he was in London early in 1792. In dedicating her work to the Frenchman, Mary proclaimed: 'If the abstract rights of man will bear discussion and explanation, those of women, by a parity of reasoning, will not shrink from the same test.' *Rights of Woman* seems to have grown out of a review Mary undertook for the *Analytical Review* of Catherine Macaulay's *Letters on Education*, though it also echoes Mary's own *Thoughts on the Education of Daughters* (1786). This earlier work had emphasized the disservice marriage did to the cultivation of a woman's intellect. The introduction to the *Rights of Woman* reiterates the same theme: 'The neglected education of my fellow-creatures is the grand source of the misery I deplore.' Mary attacks Rousseau's view of women in *Emile*, claiming not unreasonably: 'I have, probably, had an opportunity of observing more girls in their infancy than J. J. Rousseau.' Education, she believes, will make for happier marriages: 'It is vain to attempt to keep the heart pure, unless the head is furnished with ideas.' She is not against marriage, and has no wish to breed a generation of independent and unattached woman like herself. Her aim is not 'heroines' but 'rational creatures' who will make good mothers. And she adds sternly: 'Whatever tends to incapacitate the maternal character takes woman out of her sphere.' The appeal of the book nevertheless lay in Mary's complaint that, in Rousseau's scheme, 'The rights of humanity have been thus confined to the male line from Adam downwards.'[11]

Rights of Woman went into a second London edition almost at once, and was published in both Boston and Philadelphia. Reviews were favourable, as in the *New York Magazine*, though London's *Gentleman's Magazine* ignored it. Hannah More told Horace Walpole that she was determined *not* to read it, finding 'something fantastic and absurd in the very title'. Walpole (who in a famous phrase described Mary as a 'hyena in petticoats') agreed, referring to what he called 'the philosophizing serpents we have in our bosom, the Paines, the Tookes and the Wollstonecrafts'. The American Aaron Burr, while recognizing *Rights of Woman* as 'a work of genius', confessed that he had 'not yet met a single person who had discovered or would allow the merit of the work.' It was burlesqued by 'Launcelot Light' of Westminster School as *A Sketch of the Rights of Boys and Girls*, though Robert Southey (expelled from Westminster in 1792) read *Rights of Woman* at Oxford, and later dedicated his poem *The Triumph of Woman* (1795) to Mary. Coleridge was also an admirer.[12]

Coleridge read not only *Rights of Woman*, but also Gilbert Imlay's *Topographical Description of North America*, published in the same year (1792). Calling himself on the title page, 'Captain in the American Army during the late War, and a Commissioner for laying out Land in the Back Settlements', Imlay disclaims any intention to entertain: 'I have not aimed so much at being agreeable as to convey information.' But the book is not all topography. There is a Rousseauesque flavour in the introductory 'letter' or chapter, where he welcomes the opportunity of 'contrasting the simple manners, and rational life of the Americans, in these back settlements, with the distorted and unnatural habits of Europeans'. He does describe the topography of the Ohio, where 'Nature in her pride has given to the regions of this fair valley a fertility so astonishing that, to believe it, ocular demonstration becomes necessary.'[13]

By way of demonstration, Imlay cites tracts of land along the Ohio, which he decides are 'capable of being made into extensive and luxuriant meadow ground'. He is equally impressed with the plateau above Limestone (300 miles down-river from Pittsburgh) 'where I found nature robed in all her charms'. He continues:

> Flowers full and perfect, as if they had been cultivated by the hand of a florist, with all their captivating odours, and with all the variegated charms which colour and nature can produce, here, in the lap of elegance and beauty, decorate the smiling groves...The sweet songsters of the forests appear to feel the influence of this genial clime, and, in more soft and modulated tones, warble their tender notes in unison with love and nature.

Well might Imlay add apologetically: 'You must forgive what I know you will call a rhapsody, but what I really experienced after travelling across the Allegany mountain in March.' Poetic flourishes apart, Imlay shows that he is alive to commercial possibilities. He recognizes the importance of the sugar-maple, claiming that 'the country is not only equal to supply itself with sugar, but might with increase of hands supply the inhabitants of the globe.' And, properly managed, the salt springs of Kentucky are 'sufficient to produce salt for all the inhabitants which the western territory could support.'[14]

When he turns his attention to natural history, Imlay makes passing reference to some bones which have been sent to Europe: 'Buffon has called them the Mammoth.' He notes that 'the buffalo are mostly driven out of Kentucky,' adding: 'Deer abound in the extensive forests; but the elk confines itself mostly to the hilly uninhabited places.' Among the attractions of the Ohio valley are that 'the native strawberry is found in these plains in the greatest abundance, as are likewise plums of different sorts'; and he decides that 'no climate or soil in the world is more congenial to the vine'. He lists the common names of plants with their Linnaean equivalents, and the common animals and birds, together with the latitudes where they are to be found, noting somewhat smugly: 'Such errors as Buffon has been drawn into, Mr Jefferson has ably confuted.'[15]

Imlay makes frequent reference to Jefferson's *Notes on Virginia* (1784) and appeals to Jefferson when seeking to explain continental extremes of temperature. Like the Virginian, Imlay comments on political institutions. He admires America's new republican constitution, which 'from its simple construction, and the unity and efficiency of its action, is not less remarkable in the political, than its natural history is to the physical world'. And in an extended comparison between America and Europe, Imlay draws a bold contrast:

> We have more of simplicity, and you more of art. We have more of nature, and you more of the world. Nature formed our features and intellects very much alike; but while you have metamorphosed the one and contaminated the other, we preserve the natural symbols of both. You have more hypocrisy – we are more sincere.

The new America's laws and government, Imlay concludes, 'have for their basis the natural and imprescriptible rights of man'. Yet he is ready to challenge the judgment of the author of the Declaration of Independence. Imlay defends the state constitution of Kentucky, with its two houses in the legislature, whereas Jefferson had censured a similar arrangement in Virginia as unnecessary duplication. Resenting Jefferson's likening of the bicameral constitution to that of the Venetian Republic, Imlay retorts that the Venetians had not received an enlightened education.[16]

He also differs from Jefferson on the issue of negro slavery. He quotes the reasons Jefferson gives for his reluctance to grant citizenship to slaves: 'The deep-rooted prejudices of the whites, and the recollection of past injuries by the blacks, would be productive of continual feuds which would probably never end but in the extermination of one or the other race.' Imlay counters this reasoning with the reminder that slavery is 'contrary to our own bill of rights as well as repugnant to the code of nature.' He proposes *gradual* emancipation 'as it has been in Pennsylvania'. Less convincingly, he speculates that the negro's blackness 'is not fixed by nature, but is the mere effect of climate'. He concludes 16 pages devoted to the rebuttal of Jefferson's arguments with the assertion that the mind of the champion of liberalism is 'so warped by education and the habit of thinking, that he has attempted to make it appear that the African is a being between the human species and the oran-outang'.[17]

Despite such political comment, Imlay's *Topographical Description* (which ran to three English editions, a German edition and an American reprint) was chiefly aimed at encouraging transatlantic emigration. He assures his readers that 'a log house is very soon erected' and that 'this extraordinary fertility of the soil' enables the settler-farmer with little capital 'to increase his wealth in a most rapid manner'. Warming to his theme Imlay uses the eulogistic language of the estate agent:

> Such has been the progress of the settlement of this country, from dirty stations or forts, and smoky huts, that it has expanded into fertile fields, blushing orchards, pleasant gardens, luxuriant sugar groves, and commodious houses, rising villages and trading towns.

Perhaps again sensing the reader's scepticism, Imlay adds that to believe in the American miracle 'it is first necessary to be (as I have been) a spectator of such events.'[18]

When it comes to the season of sugar-making, Imlay evokes images worthy of the Romantic poets:

> The season of sugar occupies the women, whose mornings are cheered by the modulated buffoonery of the mocking-bird, the tuneful song of the thrush, and the gaudy plumage of the parroquet. Festive mirth crowns the evening. The business of the day being over, the men join the women in the sugar groves where enchantment seems to dwell....

We perhaps hear echoes in Coleridge's sonnet 'Pantisocracy':

> Wisely forgetful! O'er the ocean swell
> Sublime of Hope, I seek the cottag'd dell
> Where Virtue calm with careless step may stray,
> And dancing to the moonlight roundelay,
> The wizard Passions weave an holy spell.

The first draft of the sonnet was sent to Southey from Cambridge in September 1794, only a matter of days after Coleridge had read Imlay's *Topographical Description* in London.[19]

Imlay offers would-be emigrants practical advice as well as poetic images. Settlers are advised to take 'two or three camp kettles', to carry their own tea or coffee, but not (rather obviously) sugar. Apart from the free availability of various fish and the 'soft turtle' in the rivers, provisions are cheap: 'Dunghill fowls are from 4d to 6d each; duck 8d; geese and turkeys 1s.' From the various prices he quotes, Imlay is confident that the cost of transporting a family from Baltimore to the upper Ohio 'may be computed with tolerable exactitude'. He takes it for granted that emigrants will proceed to regions that are already settled, 'as I apprehend no European would be hardy enough to form a settlement in a wilderness'. The moral advantages of the New World will nevertheless be open to all: 'Rational pleasures meliorate the soul; and it is by familiarizing man with uncontaminated felicity, that sordid avarice and vicious habits are to be destroyed.'[20]

Imlay's novel *The Emigrants* (1794) is a fictional development of the same theme. Judging from the preface, the novel seems to have as its target the hardship imposed on women by the English divorce laws, which 'too often precipitate women of the most virtuous inclinations into the gulf of ruin'. The story opens (as befits its title) with the arrival of an English emigrant family at Philadelphia in the autumn of 1782. *The Emigrants* is structured in the form of letters, and abounds in quotations from the *philosophes*. There are numerous verse extracts, some apparently written by the novelist. Even when writing in prose, the author employs poetic imagery, as when the family departs from Philadelphia:

> The lovely Caroline's face diffused the soft effulgence of an opening rose when heaven impearls it with the morning dew – and as you have seen the aether of a western sky brighten the horizon in the evening showers of June, so shot the aethereal sparks from her half-closed eyes – With her heart beating high in the transports of nature her lovely bosom seemed to palpitate with emotions which threatened the confines of her delicate frame; and when she was severed from the arms of her more fortunate sister, it appeared as if the fibres of her tender heart would burst with the agonies of sorrow.[21]

Caroline's 'more fortunate sister' is Eliza – coincidentally the name of one of Mary Wollstonecraft's sisters. Caroline herself is captured by Indians, but is rescued by her lover who is, like Imlay, an army captain. The action of the novel takes place against the very American landscapes described in Imlay's *Topographical Description*, and the additional scenes come, not from personal observation, but from a topographical description of four American states, published in London in 1778. This curious circumstances has led one critic to suggest that both books, though bearing Imlay's name, were written by Mary who had just reviewed the French edition of Brissot's *Travels*. Imlay displays no other evidence of literary accomplishments or feminist sympathies, and the author's language carries a decidedly Wollstone-craftian stamp. There are similarities between Eliza of *The Emigrants* and the heroine of Mary's later and unfinished novel, *Maria, or the Wrongs of Woman*. And Caroline mirrors Mary herself, chafing at social restraints and anticipating 'the most exquisite pains and plea-sures' of sexual desire. Like Mary, Caroline insists that women should be educated so as to become the companions, not merely the lovers of men; and she advises Eliza to desert her 'vitiated' husband – as Mary persuaded the real-life Eliza to do. Yet many of the characters in the story are based on Imlay's American friends, whom Mary had never met. Whatever the balance of authorship, the novel's ending, with the lovers settling happily in an ideal community on the banks of the Ohio, matches not only Brissot's vision for emigrants, but also the hopes that Imlay and Mary had cherished for themselves.[22]

The reality was rather different. Imlay departed for Le Havre leaving Mary pregnant in Paris. He was motivated (in William God-win's perhaps too charitable words) 'by the prospect of a family, and this being a favourable crisis in French affairs for commercial spec-ulation'. Despairing of his return, Mary followed him to Le Havre, arriving there in January 1794. Their daughter, Fanny, was born in May. Imlay promptly left for London, despatching Mary back to Paris – though her coach apparently overturned four times before reaching the capital. By the time Imlay finally sent his servant to escort Mary to London, he had found himself another lover. Mary sought to retain his affections by travelling to Sweden, where the Gothenburg mer-chant, Elias Backman, acted as Imlay's agent. Backman ran a large import/export trade, including (it seems) gun running under a neutral flag to wartime France. But in the autumn of 1795, when it was clear that Imlay intended to abandon her, Mary tried to drown herself in the Thames by jumping off Putney Bridge. Well might Godwin describe her as 'a female Werter'.[23]

Mary had first met Godwin in late 1791 at a dinner given by Johnson, her publisher. Now, in April 1796, she boldly called on Godwin in London. Describing this second meeting, Godwin wrote: 'From that time our intimacy increased, by regular, but almost imperceptible degrees.' As might be expected of Godwin the the philosopher, the attraction seems to have been as much intellectual as physical. He remarked of Mary's *Letters written during a Short Residence in Sweden,*

Norway and Denmark (1796): 'If ever there was a book calculated to make a man fall in love with its author, this appears to me to be the book.' The relationship was sufficiently physical for Mary to find herself pregnant. She married Godwin, and at the end of 1797 bore him the daughter who would win fame as Mary Shelley. Within a few days of the birth, septicaemia set in, and a week later the mother was dead. Godwin wrote to a friend the same day: 'I have not the least expectation that I can ever know happiness again.' His more lasting tribute was to publish her memoirs, with a four-volume edition of her unpublished writings entitled *Posthumous Works* (1798). These included her unfinished novel *Maria*, together with her letters to Imlay. Southey censured Godwin for 'stripping his dead wife naked', and the reviewers were hostile. The *Monthly Review* deplored the fact that Godwin 'neither looks to marriage with respect, nor to suicide with horror', while the newly founded *Anti-Jacobin* hailed Mary's conduct as an example of 'Jacobin morality'. Predictably, the work was translated into French, but it also appeared in German; and an American edition was published in Philadelphia in 1799.[24]

By then, Mary's brother James had lost his French citizenship and been imprisoned in the Temple, from which Mary had seen Louis XVI driven to his trial six years before. But her youngest brother, Charles the emigrant, having tried his hand first at farming, and then at the calico business, enlisted in the American artillery. After ten years as captain, he was promoted brevet-major, thus out-ranking Imlay. Nothing more is heard of Imlay, but Charles's second wife, though disapproving of her sister-in-law's religious views, nevertheless wrote an article for the *Boston Monthly Magazine* in 1825 entitled 'the National Rights of Woman'. The Wollstonecraft revolution had crossed the Atlantic after all.

15 Poets' Utopia: Coleridge, Southey and the Susquehanna

The Lakeland poets Robert Southey and Samuel Taylor Coleridge both married Bristol girls in the same year – 1795. Their weddings took place at St Mary Redcliffe, the city's principal parish church: on 4 October Coleridge married Sara Fricker, and on 14 November Southey married Sara's sister Edith. The marriages were meant to be followed by emigration to America. The two brides would be founder-members of the pantisocratic community to be established on the banks of the Susquehanna river in Pennsylvania. Besides their husbands, the girls would be accompanied by their widowed mother, their brother and three other sisters, together with various members of the Southey family and sundry of their husbands' school and university friends.

There would be some 20 emigrants in all, and each male would contribute his share of the £2000 needed to finance the venture. Once in America, they would hold property in common, would respect one another's religious beliefs and would educate their own children. Before they left England, Coleridge warned them, those men who were not used to manual labour would have to 'learn the theory and practice of agriculture and carpentry', though they would need a good library too. In this idyllic fusion of labour and literature, Southey predicted, 'when Coleridge and I are sawing down a tree, we shall discuss metaphysics; criticize poetry when hunting buffalo and write sonnets whilst following the plough.' Thomas Poole, their new friend at Nether Stowey, took a less romantic view. Like the young poets, he looked on America of the 1790s as 'the only asylum of peace and liberty', and agreed that, if Coleridge and Southey achieved their aims, 'they would indeed realize the age of reason.' But he had his doubts: 'However perfectible human nature may be, I fear it is not perfectible enough.'[1]

Nothing came of this transatlantic plan. Southey's departure for Spain and Portugal at the end of 1795, immediately after his marriage, was seen by Coleridge as betrayal of the cause. Coleridge himself was now reduced to settling in Somerset. In a poem written in 1794, he pictured the ideal rural community in which:

> each heart
> Self-governed, the vast family of Love
> Raised from the common earth by common toil
> Enjoy the equal produce.

Well might Charles Lamb caution Coleridge that 'you are not in Arcadia when you are in the West of England.' The poets' vision of an American Arcadia has attracted much ridicule, partly because the dream of a transatlantic commune dwindled into the bathos of gardening beside the Bristol Channel. The coining of Greek-derived terms – *pantisocracy* (government by all) and *aspheterism* (property sharing) – to describe the proposed settlement, increased the sense of unreality. Worse still, Coleridge and Southey were young. They had met at Oxford in June 1794. Southey was in his second year at Balliol, and Coleridge, who two years before had won the Brown Gold Medal at Cambridge for his Greek 'Ode on the Slave Trade', was passing through Oxford on a walking tour with a Cambridge friend. Coleridge was not impressed with Oxford, but he took instantly to Southey, whom he called 'a nightingale among owls'.[2]

Southey had been reading Gibbon, Rousseau and Goethe's *Werther*, confessing to a friend that he was attracted by the idea of retiring with his books to a cottage in America 'where society was on a proper footing, and man was considered more valuable than money; and where I could till the earth and provide by honest industry the meat which my wife would dress with pleasing care'. Bristol Library still has records of Southey's borrowings from its shelves in his student days at Oxford. In the last weeks of 1793, he took out William Godwin's two-volume work *On Political Justice* (published that February) and soon followed it with *Rights of Woman* (1792) by Mary Wollstonecraft, whom Godwin later married. By September 1794 Southey was borrowing Cartwright's *Labrador Journal*, together with *Child of Nature* by Helvétius – the French Utilitarian. The would-be emigrant started 1795 with *Farther Observations on the Discovery of America* by John Williams, and in mid-April was reading part of Abbé Raynal's history of the European settlements in North America.[3]

John Williams's book is a curiosity, since it seeks to prove that America was discovered by Prince Madoc 'about the year 1170', and that Madoc's descendants were to be found in 'a tribe or tribes of Indians who speak the Welsh language'. The claim that Madoc had discovered 'large Countries in the Mayne Ocean' appeared in Richard Hakluyt's *Discourse of Western Planting* (1584) and was enshrined in his more famous *Principal Navigations... of the English Nation* (1589). In 1792 John Evans had crossed the Atlantic in search of Madoc's descendants, and it was not until 1797 that he wrote mournfully from St Louis: 'There is no such people as the Welsh Indians'. The impact made by Williams's book on an impressionable Southey nevertheless explains the writing of the poet's epic *Madoc*, started in 1794 though left unfinished until 1805.[4]

In a different class from Williams's Welsh mythology was William Godwin's magisterial work *On Political Justice*, which so captivated Southey that he persuaded Coleridge to honour Godwin in a sonnet. Godwin had been a Unitarian minister – a calling Coleridge would have followed, but for the generosity of the Wedgwoods, who provided him with an annuity. Like those other Unitarian ministers, Richard Price and Joseph Priestley, Godwin espoused the cause of American independence, which he saw as a 'question involving eternal principles'. Two years before the fall of the Bastille, he came close to announcing the concept of the Atlantic Revolution. Writing of revolutionary events in Holland between 1784 and 1787, Godwin predicts:

> A new republic of the purest kind is about to spring up in Europe; and the flame of liberty, which was first excited in America, and has since communicated itself to so many other countries, bids fair for the production of consequences no less extensive than salutary.

And in *Political Justice* Godwin claims that government is in itself an evil and that 'we should therefore have as little of it as the general peace of human society will permit.' He proposes instead small face-to-face communities where 'the voice of reason would be secure to be heard'.[5]

Godwin specifically repudiates 'romantic notions of pastoral life and the golden age', and criticizes those who would return in imagination to 'the forests of Norway or the bleak and uncomfortable Highlands of Scotland in search of a purer race of mankind'. For Godwin, it is the free American, with space and leisure to cultivate the intellect, who is to be the model, rather than Rousseau's noble savage. *Political Justice* goes further than the pantisocrats in recommending not only the joint ownership of property and the equalization of labour, but the sharing of wives. Before their joint lapse into the respectability of matrimony, Godwin's own wife, Mary Wollstonecraft, had taken an American lover, and Gilbert Imlay's *Topographical*

Description of North America (1792) was one of three books Coleridge read while in London in September 1794, lodging in Newgate Street and discussing pantisocracy with past and present pupils of nearby Christ's Hospital, his old school.[6]

Two other books read by Coleridge during this stay in London were Thomas Cooper's *Some Information Respecting America* (1794) and Jean-Pierre Brissot's *New Travels in the United States of America* (1792). Priestley, who was himself preparing to emigrate to America had asked Cooper to explore the most suitable site for settlement. Two of Priestley's sons accompanied Cooper across the Atlantic, and the result of their six-month stay was *Some Information Respecting America*. Having considered sites from New England to the Carolinas, Cooper chose Loyalsock Creek on the Susquehanna, where he called his settlement Cooper's Town. Priestley and his wife arrived in nearby Northumberland in mid-1794. Cooper's *Information* recommends intending emigrants to join his community on the Loyalsock lands, and George Dyer, one of the Christ's Hospital men Coleridge talked to in London, seemed convinced that the pantisocrats could join the Priestleys on the Susquehanna.

Another Christ's Hospital man just returned from America, in the hope of selling land to emigrants, also commended the Susquehanna and provided further information, which Coleridge relayed to Southey:

> He recommends the Susquehanna from its excessive beauty, and its security from hostile Indians. Every possible assistance will be given us. We may get credit for the land for ten years or more as we settle on it – That literary characters make *money* there, that etc. etc. He never saw a *bison* in his life, but has heard of them. They are quite backwards. The mosquitoes are not so bad as our gnats – and after you have been there a little while, they don't trouble you much...

And to Charles Heath of Monmouth, Coleridge wrote: 'At present our plan is to settle at a distance, but at a convenient distance, from Cooper's Town on the banks of the Susquehanna. This, however, will be the subject of future investigation. For the time of emigration we have fixed on next March.'[7]

The third book Coleridge read while preparing for his American venture was Brissot's *Travels*, published in an English edition in 1792. The *Travels* includes a proposal from Etienne Clavière, one of Brissot's sponsors, for the framing of a prospectus for intending emigrants:

A prospectus, sufficiently detailed, should inform the public of the nature of the enterprise, the principal object of which should be to realize a republic, founded on the lessons of experience and good sense, on the principles of fraternity which ought to unite mankind.

But there seems to be a closer link between Brissot's *Travels* and the pantisocracy of Coleridge and Southey. In his description of the Ohio valley, Brissot remarks that 'a man in that country works scarcely two hours in a day, for the support of himself and his family; he passes most of the time in idleness, hunting or drinking. The women spin and make clothes for their husbands and families.' This optimistic picture is echoed in Poole's account of the pantisocratic plan as expounded to him by Southey and Coleridge:

> Their opinion was that they should fix themselves at – I do not recollect the place, but somewhere in a delightful part of the new back settlements; that each man should labour two or three hours a day, the produce of which labour would, they imagine, be more than sufficient to support the colony.[8]

Does this mean that the two poets had been introduced to Brissot's *Travels* before Coleridge read it in September 1794 – by which time the main outlines of pantisocracy had already been drawn? We know that Poole had read Brissot in the French edition of 1791. He wrote to a neighbouring clergyman when sending a parcel of 'Book Society books':

> As for Brissot's book, I have read it in French; the translation has as much of the spirit and beauty of the original as a translation can possess, and as you ... are fond of French literature, you will, I trust, be pleased with it, not only on account of its being French, but more particularly as every page is the picture of a benevolent heart.

And as early as 1793, when news of Brissot's execution reached England, Southey had written: 'I am sick of the world and discontented with everyone in it. The murder of Brissot has completely harrowed up my faculties.'[9]

By 1795 Coleridge could take a more dispassionate view. In the first of his Bristol lectures given that year, he observed that Brissot was 'rather a sublime visionary, than a quick-eyed politician; and his excellences equally with his faults rendered him unfit for the helm in the stormy hour of Revolution'. Yet the Frenchman's visionary schemes appealed to Coleridge the pantisocrat. In the preface to his *Travels* Brissot explains that the reason why liberty flourishes beyond the Atlantic is because 'America borders on a state of nature.' Americans were not dependent on the luxuries demanded by the citizens of Paris. Coleridge was evidently impressed by a long passage in the preface, where Brissot argues that true patriots must spurn luxury no less than privilege. Coleridge quoted it in full in the printed version of his first Bristol lecture, published as *A Moral and Political Lecture* (1795).[10]

Coleridge, like Wordsworth and Southey, later tried to play down his youthful enthusiasm for the French Revolution. But in the autumn of 1794, the example of republican America and events in republican France were still closely intertwined. Coleridge had gone to London that September to try to find a publisher for *The Fall of Robespierre*, the verse drama that he and Southey had written together. They hoped that sales of the play would supply the vital funds needed for the Susquehanna enterprise. No London publisher would accept the work, and so Coleridge shifted the search to Cambridge. Writing from his old university to Southey in mid-September, Coleridge exclaimed:

> Pantisocracy! Oh, I shall have such a scheme of it! My head, my heart, are all alive. I have drawn up my arguments in battle array; they shall have the *tactician* excellence of the mathematician with the enthusiasm of the poet.

He enclosed an early version of his sonnet 'Pantisocracy', which seems to owe something to his recent reading of Imlay.[11]

In the same letter Coleridge gave his initial response to Southey's decision to take his servant 'Shad' to America: 'SHAD GOES WITH US. HE IS MY BROTHER!' A few weeks later, however, Coleridge was having second thoughts, and wrote to Southey: 'You will *perceive* the error into which the tenderness of your nature had led you.' But Southey did not perceive it, and Coleridge had to write again, reluctantly accepting 'the introduction of servitude into our society.' He tells Southey that he cannot see 'even the temporary *convenience*' of the proposal, and asks: 'To be employed in the toil of the field, while *we* are pursuing philosophical studies – can earldoms or emperorships boast so large an inequality?' Aptly enough, Coleridge reports a furious six-hour discussion at Cambridge (where pantisocracy was 'the universal topic at this University') during which at least some of his audience 'declared the system impregnable, supposing the assigned quantity of virtue and genius in the first individuals'.[12]

Southey tried unsuccessfully to persuade Coleridge to return to Bristol, and in December 1794 Coleridge had to write to reassure him that he was not weakening in his resolve to go to America – or to marry Sara Fricker. Perhaps a letter that reached him in Cambridge that October from his former sweetheart, Mary Evans, had given Coleridge pause. Warning him that 'there is an eagerness in your nature which is ever hurrying you in the sad extreme,' Mary added that if he really was proposing to leave England 'on a plan so absurd and extravagant', she would be forced to exclaim, 'O what a noble mind is here *o'erthrown*, blasted with ecstacy.' But the real trouble was undoubtedly money. Benjamin Flower of Cambridge agreed to print *The Fall of Robespierre*, with Coleridge's name alone on the title page, in order (Southey was told) to foster sales in Coleridge's university. It remained an unpromising publishing venture, and any financial advantage was heavily outweighed by the news that Southey's aunt had expressed her distaste for pantisocracy by disinheriting him. At the end of the year, Southey was proposing a plan, suggested by a Welsh friend and supported by at least one of the pantisocrats, under which the men would go shares in a Welsh farm and there learn agricultural skills before departing for America.[13]

Coleridge at first reacted angrily: 'As to the Welsh scheme – pardon me – it is nonsense. We must go to America, if we can get Money enough.' He added that Southey seemed to be a man 'aweary of the world because it accords not with his ideas of perfection'. But by January 1795 they were proposing their course of public lectures at Bristol to raise the £300 needed to settle in Wales. In the event the takings barely covered Coleridge's rent. Hopes rose when Southey was promised an annuity by a friend, but when Southey proposed keeping this windfall to himself – while still expecting the Welsh farm to be run on communal lines – Coleridge wrote bitterly: 'This was the mouse of which the Mountain of Pantisocracy was at last safely delivered.'[14]

Just as pantisocracy has too often been dismissed as student escapism, rather than recognized as one strand in a widespread contemporary idealization of the New America, so Coleridge's 1795 Bristol lectures have too often been ridiculed as the confused rhetoric of juvenile Jacobinism. Coleridge was certainly young, embarking on his lecture programme at the age of 22. Indeed his first lecture begins with an apology for his youthful presumption. But his aim in the lecture, he goes on to explain, is 'not so much to excite the torpid as to regulate the feelings of the ardent', and above all to provide a proper foundation or 'bottoming' of unchanging political principles. The example of France, he concedes, is a 'Warning to Britain'. Yet the proper response to the excesses of the French Revolution should be to seek to determine how such excesses arose. For Coleridge, 'French freedom is the beacon, which while it guides to equality, should show us the dangers that throng the road.' For him the fault lies not in the principles of the European Enlightenment or the ideas of 1789, but in the failure to diffuse those principles throughout the whole population:

> The Annals of the French Revolution have recorded in Letters of Blood, that the Knowledge of the Few cannot counteract the Ignorance of the Many; that the Light of Philosophy, when it is confined to a small Minority, points out the Possessors as the Victims, rather than the Iluminators of the Multitude.[15]

Coleridge does not share the Jacobin commitment to universal suffrage. The hope he professes in this first Bristol lecture is that 'the purifying alchemy of Education may transmute the fierceness of an ignorant man into virtuous energy' and that the future may belong to 'thinking and disinterested Patriots'. Such true patriots, he claims, are 'accustomed to regard all the affairs of men as a process, they never hurry and they never pause'. By contrast, he argues, 'a system of fundamental Reform will scarcely be effected by massacres mechanized into Revolution'. What he calls 'general illumination' must precede revolution. This optimistic belief in the power of education was characteristic of the Enlightenment, and is closer to Godwinism than to Jacobinism. In *Political Justice* Godwin had written: 'The complete reformation that is wanted is not instant but future reformation. It can scarcely be considered as the nature of action. It consists in a universal illumination.' Coleridge disliked Godwin's atheism, and was critical of the way in which he 'proposes an end without establishing the means'. But he shared Godwin's gradualist approach to reform.[16]

So, when Coleridge later admitted to a correspondent that his rhetoric had carried him away in his Bristol lectures, and that he had 'aided the Jacobins, by witty sarcasms and subtle reasonings and declamations full of genuine feeling against all established forms', which lectures was he thinking of? Probably not the political lectures given in the early months of 1795, though by attacking the war with Revolutionary France they provoked what Coleridge called (with some relish) 'Mobs and Mayors, Blockheads and Brickbats, Placards and Press gangs'. Nor can he have meant the six Lectures on Revealed Religion, delivered during May and June, though they attacked the Established Church and claimed that Christianity was an egalitarian creed. Nor even the Lecture on the Slave Trade – a bold choice for Bristol – which followed in mid-June and proposed direct action by boycotting sugar and rum. Though all these lectures employed colourful invective, his most vituperative denunciations were uttered in November 1795, after his first meeting with Wordsworth, and just after his own marriage. It was the repressive policy of Pitt's government that so swiftly drew the newly married Coleridge out of retirement to:

> join head, heart and hand
> Active and firm, to fight the bloodless fight
> Of Science, Freedom and the Truth in Christ.[17]

It was in late November that Coleridge gave his 'Lecture of the Two Bills', subsequently printed as *The Plot Discovered*. The two bills were the so-called 'Treason Bill' designed to secure the King and his ministers 'against Treasonable and Seditious Practices and Attempts', and the 'Convention Bill' directed against seditious meetings and assemblies. Coleridge argues that, if Pitt's ministry succeeds in suspending the right to hold meetings and the freedom to publish (as the two bills proposed), 'the cadaverous tranquility of despotism will succeed the generous order and graceful indiscretions of freedom', with the result that 'our assemblies will resemble a silent and sullen mob of discontented slaves who have surrounded the palace of some eastern tyrant.' As for the other Bill, curtailing public meetings, Coleridge claims that it means two things: 'First that the people of England should possess no unrestrained right of consulting in common on common grievances: and secondly that Mr Thelwall should no longer give political lectures.' Before the two Bills became law, John Thelwall's London lectures continued to attract audiences of 500 a night, while his attacks on government policy cited Coleridge and Godwin in support. In his own pamphlet attacking the Two Bills, Godwin also censured Thelwall's tactics, remarking: 'The system of political lectures is a hot-bed, perhaps too well adapted to ripen men for purposes, more or less similar to those of the Jacobin Society of Paris.'[18]

Despite the robust invective of his November lecture, Coleridge followed the Godwin line. Turning to journalism, he proclaimed in the prospectus to his newly founded *Watchman* that he had set himself to 'preserve Freedom and her Friends from the attacks of Robbers and Assassins'. But the first issue prudently conceded that the Two Bills might usefully cool the language of political publications and perhaps 'confine us for a while to the teaching of first principles, or the diffusion of that general knowledge which should be the basis or substratum of politics'. The *Watchman* folded after ten issues, but its editor did not finally abandon faith in Revolutionary France until the Directory's invasion of republican Switzerland in 1798. In February of that year Coleridge signalled his disillusionment by writing 'Recantation', later renamed 'France: an Ode'. The last of its five stanzas apostrophizes Liberty:

> The guide of homeless winds, and playmate of the waves!
> And there I felt thee! – on that sea-cliff's verge
> > Whose pines scarce travelled by the breeze above,
> Had made one music with the distant surge!
> Yes, while I stood and gazed, my temples bare,
> And shot my being through earth, sea and air,
> > Possessing all things with intensest love,
> > > O Liberty! my spirit felt thee there.

The sentiments foreshadow Wordsworth's 'Lines Written above Tintern Abbey', composed later that year and dated 13 July – the eve of Bastille Day.[19]

Wordsworth had been in France and joined in the first Bastille Day celebrations in 1790. On a second visit in 1791, he had pocketed a fragment of the Bastille, attended a session of the Legislative Assembly and may possibly have lodged with Brissot before finding himself among the Jacobins of Orléans. Here he wrote *Descriptive Sketches* with lines seemingly celebrating revolutionary violence:

> But foes are gathering – Liberty must raise
> Red on the hills her beacons far-seen blaze;
> Must bid the tocsin ring from tower to tower:
> Nearer and nearer comes the trying hour!
> Rejoice, brave Land, though pride's perverted ire
> Rouse hell's own aid, and wrap thy fields in fire:
> Lo from the flames a great and glorious birth
> As if a new-made heaven were hailing a new earth!

This is not quite yet Robespierre's 'Virtue through Terror', but the young Wordsworth speaks in the authentic accents of Jacobinism. By contrast, the revolutionary principles of the young Coleridge, flowing from the more distant and less turbulent source of the American Revolution, became more subtly transmuted and never lost the

Utopian current that ran from Godwin, through pantisocracy, to the Bristol lectures of 1795.[20]

At the end of 1796, after the birth of their first son, Hartley, the Coleridges forsook their rented cottage at Clevedon to settle permanently at Nether Stowey. It was here that Coleridge wrote to Thelwall the famous words: 'I am not fit for *public* life; yet the light shall stream to a far distance from the taper in my cottage window.' And shortly before moving from Clevedon to their new home, he proclaimed: 'I would rather be an expert, self-maintaining gardener than a Milton, if I could not unite both.' Charles Lamb was startled by Coleridge's expressed wish that his children should grow up 'in the simplicity of peasants', and asked about his plans for Hartley: 'I did not distinctly understand you, – you don't mean to make an actual ploughman of him?' Lamb hoped that Coleridge would write an epic poem:

> Nothing but it can satisfy the vast capacity of the true poetic genius. You have learning, you have fancy, you have enthusiasm – you have strength and amplitude of wing enow for flights like those I recommend. In the vast unformed and incultivated; search there, and realize your favourite Susquehanna scheme.

Pantisocracy was to be refined into poetry.[21]

The arrival of the Wordsworths at nearby Alfoxden in 1797 ensured that Coleridge would be poet rather than ploughman. But even in the Quantocks, revolutionary echoes pursued them. That summer, as Coleridge and the Wordsworths roamed the hills with camp-stools and sketch-books, they were mistaken for French spies. They had particularly aroused suspicion by asking about the river, which reached the sea at Bridgwater. The episode, as reported by Coleridge in *Biographia Literaria*, reads as pure farce. But James Walsh – 'Spy Nozy' in Coleridge's account – who came down to Somerset to investigate these supposedly seditious activities, was an experienced government spy who had kept a watch on Thelwall's London lectures. Walsh knew a French spy when he saw one, and was quick to dismiss the newcomers as nothing but 'a mischievous gang of disaffected Englishmen'. Yet less than six months before, the French had contrived to land 1200 soldiers on the Pembrokeshire coast, and had intended landing on the Somerset side with a view to attacking Bristol. No wonder the Home Office and the inhabitants of Nether Stowey were nervous. Thelwall now decided to cross the Bristol Channel and buy a farm in Wales, while Wordsworth and Coleridge prepared for the publication of *Lyrical Ballads*. There would be echoes of America and of pantisocracy in Wordsworth's poem 'Ruth', with its 'youth from Georgia's shore':

'How pleasant,' then he said, 'it were
A fisher or a hunter there,
In sunshine or in shade
To wander with an easy mind
And build an household fire and find
A home in every glade.'[22]

Southey, who was still a schoolboy at Westminster when the Bastille fell, later wrote of that period: 'Few persons but those who have lived in it can conceive or comprehend what a visionary world seemed to open up. Old things seemed passing away and nothing was dreamt of but the regeneration of the human race.' So idealized a view of revolution now seems ridiculous, and Coleridge himself would refer dismissively to their plan 'of trying the experiment of human perfectibility on the banks of the Susquehanna'. Yet it was six months after the execution of Brissot that Southey could still be moved by his reading of Godwin to exclaim: 'I am studying such a book! I am inclined to think that man is capable of perfection.' But it was not only college students who believed in perfection: in the 1790s, thanks to Godwin and the American Revolution, human perfectibility seemed an attainable goal.[23]

16 North American Naturalists: Bartram and Audubon

For the first two years of the War of Independence, while the battles of Lexington, Concord and Bunker Hill were being fought, William Bartram was searching the southern states of North America for undiscovered plants. At the beginning of the account of his adventures, published under the title *Travels through North and South Carolina, Georgia, East and West Florida,* Bartram explains that he had been asked by Dr John Fothergill of London to undertake an expedition for 'the discovery of rare and useful productions of nature, chiefly in the vegetable kingdom'. His picturesque descriptions include paddling through 'innumerable millions' of mating mayflies, hailing the yellow bream or sun-fish as 'a warrior in a gilded coat of mail', and noting that the noise of a beautiful green frog 'exactly resembles the barking of little dogs, or the yelping of puppies'. Among his botanical discoveries was a rare flowering tree, which he had first seen with his father, John Bartram, during an expedition in the 1760s. William now named the tree the Franklinia, after Benjamin Franklin, who had obtained for the elder Bartram the salaried post of King's Botanist. During the war, Franklin wrote from Paris encouraging the Bartrams to send botanical specimens to France: 'If you incline, you may send the same number of boxes here that you used to send to England. Enclosed is a list of the sorts wished for here. I will take care of the sale and returns.'[1]

William never went to Europe, and although the account of his plant-hunting expedition was sent to Fothergill, it did not appear in the European scientific periodicals as Bartram had hoped. It was not until 1791 that the *Travels* was published in America, with pirated editions appearing in London in 1792 and Dublin in 1793. Coleridge quoted from the *Travels* in his *Biographia Literaria,* applying some of Bartram's descriptions 'as a sort of allegory or connected simile and metaphor of Wordsworth's intellect and genius'. Wordsworth himself lost his own copy of the *Travels* on a trip to Germany, and immediately wrote home to ask for a replacement. At least one literary historian has traced lines in *Kubla Khan*, with its 'caverns measureless to man', to Bartram's descriptions of the underground waterways of Florida. And it does seem that the opening lines of Wordsworth's *Ruth* were suggested by Bartram's account of his meeting with a Cherokee chief.[2]

Bartram is indeed fascinated by the Indian tribes. His first chapter describes an encounter in the forest with a Seminole Indian, who looks in murderous mood, but ends by shaking the naturalist's hand. Bartram later reflects that life in the forest is 'like that of the primitive state of man, peaceable, contented and sociable'. The theme of the noble savage recurs in Bartram's account of the vast territories of the Seminoles, who 'contented and undisturbed' appear 'as blithe and free as the birds of the air, and like them as volatile and active, tuneful and vociferous'. He admits that the Seminoles are war-like, but adds: 'I cannot find, upon the strictest inquiry, that their bloody contests at this day are marked with deeper stains of inhumanity or savage cruelty than what may be observed among the most civilized nations.'[3]

Part II of the *Travels* begins: 'April 22d, 1776, I set off from Charleston for the Cherokee nation'. His enjoyment of half-an-hour's hospitality at the hands of a Cherokee chief prompts the rhapsodic reaction: 'O divine simplicity and truth, friendship without fallacy or guile, hospitality disinterested, native, undefiled, unmodified by artificial refinements.' Accompanied by a young trader, he observes Cherokee virgins gambolling amid the azaleas and strawberry fields or 'bathing their limbs in the cool fleeting streams'. Well might he decide that 'the sylvan scene of primitive innocence was perhaps too enticing for hearty young men long to continue as idle spectators.' In 'Ruth', Wordsworth's Georgian youth:

> told of girls – a happy rout!
> Who quit their fold with dance and shout,
> Their pleasant Indian town,
> To gather strawberries all day long;
> Returning with a choral song
> When daylight is gone down.

Bartram finds the Cherokees 'frank, cheerful and humane' and 'tenacious of the liberties and natural rights of man'. The naturalist concludes: 'As moral beings they certainly stand in no need of European civilization.' Indeed it was for Europe to learn from the native Americans.[4]

In 1791, the year in which Bartram finally published his *Travels*, the future transatlantic naturalist John James Audubon was six, and living in the French city of Nantes. He was there during the unsuccessful attempt of royalist Vendeans to take the city, and during the brutal reprisals that followed. It was a time, Audubon later wrote to his sons, when 'the Revolutionists covered the earth with the blood of man, woman and child.' His own father nevertheless signalled his republicanism by enlisting in the Nantes National Guard. Audubon's father, Jean, had been born in the Vendée, and went to sea at the age of 13. He served in the merchant marine, first in the Newfoundland trade and then in the lucrative commerce between France and Santo Domingo, besides spending a brief spell in the French navy. He was imprisoned twice by the British, and when released for the second time, openly championed the American cause. He was given command of a corvette, which joined the French fleet off Yorktown. When peace came, he settled in Santo Domingo – without his wife – determined to make a fortune in the transatlantic trade, now thrown open by the British defeat. By 1789 he had prospered sufficiently to visit the United States and purchase the farm of 'Mill Grove', near Philadelphia. Promptly leasing it to the vendor, he returned to Santo Domingo.[5]

It was in Santo Domingo that his son, John James, was born in the spring of 1785. His mother was a local woman of French parentage – a créole, like the future Empress Josephine. Two years later, another créole woman bore Jean Audubon a daughter. John James would later boast that he had 'received light and life in the New World', and that he came to France to be educated. His father brought both children back to France in 1789. They started their transatlantic journey knowing that the States-General was in session, but not knowing that the Bastille had fallen. Jean's forbearing French wife, a widow who was nine years his senior and childless, apparently welcomed these New World offspring. They were formally adopted into the Audubon family in March 1793. Thus John James Audubon cannot himself be regarded as one of the Revolutionary generation, but he is at least a child of the French Revolution, who helped to foster the romantic image of Revolutionary America.[6]

The younger Audubon never mastered written French, but he was nevertheless a pupil of the Enlightenment, and was influenced as much by Rousseau as by Buffon. Educated at the military school at Rochefort (where he learned elementary mathematics, geography, fencing and music), John James also learned to dance – an accomplishment, his first biographer remarks, 'which in after years he had more opportunities of practising among bears than among men'. At the age of 17, his drawing skills were improved under the tutelage of Jacques Louis David in Paris. At 18, his father sent him to Philadelphia to learn English and a useful trade. Landing at New York, he survived a bout of yellow fever, and by the spring of 1804 was safely installed at Mill Grove. It was here that he met his future wife, Lucy Bakewell, and also took his first steps in serious ornithology. Lucy's brother, William, describes Audubon's room at Mill Grove two summers later:

> The walls were festooned with all kinds of birds eggs, carefully blown out and strung on a thread. The chimney-piece was covered with stuffed squirrels, racoons and opussums; and the shelves around were likewise crowded with specimens, among which were fishes, frogs, snakes, lizards and other varieties. Besides these stuffed varieties, many paintings were arrayed on the walls, chiefly of birds.[7]

Eighteen months earlier, Audubon had made a surprise trip home to Nantes, chiefly to allay his father's misgivings about his proposed marriage. He returned to America early in 1806, apparently to escape military service in the Napoleonic army. He was accompanied by Ferdinand Rozier, whose father (a wealthy Nantes merchant) had already invested 16 000 francs in Mill Grove. The two young men were given power of attorney to conduct the affairs of the farm. They went as emigrants. Rozier wrote to his father: 'We are determined to go into trade, to cover our expenses, and to choose for ourselves some kind of serious work that can lead us to an honourable establishment.' Audubon saw it all rather differently. 'I returned to the woods of the new world with fresh ardour,' he later wrote, 'and commenced a collection of drawings, which I henceforth continued, and which is now publishing under the title of *The Birds of America*.[8]

For the moment, however, the ornithologist found himself with Lucy's uncle, Benjamin Bakewell, who operated a wholesale importing business in New York. The Bakewells were newcomers to the New World themselves. Benjamin had come to America in 1794, the same year as Joseph Priestley, whom the Bakewells knew in England. Lucy's father, another William, had crossed the Atlantic even more recently, in 1802. Audubon was hardly an asset to the Bakewell business, escaping from the counting-room as often as he could. He and Rozier soon set out for the Kentucky town of Louisville, on the Ohio, then regarded as the western frontier. The shop they opened there was a failure. They would have done better to have invested in land. As Audubon wrote in his journal: 'We marked Louisville as a spot designed by nature to become a place of importance, and had we been as wise as we now are, I might never have published *The Birds of America*.' Leaving Rozier in Kentucky, Audubon returned to Pennsylvania to marry Lucy. The wedding was on 5 April 1808, and Lucy accompanied her husband back to Louisville – a 1000-mile journey accomplished in 12 days.[9]

Audubon was happy at Louisville, a town of barely 1000 inhabitants, where their first child, Victor, was born. But Lucy's early loneliness is reflected in her letters: 'I am sorry there is no library here or book store of any kind; for I have very few of my own, and as Mr Audubon is constantly at the store I should enjoy a book very much whilst alone.' She may not have realized how rarely her husband was in the store. As he himself admitted: 'I shot, I drew, I looked upon nature only...I seldom passed a day without drawing a bird, or noting something respecting its habits, Rozier meantime attending the counter.' It was nevertheless at the Louisville store that he met the rival ornithologist, Alexander Wilson, who was collecting subscriptions for his *American Ornithology* – a work inspired by William Bartram's listing of 215 species of birds. Audubon was about to become a subscriber himself, when Rozier (speaking in French) dissuaded him: 'My dear Audubon, what induces you to subscribe to this work? Your drawings are certainly far better'.[10]

Audubon later called on Wilson in Philadelphia and found him drawing a white-headed Eagle. But the two men were too much in competition to become friends, and each would accuse the other of plagiarism. Meanwhile Audubon and Rozier left Louisville, still hoping, in spite of evident failures, to make their fortune. They moved to the small settlement of Henderson, further down the Ohio, where the long-suffering Lucy joined them (with Victor) to live in a log cabin. Again Audubon paints a romantic picture: 'The woods were amply stocked with game, the river with fish; and now and then the hoarded sweets of the industrious bees were brought from some hollow tree to our little table.' He fished for cat-fish with live toads, which he brought back in baskets to the cabin. After six months at Henderson, Audubon and Rozier decided to venture down the Ohio to the Mississippi. Drifting down-river for nine weeks, they amused themselves by 'firing into flocks of birds'. Christmas Day 1810 was spent with some Indians who were hunting wild swan. At the end of one day they 'counted more than fifty of these beautiful birds whose skins were intended for the ladies of Europe'. It was odd sport for an ornithologist.[11]

Audubon's last business venture, with his brother-in-law Thomas Bakewell, involved setting up a steam saw-mill on the river-front at Henderson. The partners lost their own and their investors' money. Audubon records: 'I parted with every particle of property I held to my credit, only keeping the clothes I wore that day, my original drawings and my gun.' Without a dollar in his pocket, he walked to Louisville, where he was imprisoned for debt. On his release, Lucy and their two sons (a second, John Woodhouse, was born in 1812) joined him at nearby Shippingport. Audubon resorted to drawing portraits in crayon at five dollars a head; he briefly accepted an appointment at the Western Museum in Cincinnati; he even started a drawing school. He supplemented the family's economical style of living by hunting: 'Partridges are frequently in the streets, and I can shoot Wild Turkeys within a mile or so'. And here in 1820 he hit on what he called the 'Great Idea' of publishing his drawings in a comprehensive and systematic form. He would provide life-sized drawings of all American birds, setting them in their natural habitat. So he must set off again for the Mississippi, leaving Lucy and the children at Cincinnati.[12]

After five months at New Orleans, Audubon was on his way up-river on the steamboat *Columbus* when he met Mrs James Pirrie, wife of a Louisiana cotton planter. She engaged him as tutor to her daughter, on the understanding that he should live on her husband's plantation, 'Oakley', and have half his time free for hunting and drawing. He stayed for several months, and produced the originals of many of his plates. Among them was what Audubon himself called 'a very fine specimen of a rattlesnake.' The artist explains that, 'anxious to give it a position most interesting to a naturalist, I put it in that which the reptile commonly takes when on the point of striking madly with its fangs.' The accuracy of his observation would later be challenged, by those who questioned the authenticity of his much discussed 'Mocking-birds with rattlesnake'. At the time Audubon was disappointed because the heat of the day prevented him from devoting more than 16 hours to the drawing.[13]

In November 1821, he claimed to have made over 60 drawings of birds and plants since leaving Cincinnati. That winter in New Orleans was a harsh one for the family, though Lucy eventually found work as a governess. Her husband had the grace to acknowledge in his journal: 'My best friends solemnly regarded me as a madman, and my wife and family alone gave me encouragement. My wife determined that my genius shall prevail and that my final success as an ornithologist should be triumphant.' It was confidence in his ultimate success that took Audubon in 1824 to Philadelphia in search of patron or publisher. He met the leading artists and scientific men of the city, among them the 21-year-old Charles Lucien Bonaparte, nephew of Napoleon and himself an aspiring ornithologist. Charles introduced his fellow Frenchman to the Philadelphia Academy of Natural Sciences, where his drawings were exhibited. His work was generally admired, though George Ord, editor of Wilson's work, objected to Audubon's practice of introducing plants and other features into his drawings. As Audubon commented: 'Those interested in Wilson's book on American birds advised me not to publish, and not only cold water, but ice, was poured upon my undertaking.'[14]

Charles Bonaparte, however, was an enthusiastic admirer, telling his compatriot that his birds were 'superb, and worthy of a pupil of David'. Bonaparte advised that the work of engraving the plates should be undertaken in Europe, but (Audubon sadly records) 'he replied coldly to my application for aid to carry out this purpose'. Yet various letters of recommendation were forthcoming for presentation in New York. One was from Thomas Sully to the fashionable artist Washington Alston, commending Audubon's work 'which for copiousness and talent bids fair in my estimation to surpass all that has yet been done, at least in this country'. On arrival in New York the naturalist met Joseph Bonaparte, and visited the city museum, where he found 'the specimens of stuffed birds set up in unnatural and constrained attitudes'. This persuaded him that 'the world owes to me the adoption of the plan of drawing from animated nature.' He soon found that no New York publisher was interested in his ambitious project, and he felt 'clouded and depressed', adding disconsolately: 'Remember that I have done nothing, and fear I may die unknown.' But a visit to Niagara Falls revives his spirits, and he goes to bed 'thinking of Franklin eating his roll in the streets of Philadelphia'.[15]

He spends a month at Pittsburgh, 'scouring the country for birds', and during an expedition to the Great Lakes, he crystallizes in his mind the arrangement of his proposed *Birds of America*:

Chance, and chance alone, had divided my drawings into three different classes, depending on the magnitude of the objects to be represented; and, although I did not at that time possess all the specimens necessary, I arranged them as well as I could into parcels of five plates...

He now decides to set off in a skiff down the Ohio and Mississippi, with (as he improbably puts it) 'an artist, a doctor and an Irishman'. On the way he tries unsuccessfully to sell lithographs of Lafayette in order to raise funds, while his companions soon tire of the voyage. So, selling the skiff, he makes instead for Cincinnati. From there he travels by way of Louisville to the Pirrie plantation, arriving with torn clothes and uncut hair, 'and altogether looking like the wandering Jew.' He finds his wife already up and giving a lesson to her pupils: 'Holding and kissing her, I was once more happy, and all my toils and trials were forgotten.' He was to spend the next 18 months on the plantation, teaching dancing and fencing to raise money for his trip to Europe.[16]

In May 1826 he sailed from New Orleans for Liverpool on a cotton-schooner. For the first fortnight out of port, Audubon records, 'the time was pleasantly spent shooting birds and catching dolphins and sharks, from which I made frequent sketches.' He was anxious about his prospects in Europe, but there was now no turning back, and he wrote in his journal for 23 June: 'This morning we entered the Atlantic Ocean from the Florida Straits with a fair wind. The land birds have left us. I leave America and my wife and children to visit England and Europe and publish my *Birds of America*.' He landed at Liverpool a month later, finding the smoke of the city 'so oppressive to my lungs that I could hardly breathe'. He was much helped by the Rathbone family, as he later acknowledged in his 'Rathbone Warbler', and by Lord Stanley, to whom we owe the 'Stanley Hawk'. It was Stanley who allegedly told Audubon on inspecting his drawings: 'This work is unique, and deserves the patronage of the Crown.' Within barely a week of landing, the artist was invited to exhibit his drawings at the Liverpool Royal Institution, for which he painted a wild turkey, life-size, as a mark of appreciation.[17]

In Manchester his reception was more muted, despite letters of introduction to Sir Walter Scott, Sir Humphry Davy and the American portraitist Sir Thomas Lawrence. Audubon was not impressed with the city or its inhabitants, who seemed to this keen observer 'worse off than the negroes of Louisiana'. Yet he added to his list of possible patrons, opened a subscription book, and visited the town of Bakewell. After his rebuff at Manchester, Edinburgh's enthusiastic embrace was almost unnerving: 'It is Mr Audubon here, and Mr Audubon there, and I can only hope they will not make a conceited fool of Mr Audubon at last.' Lizars the engraver quickly offered to engrave and publish the first specimen plates, which, despite Rathbone's earlier advice to scale down the drawings, appeared in double elephant folio. When exhibited at the Royal Institution of Edinburgh, the drawings created immense interest. Lord Elgin was among the visitors, and an established French critic of the day wrote:

> A magic power transported us into the forests which for so many years this genius has trod ... Imagine a landscape wholly American, trees, flowers, grass, even the tints of the sky and the waters, quickened with a life that is real, peculiar, trans-Atlantic ... It is a real and palpable vision of the New World, with its atmosphere, its imposing vegetation, and its tribes which know not the yoke of man.

Another French writer likened Audubon's reception in England to the impact Franklin had had on an earlier generation in France.[18]

Audubon thought that part of his fame was due to his long hair: 'I wear my hair long as usual. I believe it does as much for me as my paintings.' Not until 19 March 1827 does he write dolefully in his journal: 'This day my Hair was sacrificed, and the will of God usurped by the wishes of man.' By the time he exhibited his first five engraved plates at the Royal Society of Edinburgh that February, he had met the Earl of Morton – 'a small slender man, tottering on his feet and weaker than a newly-hatched partridge' – whose wife not only entered her name in the subscription book, but offered to pay in advance. Walter Scott did not visit the exhbibition, but granted Audubon an interview, confiding to his own journal his impression of the artist:

> He is an American by naturalization, a Frenchman by birth; but less of a Frenchman than I have ever seen – no dash or glimmer, or shine about him, but great simplicity of manners and behaviour ... The drawings are of the first order – the attitudes of the birds of the most animated character, and the situations appropriate ...[19]

Audubon began to contribute to scientific journals, and was soon elected to membership of the Linnaean Society. By then he was the talk of London. Meanwhile, before leaving Edinburgh, he issued his 'Prospectus'. In it he explains that he has not contented himself 'as others have done' with simple profile views, but has in many instances 'grouped his figures so as to represent the originals at their natural avocations'. Some are depicted 'pursuing their prey through the air, searching for food amongst the leaves and herbage, sitting in their nests or feeding their young'. And above all the engraved drawings 'without any exception, represent the birds and other objects of their natural size'. Few of Audubon's friends and acquaintances can have supposed that his ambitious plan involving three volumes, each of 133 plates, would ever be accomplished.[20]

In London, which seemed to him 'like the mouth of an immense monster, guarded by millions of sharp-edged teeth', Audubon had his greatest stroke of good fortune. He met the two Robert Havells, father and son. Robert Havell senior, considering himself too old at 57 to undertake so great a labour, promised Audubon to find a substitute. After scouring London, he discovered that the best candidate was his own son, who soon replaced Lizars as sole engraver of the work. Audubon was beginning to despair of raising sufficient funds, but a visit to Sir Thomas Lawrence produced an introduction to a number of purchasers, who paid between £7 and £35 for the drawings they bought. 'Without the sale of these pictures', Audubon rightly remarked, 'I was a bankrupt before my work was scarcely begun.' Two days later he was ready to pay Havell his promised £60. 'Thus,' records Audubon, 'I had passed the Rubicon.'[21]

Although the hopeful naturalist was not received by George IV, the King was shown the *Birds of America*, through the good offices of the British Museum. Audubon reported the royal reaction: 'His Majesty was pleased to call it fine, and permitted me to publish it under his particular patronage, approbation and protection; and became a subscriber on usual terms, not as kings generally do, but as a gentleman.' Audubon now had his eyes on the French court. In June 1828 he dined with Charles Bonaparte, who offered to name the birds previously unknown to ornithologists, suggesting 'upwards of fifty names'. Audubon noted with some irritation that Charles's servant insisted on addressing his master as 'Your Royal Highness'. Three months later the American backwoodsman was in Bourbon Paris. His first visit was to the distinguished botanist, Baron Cuvier, who introduced Audubon's work to the *Académie des Sciences*. Cuvier's report concluded: 'Wilson's history of the *Birds of the United States* equals in elegance our most beautiful works on ornithology. If that of Mr Audubon should be completed, we shall be obliged to acknowledge that America, in magnificence of execution, has surpassed the old world.'[22]

Meanwhile the famous flower-painter Redouté offered to obtain subscriptions from the Duke and Duchess of Orléans. Soon to become King Louis Philippe, the Duke had sought refuge in the United States during the 1790s, and now gave an affable welcome to this strange Gallo-American. In Audubon's words: 'He had my book brought in, and helped me to untie the strings and arrange the table, and began by saying that he felt great pleasure in subscribing to the work of an American; that he had been kindly treated in the United States and would never forget it.' On the eve of his departure from Paris, Audubon heard that Charles X would subscribe for six copies. Well might Audubon write home: 'I have run the gauntlet of Europe, Lucy, and may be proud of two things – that I am considered the first ornithological painter and the first practical naturalist of America.'[23]

At the end of October he returned to London and a further spell of drawing. But it was time to return home, and on 1 April 1829 his journal records: 'I went by mail to the smoky city of Portsmouth, have hoisted the anchor, am at sea, and sea-sick.' He had not seen his wife and family for three years, but he wanted to renew 50 of his earlier drawings. It would be nearly six months after landing at New York before he rejoined Lucy in Louisiana. First he went to draw birds at the Great Egg Harbour, New Jersey. Then he spent six weeks in a lumberman's cottage in the Great Pine Swamp, where he paid parti- cular attention to finches, warblers and fly-catchers, and heard the lumberman read the poems of Robert Burns. 'Was this not enough,' Audubon asks, 'to recall to my mind the early impressions that had been made upon it by the description of the golden age, which I here realized?' In October he could report that he had completed 42 drawings in four months. Not until mid-November was he finally reunited with his family. He stayed with them for three months, still hunting and drawing as actively as ever. His 'Black Vulture attacking the Herd of Deer' dates from this period. He was hardly home before writing to Richard Harlan about his plan to send turkeys, alligators, oppossums, parrakeet and plants such as begonias 'to the Zoological Gardens of London, from the Natural ones of this magnificent Louis- iana'. He might have added that it was the same Louisiana sold by Napoleon to the United States under Jefferson's Presidency. What Audubon did add was an excited postscript to say that he just found a new black falcon, which he proposed to name *Falcon Harlanii*.[24]

On the first day of 1830, he set off for Washington, where he found Congress in session. He exhibited his drawings to the House of Representatives, and was received by President Andrew Jackson. During his stay in the capital Audubon learned that he had been elected Fellow of the Royal Society. A further year would elapse before he was elected a Fellow of the American Academy of Arts and Sciences, while in March 1830 a leading Congressman, Edward Everett, told a correspondent that Audubon had 'not yet procured a single subscriber in the United States of America'. It was Everett who ensured that at least the Library of Congress subscribed for a copy. Eventually the number of American subscribers just exceeded those in Europe – 82 out of a total of 161. The last plate of the *Birds of America* was printed in June 1838, and within a year the fifth and final volume of Audubon's *Ornithological Biography* had also appeared. During the 1830s the Audubons spent more time in Europe than in America. For two-and-a-half years between 1831 and 1834 Audubon went back to search for birds in Florida, Maine and Labrador; and for 12 months in 1836–7, while planning with John Bachman their joint book on quadrupeds, Audubon and his younger son sought unsuccessfully for more species in the Gulf of Mexico. It was during this visit that he and John Woodhouse dined *en famille* with President Jackson at the White House, and drank grog with Sam Houston, President of the still independent Republic of Texas.[25]

In the summer of 1839 Audubon left Europe for the last time. On arrival in New York he issued a prospectus for what was to prove the best-selling octavo edition of the *Birds of America* (at $1000 compared with $10 000 for the original edition) and also for the newly begun three-volume *Quadrupeds of America*, the first volume only of which was to be published in his lifetime. During the last ten years of his life – all spent in America – the 'Man of the Woods' embarked on one more expedition. It was an eight-week journey up the Missouri 'undertaken for the sake of our work on the Quadrupeds of North America'. Audubon himself drew the smaller mammals, leaving John Woodhouse to draw the larger. The Journals, with Audubon's romanticized accounts of his expeditions, were not published until the 1860s, by which time the image of the United States was one of industrialization and civil war. But his drawings of birds, and the sensation he and they created on both sides of the Atlantic, helped to maintain 'natural' America's hold on the Romantic imagination until the middle years of the nineteenth century. It comes as no surprise to find that in 1839, the year after the last plate of the *Birds of America* was printed, its engraver, Robert Havell, himself set sail for America. He lived in New York State for almost 40 years, sketching and painting the awe-inspiring scenery of the Hudson River – which had impressed so many eighteenth-century European visitors to the New World.[26]

Notes

CHAPTER 1   DISCOVERY AND REDISCOVERY

1. For de Pauw, see René Pomeau in *L'Amérique des Lumières: Partie Littéraire du Colloque du Bicentaire de l'Indépendance Américaine* (Geneva and Paris, 1977) ix; for Genty, see Yves Morand in *L'Amérique des Lumières* 9.
2. For Hakluyt, see A. L. Rowse, *The Elizabethans and America* (London, 1959) 11.
3. William Bradford, *History of the Plymouth Plantation*, ed. Harold C. Syrett (New York, 1960) 16, 22; Voltaire, *Essai sur les moeurs* 2 vols (Paris: *Classiques Garnier*, 1961–3) II 381 (my translation).
4. [Thomas Nairne], *A Letter from South Carolina* ... (London, 1710) and [John Norris], *Profitable Advice for Rich and Poor* ... (London, 1712) both originally published anonymously and now reprinted in ed. Jack P. Greene, *Selling a New World: Two South Carolina Promotional Pamphlets* (Columbia: University of South Carolina Press, 1989) 33, 38.
5. Greene 66 and 139, 129, 35.
6. R. C. Simmons, *The American Colonies from Settlement to Independence* (London, 1976) 193; V. H. H. Green, *The Young Mr Wesley* (London, 1961) 250–1.
7. See Andrew Hook, *Scotland and America* (Glasgow and London, 1975) 9–12; for a typical advertisement, see George R. Mellor, 'Emigration from the British Isles to the New World, 1765–1775' in *History*, February/June 1955 (New series XL nos 138 and 139) 68–83; Hook 69.
8. Hook 51, 20, 30, 33; see also his article on Scotland and Philadelphia in ed. Richard B. Sher and Jeffrey R. Smitten, *Scotland and America in the Age of the Enlightenment* (Edinburgh, 1990). Gary Wills in *Inventing America: Jefferson's Declaration of Independence* (New York, 1978) reminds us that, at 16, Jefferson, Madison and Hamilton were all being taught by Scotsmen; Hume had championed the cause of American independence as early as 1768, and in October 1775 described himself as 'an American in my principles'; for his constitutional ideas, see Donald W. Livingston in Sher and Smitten 133–47.
9. For Jefferson's copies of works by e.g. Hume, Francis Hutcheson, Adam Smith, Robertson and Blair, see E. Millicent Sowerby, *Catalogue of the Library of Thomas Jefferson* (Washington, 1952); for Hutcheson's ideological links with seventeenth-century 'Commonwealth Men' like Harrington, see Caroline Robbins, *The Eighteenth-Century Commonwealthman* (Cambridge, Mass., 1959); for Blair's influence on the federal constitution, see David Daiches in Sher and Smitten 210. Yale had Blair's *Lectures* in use as a textbook by 1785, and the lectures may have circulated as manuscript notes in the 1770s.
10. Peter Kalm, *Travels into North America containing its Natural History, and a circumstantial account of its Plantations and Agriculture in general, with*

the civil, ecclesiastical and commercial state of the country, the manners of the inhabitants, and several curious and important remarks on various subjects 2nd English edn 2 vols (London, 1772) I v–vi, 37, 41, 46, 51, 66.

11. Kalm I 67, 82, 77, 79, 233; II 65.

12. *Account of the European Settlements in America* 2 vols 5th edn (London, 1770) 1, 4–5, 175, 199.

13. René Pomeau (Preface) and Claudine Hunting in *L'Amérique des Lumières* ix; 97, 99 (my translation).

14. Pierre Charlevoix, *Letters to the Duchess of Lesdiguières giving an Account of a Voyage to Canada* ... (London, 1763) 57, 165; 182, 185–6. This separate English translation is shorter by two chapters than the two-volume (London, 1761) edition entitled *Journal of a Voyage to North-America*. All references here are to the 1763 one-volume edition, though using the 1761 title of *Journal*.

15. Charlevoix xvi, 129, 220, 62, 183; for the passage in Raynal, see chapter 12 below.

16. René Pomeau (Preface) and Lillian Willens in *L'Amérique des Lumières* x, 63n, 72 (my translation); Voltaire, *Letters Concerning the English Nation* (*Lettres philosophiques*), ed. Nicholas Cronk (Oxford and New York, 1994) 24.

17. Daniel Boorstin, *The Americans: The Colonial Experience* (New York, 1964) 108, 122, 110; Jacques Godechot, *France and the Atlantic Revolution of the Eighteenth Century, 1770–1799* (New York and London, 1965) 22; for a discussion of the religious issues at stake see J. C. D. Clark, *The Language of Liberty 1660–1832: Political Discourse and Social Dynamics in the Anglo-American World* (Cambridge University Press, 1994).

18. Charles Chauncy, *Seasonable Thoughts on the State of Religion in New England* (Boston, 1743) and his sermon, *Civil Magistrates Must be Just, Ruling in the Fear of God* (Boston, 1747), both quoted in Ralph B. Perry, *Puritanism and Democracy* (New York and Evanston, 1964) 77, 202.

19. See Increase Mather's preface to *A Discourse Concerning Faith and Fervency in Prayer, and the Glorious Kingdom of the Lord Jesus Christ, on Earth, Now Approaching* in Ruth H. Bloch, *Visionary Republic: Millenial Themes in American Thought* (Cambridge University Press, 1985) 11, 12; 'Notes on the Apocalypse' in *The Works of Jonathan Edwards*, ed. Perry Miller and others (Yale, 1957–97) V 136; Clark 40; Bloch 80, 85.

20. For Dutch recognition of American independence, see chapter 4 below and Barbara Tuchman, *The First Salute* (London, 1989); Simon Schama, *Patriots and Liberators: Revolution in the Netherlands 1780–1813* 2nd edn (London, 1992) 71; for the Free Corps, see Schama 80–121.

21. For D'Alembert, see *The Encyclopédie of Diderot and D'Alembert* (selected articles), ed. John Lough (Cambridge University Press, 1969) 95; Jean-Jacques Rousseau, *The Social Contract and Discourses* (London: Dent Everyman, 1913) 144–53; for Rousseau and the Genevan Revolution, see R. R. Palmer *The Age of the Democratic Revolution: A Political History of Europe and America 1760–1800* 2 vols (Oxford, 1959 and 1964) I 111–39.

22. Rousseau 121; Peter Gay, 'The Enlightenment' in *A Comparative Approach to American History*, ed. C. Van Wooward (U. S. Information Service, 1968: originally broadcast as talks by the Voice of America) 44; for a list of books published 1760–90, see Palmer I 244.

23. Adam Smith, *Inquiry into the Nature and Causes of the Wealth of Nations* (Oxford World Classics, 1993) 343, 363, 364; for Smith's advocacy of an Atlantic Economic Union as a way of preserving the Empire under the umbrella of free trade, see Andrew Skinner in Sher and Smitten 148–60.

24. Original text of *La Découverte du Nouveau Monde* in Rousseau, *Oeuvres Complètes: La Nouvelle Héloïse, Théatre, Poésies, Essais Littéraires* (éditions Gallimand-Pléiade: Dijon, 1964) where variations from the 1776 edition are noted; for Freneau and Barlow, see Kirkpatrick Sale, *The Conquest of Paradise* (London, 1991) 334–40.

25. Sale 336–40.

26. For Brissot's *New Travels in the United States of America* (1792) see chapter 9 below.

CHAPTER 2 PORCELAIN AND REVOLUTIONARY PRINCIPLES

1. *Mount Vernon China* (Mount Vernon Ladies Association of the Union, 1962) 39–41.

2. *Mount Vernon China* 32; the Royal Society of Arts in London still awards a Franklin Medal.

3. *The Autobiography of Benjamin Franklin*, ed. Leonard W. Labaree and others (Yale, 1964) 58, 130–1.

4. For the importance of Franklin's scientific discoveries, see I. Bernard Cohen *Science and the Founding Fathers: Science in the Political Thought of Jefferson, Franklin, Adams and Madison* (London and New York, 1995) 138–88; *Ephémérides du Citoyen* (Paris, 1765–72) IX 68 and X 75; Bernard Fay, *Esprit révolutionnaire* (Paris, 1925) 36.

5. *The Writings of Benjamin Franklin*, ed. Albert Henry Smyth 10 vols (New York, 1905–7) VII 347; Page Smith, *John Adams* 2 vols (New York, 1962) 377.

6. Bernard Bailyn, *The Ideological Origins of the American Revolution* (Harvard, 1967) 45; John Adams, *Thoughts on Government* (Philadelphia, 1776) in *The American Enlightenment*, ed. Adrienne Koch (New York, 1965) 247; 21 February 1769 Palfrey to Wilkes in Bailyn 112.

7. John Dunn, 'The politics of Locke in England and America in the eighteenth century' in *John Locke: Problems and Perspectives*, ed. John W. Yolton (Cambridge University Press, 1969) 75; see Yolton 69–80 for an assessment of the impact of Locke's ideas on America.

8. *The Works of John Adams*, ed. Charles Francis Adams 10 vols (Boston, 1851) III 22–3; John Adams, *Dissertation on Canon and Feudal Law* (Boston, 1768) in *American Enlightenment* 239–40.

9. John Adams, *Novanglus* (Boston, 1774–5) in *American Enlightenment* 245; John Locke, *The Second Treatise of Civil Government*, ed. J. W. Gough (Oxford, 1948) 15.

10. *The Federalist or the New Constitution. By A. Hamilton, James Madison and John Jay*, ed. Sir Max [now Lord] Beloff (Oxford, 1948) xlvi; *The Life and Selected Writings of Thomas Jefferson*, ed. Adrienne Koch and William Peden (New York, 1944) 497.

11. Paul M. Spurlin, *Montesquieu in America, 1760–1801* (Louisiana State University, 1940) 186–9.

12. *The Federalist*, ed. Jacob E. Cooke (Cleveland and New York, 1961) 324; for Hamilton's long quotation from Montesquieu, see Cooke 53–4.

13. Montesquieu, *The Spirit of the Laws* (Hafner edn: New York and London, 1949).

14. For Countess d'Houdetot's remark in the original French, see R. R. Palmer, *The Age of the Democratic Revolution* 2 vols (Princeton, 1959) I. 250; Page Smith 433; Adams, *Works* I 660–3.

15. See Carl Van Doren, *Benjamin Franklin* (new edn, New York: Viking Press, 1964) 605–6.

16. For an illustration of the sword see *History Today*, XXVII (October 1977) i; for French Support of John Paul Jones, see Thomas J. Schaeper *France and America in the Revolutionary Era: the Life of Jacques–Donatien Leray de Chaumont 1725–1803* (Oxford and Providence, 1995) 227–43; *Writings* VII 270.

17. *The Revolutionary Diplomatic Correspondence of the United States*, ed. Francis Wharton 6 vols (Washington, 1889) IV 16–17, 24–5.

18. *Works of Dr Benjn Franklin, Consisting of Essays Humorous, Moral and Literary with His Life Written by Himself* (London, 1819) 272–3; for extracts from the 1782 edn, see *American Enlightenment* 133–8.

19. *Essays Humorous* 274–5, 279–80.

20. *Writings* IX 480.

21. For Franklin and the ladies, see Van Doren 639–54.

22. Van Doren 653.

CHAPTER 3   AMERICAN ENCYCLOPÉDISTE

1. 2 March 1809 to Dupont de Nemours in *The Life and Selected Writings of Thomas Jefferson*, ed. Adrienne Koch and William Peden (New York, 1944) 595. Pierre Samuel Dupont de Nemours (1759–1817) coined the word 'physiocrat' in order to emphasize the belief that economic laws were as discoverable as laws in the physical world. He emigrated to the USA in 1799, where he was commissioned by Jefferson to prepare a scheme of national education. Jefferson's instructions for his own monument appear as the frontispiece to *Life and Selected Writings*.

2. D'Alembert, *Eléments de Philosophie* in *Mélanges de Littérature, d'Histoire et de Philosophie* 6 vols (Amsterdam, 1759) IV 3–6 [English translation in Ernst Kassirer *Philosophy of the Enlightenment* (Boston, 1955)

3–4]; 3 March 1818 to Waterhouse, and 24 June 1826 to Roger C. Weightmem in *Life and selected Writings* 687, 729

3.   12 September 1821 to Adams in *Life and Selected Writings* 702.
4.   *Life and Selected Writings* 4, 310; for Jefferson and Newtonian science see I. Bernard Cohen *Science and the Founding Fathers* (London and New York, 1995) 61–108.
5.   *Autobiography* in *Life and Selected Writings* 53.
6.   *Autobiography* in *Life and Selected Writings* 63–4.
7.   8 December 1822 to James Smith, and 19 April 1814 to Nicholas Dufief in *Life and Selected Writings* 703–4, 636.
8.   16 January 1811 to Benjamin Rush in *Life and Selected Writings* 609; see also Richard Beale Davis, *Intellectual Life in Jefferson's Virginia* (Chapel Hill, 1964) 91.
9.   The full title is given in *Life and Selected Writings* 185; see also 198.
10. *Life and Selected Writings* 209, 391; Albert Jay Nock, *Jefferson* (New, York, 1960) 82.
11. Nock 170.
12. 4 May 1786 to John Page in *Life and Selected Writings* 394; Nock 84–5.
13. Nock 86–7, 83.
14. Jefferson, *Essay on Anglo Saxon* in *Life and Selected Writings* 170.
15. 23 September 1800 to Rush in *Life and Selected Writings* 558; *Autobiography* in *Life and Selected Writings* 67.
16. 18 August 1785 to Elizabeth Trist, and 25 January 1786 to Archibald Stuart in *Life and Selected Writings* 372, 390; *Autobiography* in *Life and Selected Writings* 88–9.
17. *Autobiography* in *Life and Selected Writings* 91–2.
18. *Autobiography* in *Life and Selected Writings* 94; 6 May 1789 to Lafayette in *American Enlightenment* 327–8.
19. *Life and Selected Writings* 470–1.
20. *Autobiography* in *Life and Selected Writings* 96; *Letters of Lafayette and Jefferson*, with an introduction and notes by Gilbert Chinard (Baltimore and Paris, 1929) 130.
21. *Autobiography* in *Life and Selected Writings* 107–9.
22. *Autobiography* in *Life and Selected Writings* 100–1.
23. 13 September 1789 to Paine in *Papers of Thomas Jefferson*, ed. Julian P. Boyd and others 26 vols (Princeton, 1950–95) XV 424; to Lafayette 2 April 1790 in *Life and Selected Writings* 495.
24. 5 September 1790 Short to Jefferson in Boyd XVII 492; for comments on Short's despatches from Paris, see Conor Cruise O'Brien, *The Long Affair: Thomas Jefferson and the French Revolution* (London, 1996) [O'Brien's critique of Jefferson's defence of revolutionary violence is more questionable]; 3 January 1793 to Short in *Life and Selected Writings* 522.
25. 1 May 1794 to Tench Coxe in *Life and Selected Writings* 528.
26. 14 February 1815 to Lafayette, and 16 October 1815 to Albert Gallatin in *Life and Selected Writings* 655, 657; *Autobiography* in *Life and Selected Writings* 109.
27. 4 June 1819 to Jean Baptiste de la Porte in *Life and Selected Writings* 692.
28. 11 June 1790 to John Garland Jefferson, and 21 September 1814 to Samuel H. Smith in *Life and Selected Writings* 498, 652.

CHAPTER 4   RELUCTANT PHILOSOPHE

1. For the interview see Page Smith, *John Adams* 2 vols (New York, 1962) 628–9; *Autobiography* in *Works of John Adams, Second President of the United States, with a Life of the Author*, ed. Charles Francis Adams 10 vols (Boston, 1856) III 391.
2. Page Smith 19; 3 June 1778 and 30 August 1777 to Abigail in *Familiar Letters of John Adams and his wife Abigail Adams, during the Revolution*, ed. Charles Francis Adams (New York, 1876) 334, 302; 25 July 1782 from Abigail in Smith 529.
3. *Diary and Autobiography of John Adams*, ed. L. H. Butterfield 4 vols (Harvard, 1961) I 35.
4. Smith 55; *Works* III 448, 459–60.
5. Smith 104; 28 April 1776 to Abigail in *Familiar Letters* 165; Smith 229.
6. 14 March 1776 from Ward in *Familiar Letters* 146; *Warren-Adams Letters. Being chiefly a correspondence among John Adams, Samuel Adams and James Warren* 2 vols (Boston, 1917, 1925) I 242; *The American Enlightenment*, ed. Adrienne Koch (New York, 1965) 246–7; for Paine's dismayed reaction to Adams's defence of the British constitution see John Keane, *Tom Paine: A Political Life* (London, 1995) 126.
7. *Sources and Documents Illustrating the American Revolution 1764–1788 and the formation of the Federal Constitution*, ed. Samuel Eliot Morison (Oxford, 1965) 148; Smith 261; 3 July 1776 to Abigail in *The Book of Abigail and John: Selected Letters of the Adams Family*, ed. with introduction by L. H. Butterfield and others (Harvard, 1975) 142.
8. *Warren-Adams Letters* I 307.
9. 20 August 1777 to Abigail in *Familiar Letters* 293; 28 November 1777 from James Lovell in Smith 350.
10. 22 February 1790 to Benjamin Rush in Zoltán Haraszti, *John Adams and the Prophets of Progress* (Harvard, 1952) 20.
11. Haraszti 48; *Diary and Autobiography* II 292.
12. 9 July 1778 to Patrick Henry in Smith 366–7; Smith 383, 377.
13. For an account of the crossing, see *Diary and Autobiography* III 381–400.
14. For a discussion of Adams's work on the Massachusetts Constitution, see Smith 440–4.
15. For Adams's Instructions, see Smith 452; 9 May 1780 to Vergennes in *The Revolutionary Diplomatic Correspondence of the United States*, ed. Francis Wharton 6 vols (Washington, 1889) III, 665; 30 June 1780 from Vergennes, 13 July 1780 to Vergennes and 20 July 1780 from Vergennes in Wharton III 828, 855, 871.
16. Smith 494.
17. 8 July 1781 to Vergennes in Wharton IV 590.
18. 15 October 1781 to President of Congress and again on 25 October 1781 in Wharton IV 780, 812; 18 December 1781 to Abigail in *Familiar Letters* 402; 5 May 1782 from Jacob Roorde in Smith 539; Smith 512.
19. 13 November and 25 October 1782 from Abigail in *Familiar Letters* 407–8; 23 May 1785 from Jefferson in *The Adams-Jefferson Letters. The*

Complete Correspondence between Thomas Jefferson and Abigail and John Adams, ed. Lester J. Cappon 2 vols (Chapel Hill, 1959) I 23; *Diary and Autobiography* III 187.

20. 22 March 1778 Turgot to Price in *Richard Price and the Ethical Foundations of the American Revolution*, ed. Bernard Peach (Durham, North Carolina, 1979) 218.

21. John Adams, *A Defence of the Constitutions of Government of the United States of America against the attack of M. Turgot in his Letter to Dr Price dated the twenty-second day of March 1778* 3 vols (London, 1794) I iv, ix, xix–xx, xxvii.

22. On adaptations of Coxe, see Haraszti 156–7 and *Defence* I 33–34; *Defence* I 83.

23. *Defence* I 325–6; 22 November 1786 Abigail to John Quincy in Smith 692; Smith 697.

24. *Defence* I 169, 208, 368.

25. *Defence* II 1, 135; III 157.

26. 25 August 1787 to Jefferson in *Adams-Jefferson Letters* I 191–2; *Thoughts on Government* in *American Enlightenment* 247; *Defence* III 387.

27. *Defence* III 503–4; 505–27.

28. 14 June 1787 from Barlow, and 2 July 1788 from Rush in Smith 699.

29. Haraszti 241; *Oeuvres de Condorcet*, ed. A. C. O'Connor 12 vols (Paris, 1847–9) VIII 13, 94.

CHAPTER 5   BRIDGING THE ATLANTIC

1.   Cobbett-Bonneville manuscripts in Moncure Daniel Conway *The Life of Thomas Paine* 2 vols (New York, 1892) II 454–5; 1 May 1790 to George Washington in Philip S. Foner, *The Complete Writings of Thomas Paine* 2 vols (New York, 1945) II 1303. Thomas Brand Hollis took the key across the Atlantic.

2.   *Common Sense* in *Complete Works of Thomas Paine: Political and Controversial* (London, 1850) 11–12, 15; Paine refers to the success of *Common Sense* in *Rights of Man* in *Complete Works* 390; for Paine's Quaker and Methodist background, see John Keane, *Tom Paine: A Political Life* (London, 1995) 15–25, 45–9.

3.   *Complete Works* 21, 29.

4.   Foner I xii; *American Crisis* No. XIV in *Complete Works* 154.

5.   *Crisis* XIV and I in *Complete Works* 154–5, 41.

6.   *Complete Works* 44, 46.

7.   *Complete Works* 47, 51, 55; *Journal of John Wesley*, ed. Nehemiah Curnock 8 vols (London, 1938) VIII 325–8.

8.   *Crisis* III in *Complete Works* 74, 57–8, 60–1, 74.

9.   *Crisis* V in *Complete Works* 77, 83.

10. Marquis de Chastellux, *Travels in North America in the Years 1780, 1781, and 1782* 2 vols (London, 1787) I 311; 3 August 1796 to Washington in *Complete Works* 502.

11. For Paine's account, see his letter 14 February 1808 to Congress in *Complete Works* 726. Paine offers to show Deane (or any of his friends in Congress) 'in a handwriting which Mr Deane is well acquainted with, that the supplies he so pompously plumes himself upon, were promised and engaged, and that as a present, before he ever *arrived* in France.' (Foner II 121); 21 January 1808 'To the Honourable Senate of the United States' in Foner II 1490.

12. Paine, *Letter Addressed to the Abbé Raynal on the Affairs of North America* in *Complete Works* 204; letter 3 February 1783 in Frank Smith, *Tom Paine, Liberator* (New York, 1938) 100.

13. *Crisis* XIV in *Complete Works* 151–53. The piece that misleadingly appears in the collected works as *A Supernumerary Crisis* was entitled 'To the People of America' and published in the *Pennsylvania Gazette* for 17 December 1783.

14. 6 January 1789 to Kitty Nicholson Few in Paine, *Letter to George Washington* in *Complete Works* 502; 6 June 1786 to Franklin in Foner II 1027.

15. Samuel Smiles, *Lives of the Engineers* 5 vols (London, 1874) III 175; for a drawing of the Sunderland bridge (though wrongly captioned), see Allan Braham, *The Architecture of the French Enlightenment* (London, 1980) 253; Cobbett-Bonneville manuscripts in Conway II 445; see also Paine, *The Age of Reason*, with a biographical introduction by John M. Robertson (London, 1912) x; also Keane 267–82.

16. Foner II 1031–4.

17. 16 March 1790 to Benjamin Rush in David Freeman Hawke, *Paine* (New York, London etc, 1974) 202; 3 January 1803 Paine's memoir 'To the Congress of the United States' in *Complete Works* 644; 25 November 1791 to John Hall (referring to second part of *Rights of Man*) Foner II 1321.

18. *Complete Works* 302, 299; Foner II 1315–18.

19. *Complete Works* 366, 359, 419, 384; for *Le Républicain* see Keane 317.

20. Paine, *Letters to the Citizens of the United States of America after an absence of Fifteen Years* (1802) in *Complete Works* 529; *Le Moniteur* 28 August 1792 (trans. in 'Paine and France', Gimbel Collection, American Philosophical Society).

21. Hawke 252; 13 September 1792 J. Mason to J. B. Burgess in J. B. Fortescue, *The Manuscripts of J. B. Fortescue Preserved at Dropmore* 10 vols (London, 1892–1927) II 316–17, quoted Hawke 255.

22. Paine, *To the People of France* (Paris, 1792) in *Complete Works* 614–15.

23. Paine, *On the Propriety of Bringing Louis XVI to Trial* (Paris, 1792) in *Complete Works* 617–18.

24. Paine, *Reasons for preserving the Life of Louis Capet as delivered to the National Convention* (Paris, 1793) in *Complete Works* 622; Paine, *To Forgetfulness* in *Complete Works* 640.

25. *To Forgetfulness* in *Complete Works* 640–1.

26. Paine, *Letter to George Washington* (Paris, 1796) in *Complete Works* 505; 18 September 1794 from James Monroe in *Complete Works* 506.

27. 20 January [or June] 1796 Monroe to Madison in ed. Stanislas Murray Hamilton, *Writings of James Monroe* 7 vols (New York, 1898–1903) II 440; *Letter to George Washington* in *Complete Works* 511, 521.

28.   W. E. Woodward, *Tom Paine: America's Godfather, 1737–1809* (London, 1945) 297.
29.   Cobbett-Bonneville manuscripts in Conway II 446.
30.   Paine, *Agrarian Justice* in *Complete Works* 479.

CHAPTER 6   BURKE'S GRASSHOPPERS

1.   Joseph Priestley, *A Discourse on Occasion of the Death of Dr Price* (London, 1791) 8–9, 13.
2.   Edmund Burke, *Reflections on the Revolution in France* (London: Everyman, 1910) 4.
3.   Price, *A Discourse on the Love of our Country* 5th edn (London, 1790) appendix 11–13.
4.   *Love of our Country* 11–12, 26, 49, 51.
5.   Burke 10, 14; *Love of our Country* 32.
6.   Burke 15, 23–4.
7.   Burke 8, 82.
8.   *Richard Price and the Ethical Foundations of the American Revolution*, ed. Bernard Peach (Durham, North Carolina, 1979) 312n. This is a collection of Price's American pamphlets, together with a selection of letters; for Price's actuarial work see Nicolas Lane 'Life Insurance and the War of Independence' *History Today* IX (August 1959).
9.   Price, *Observations on the Nature of Civil Liberty, the Principles of Government and the Justice and Policy of the War with America* (London, 1776) in Peach 65, 69, 74.
10.   Peach 70; for the text of the Articles of Confederation see Samuel Eliot Morison, *Sources and Documents Illustrating the American Revolution and the Formation of the Constitution* paperback edn (London and New York, 1965) 178–86.
11.   Peach 84–5.
12.   Peach 90, 110, 114.
13.   Peach 115–16, 118.
14.   Peach 87–88; *Journal of John Wesley*, ed. Nehemiah Curnock 8 vols (London, 1938) VI 100. A shortened version of the tract is printed as an appendix to Peach, 245–52.
15.   Price, *Additional Observations on the Nature and Value of Civil Liberty and the War with America* (London, 1777) in Peach 139n, 148, 174.
16.   Price, *General Introduction and Supplement to the Two Tracts on Civil Liberty, the War with America, and the Finances of the Kingdom* 2nd edn (London, 1778) in Peach 54–5; for Burke's letter and the Archbishop's sermon see Peach 273, 261.
17.   Price, *Observations on the Importance of the American Revolution, and the Means of Making it a Benefit to the World. To which is added, a Letter from M. Turgot, Late Comptroller-General of France* (London, 1785) in Peach 182–3.
18.   Peach 187–8.
19.   Peach 190–1, 196, 199–200.

20. Peach 201, 203, 211, 213.
21. Peach 220.
22. Peach 221–2.
23. Peach 224; for John Adams's objections in *Defence of the Constitutions*, see chapter 4 above; for his letter to Price 19 April 1790, see *The American Enlightenment*, ed. Adrienne Koch (New York, 1965) 199.
24. 22 December 1780 and 6 April 1784 to Franklin in Peach 319, 321–3.
25. 7 August 1785 Jefferson to Price, and 30 July 1786 Price to Rush in Peach 333, 337.
26. 26 September 1787 to Franklin in Peach 341.
27. Priestley, *Death of Dr Price* 9, 14; *Gentleman's Magazine* April 1791.

CHAPTER 7   FLAMMABLE GAS

1. Priestley, *Essay on the First Principles of Government* 2nd edn (London, 1771) 9–10.
2. *First Principles* 13; *Works of Jeremy Bentham, Published under the supervision of his Executor, John Bowring* 11 vols (Edinburgh, 1843) X 142.
3. 18 January 1800 from Jefferson in *Life and Correspondence of Joseph Priestley, LL. D., FRS*, ed. J. T. Rutt 2 vols (London, 1831) II 435.
4. *Life and Selected Writings of Thomas Jefferson*, eds Adrienne Koch and William Peden (New York, 1944) 555, 562; *Memoirs of Dr Joseph Priestley, with a Journal of his travels*, printed with introduction and notes by Jack Lindsay as *Autobiography of Joseph Priestley* (Bath, 1970) 134.
5. *American Daily Advertiser* 5 June 1794; for Addresses and Priestley's replies see appendix to Henry Wansey, *Journal of an excursion to the United States of North America in the Summer of 1794* (Salisbury, 1796) 262–83.
6. Wansey 269–70, 281–3.
7. William Cobbett, *Observations on the emigration of Dr J. Priestley, and on the several addresses delivered to him on his arrival at New York* (London, 1794) 4, 6, 23, 29, 36; for a shortened version of the text see *Peter Porcupine in America*, ed. with introduction by David A. Wilson (New York and London, 1994) 52–88. The phrases 'apostle of sedition' and 'admirer of the woeful revolution in France' come from Cobbett, *Remarks on the Explanation, lately published by Dr Priestley, respecting the intercepted Letter of his Friend and Disciple, John H. Stone* (London, 1799) and quoted in Appendix to *Anti-Jacobin Review and Magazine* II (January-April 1799) 545.
8. *Autobiography* 89.
9. Priestley, *An Address to Protestant Dissenters of All Denominations on the Approaching Election of Members of Parliament* (London, 1774) in *Theological and Miscellaneous Works of Joseph Priestley LL. D., FRS etc*, ed. J. T. Rutt 25 vols (London, 1817–31) XXII 491.
10. *Theological and Miscellaneous* XXII 492–3.
11. *Theological and Miscellaneous* XXII 493–4.
12. *Theological and Miscellaneous* XXII 494–7.

13. *Theological and Miscellaneous* XXII 498.
14. 19 September 1772 Franklin to Priestley (urging him to accept the appointment) in *The American Enlightenment*, ed. Adrienne Koch (New York, 1965) 89.
15. *Autobiography* 111, 116; Carl Van Doren, *Benjamin Franklin* (New York: Viking Press, 1964) 422.
16. *Autobiography* 117.
17. 7 July 1775 from Franklin in *Life and Correspondence* I 271; *The Papers of Benjamin Franklin*, ed. Leonard Labaree 29 vols (Yale, 1959–92) VIII 9–10, 451–3; *The Writings of Benjamin Franklin*, ed. Albert Henry Smyth 10 vols (New York, 1905–7) IX 255.
18. 19 July 1791 to 'The Inhabitants of the town of Birmingham. My Late Townsmen and Neighbours' in *Autobiography* 29; *Life and Correspondence* II 130–1.
19. *Autobiography* 131.
20. Priestley, *The Present State of Europe compared with ancient Prophecies. A Sermon preached at the Gravel-pit Meeting, in Hackney February 28, 1794, Being the Day appointed for a general fast* (London, 1794) in *Theological and Miscellaneous Works* XV 520, 523–4; *Autobiography* 132.
21. *Theological and Miscellaneous* XXII 177; preface to Fast Sermon 1794 in *Theological and Miscellaneous* XV 532.
22. 11 June 1801 and 1 January 1803 to Lindsey in *Life and Correspondence* II 463, 501.
23. 19 February 1802 to J. H. Stone in *Life and Correspondence* II 476; 25 January 1804 to Dr George Logan in Philadelphia *Aurora* 2 March 1804.

CHAPTER 8 LAND-AGENT OF LIBERTY

1. Thomas Cooper, *Letters on the Slave Trade* (Manchester, 1787) 8, 25.
2. Thomas Walker, *Review of the Political Events in Manchester* (Manchester, 1794) 55.
3. *Manchester Chronicle* 5 March 1791.
4. Appendix to Cooper, *A Reply to Mr Burke's invective against Mr Cooper and Mr Watt, in the House of Commons on the 30th April, 1792* (Manchester, 1793) 86–7.
5. *Reply to Burke* 88; Dumas Malone, *The Public Life of Thomas Cooper 1783–1839* (Yale and Oxford, 1923) 39.
6. Malone 44; *Reply to Burke* 6–7, 10.
7. *Reply to Burke* 9–13, 29; for Price's sermon and Burke's response, see chapter 6 above.
8. *Reply to Burke* 62, 64, 93, 98; for Priestley and Bentham, see chapter 7 above.
9. Malone 53; *Annual Register* 27 September 1792.
10. Mary Cathryne Park, *Priestley and the Problem of Pantisocracy* (University of Pennsylvania, 1947) 16; for Coleridge and the Susquehanna, see chapter 15 below.

11. Cooper, *Some Information Respecting America* (London, 1794) iii, 52.
12. *Information* 7–16, 74.
13. *Information* 81–4.
14. *Information* 209; for Franklin's pamphlet, see chapter 2 above.
15. For Adams's letter to Pickering, see *The Works of John Adams*, ed. Charles Francis Adams 10 vols (Boston, 1850–6) IX 6; Henry Wansey, in *Journal of an excursion to the United States of North America in the summer of 1794* (Salisbury, 1796) 77, notes that Priestley had intended to join the Loyalsock settlement, but that 'owing to the absence of Mr Cooper, who went to England to fetch his family, the scheme is since given up.'
16. Cooper, *Political Essays* 2nd edn (Philadelphia, 1800) 55–6; Malone 100.
17. Malone 120–7; Cooper, *Account of the Trial of Thomas Cooper* (Philadelphia 1800) 50–1.
18. *Aurora* 7 November 1800 and 1 June 1805; *Argus* 16 August 1805.
19. 27 June 1810 Jefferson to Cabell in Malone 198; Malone 206.
20. Minutes of the Board of Trustees 27 November 1833.
21. Cooper, *Narrative of Proceedings against Thomas Cooper, Esquire, President Judge of the Eighth Judiciary District of Pennsylvania on a Charge of Official Misconduct* (Lancaster, 1811) 6; 16 March 1826 to Senator Mahlon Dickerson in *American Historical Review* VI 729.
22. *Memoirs of Dr Joseph Priestley* (London, 1806) appendix 3; Cooper, *Consolidation, An Account of Parties in the United States from the Convention of 1787, to the Present Period* 2nd edn (Columbia, South Carolina, 1830) 3, 6.
23. Cooper, *On the Constitution of the United States and the questions that have arisen under it* (Columbia, South Carolina, 1826) 21–8; Malone 309.
24. Malone 321; *Telescope* tribute copied by *Mercury* and *Courier* for 21 May 1839.

CHAPTER 9   SLAVES, QUAKERS AND 'FREE AMERICANS'

1. J. P. Brissot de Warville, *New Travels in the United States of America* (London, 1792) xliii. The English translation contains only two of the three volumes of the French edition of 1791. The third volume was a reprinting of *De la France et des Etats Unis, ou De l'importance de la Révolution de l'Amérique pour le bonheur de France* (1787) by Brissot and Clavière, which had appeared in English (London, 1788) as *Considerations on the Relative Situation of France and the United States of America: showing the importance of the American Revolution to the welfare of France* ...
2. Brissot, *Travels* 46, 54–5, 57, 60–1, ix.
3. See Brissot to Calonne in Brissot, *Correspondance et Papiers*, ed. with a biographical introduction by C. Perroud (Paris, 1912) 91 (my translation).

4. Brissot, *Examen critique des Voyages dans l'Amérique septrionale de M. le marquis de Chastellux, dans laquelle on réfute principalement ses opinions sur les Quakers, sur les nègres, sur le peuple et sur l'homme* (London, 1786) 2, 4, 12, 17–19 (my trans.); for Crèvecoeur's *Letters*, see chapter 13 below. Brissot is quoting from *Lettres d'un Cultivateur Américan* (Paris, 1784) which is a reworking of the English materials, and not simply a French translation of the 1782 edition.

5. *Chastellux* 84, 86, 88, 95, 107; for Chastellux on the negroes see chapter 11 below.

6. *Correspondance et Papiers* 92–3, 109, 113. In 1786 Brissot translated William Mackintosh's *Travels*, published as *Voyages en Europe, en Asie et en Afrique...commencés en 1777 et finis in 1781, par M. Mackintosh. Suivis des Voyages du Colonel Capper, dans les Indes, au travers de l'Egypte et du grand désert, par Bassora in 1779*. It was republished in 1792.

7. *Correspondance et Papiers* 114–16, 118.

8. *Correspondance et Papiers* 121, 124–5, 133; for the French text of the letters to Lafayette and Jefferson, see 126–7; for Adams's *Defence of the American Constitutions*, see chapter 4 above.

9. *Correspondance et Papiers* 135, 143; for Cooper on the slave trade and for his Susquehanna scheme, see see chapter 8.

10. *Correspondance et Papiers* 458–60.

11. *Correspondance et Papiers* 165–6, 175; Valady later became Lafayette's aide-de-camp.

12. *Correspondance et Papiers* 176–7.

13. *Correspondance et Papiers* 192, 193; for the contract, see 180–1.

14. *Correspondance et Papiers* 205, 207.

15. Brissot, *Plan de conduite des députés du peuple aux Etats-Généraux de 1789* (Paris, 1789) 240–2; English translation in R. R. Palmer *The Age of the Democratic Revolution* 2 vols (Oxford and Princeton, 1959) I 262.

16. Brissot *Travels* 107, 423.

17. *Travels* 115, 119, 429, 291.

18. *Travels* 215, 216–7, 221–2, 236. Before publication, Brissot was able to insert the text of Mirabeau's speech proposing that the National Assembly should go into mourning to mark Franklin's death; it was printed together with Brissot's own tribute from the *Patriote francaise* (*Travels* 230–1 and appendix).

19. *Travels* 106, 113, 327, 212, 202, 204, 207, 272–3.

20. *Travels* 433, 150, 244–5.

21. *Travels* 312, 97, 200.

22. *Travels* 409, 169, 432.

23. *Travels* 132, 260–1, 336. Dr Antoine Saugrain was persuaded by Franklin to settle on the Ohio in order to minister to the Indians. His niece was to follow with her husband, Dr Ignace Guillotin (inventor of the guillotine); but Saugrain sent back discouraging reports, and the newly-weds stayed in France. For the connection between Brissot's *Travels* and the pantisocratic scheme of Southey and Coleridge see chapter 15 below.

24. *Travels* 348, 368, 330.

25. *Travels* 93, 418–19, 420; Coleridge quoted Brissot in the first of his 1795 Bristol lectures. See chapter 15 and S. T. Coleridge *Essays on his Own Times* 3 vols (London, 1850) I 119. In his autobiography (see bibliography) Brissot would write that, if he could have chosen his birthplace, it would have been 'under the simple and rustic roof of an American husbandman'.

CHAPTER 10   HERO OF TWO WORLDS

1. David Loth, *Lafayette* (London, 1952) 183. For the sake of consistency, the later 'democratic' spelling of Lafayette has been preferred, except where it appears as La Fayette in contemporary quotations.
2. For Jefferson's account, see chapter 3 above and *Life and Selected Writings of Thomas Jefferson*, eds Adrienne Koch and William Peden (New York, 1944) 108–9; Maurice de la Fuye and Emile Babeau, *The Apostle of Liberty: a Life of Lafayette* translated Edward Hyams (London, 1956) 87.
3. Peter Buckman, *Lafayette* (New York and London, 1977) 148; Loth 170. The National Guard uniform was later adopted (with minor modifications) for the new mass armies of the French republic.
4. Loth 47; 19 April 1777 to William Carmichael in Loth 57; 9 March 1777 to Duc d'Ayen in Olivier Bernier, *Lafayette: Hero of Two Worlds* (New York, 1983) 29–30.
5. Loth 62–3; Buckman 47.
6. Loth 82, 74; Buckman 59, 55.
7. W. E. Woodward, *Lafayette: a biography* (London, 1939) 98.
8. Loth 103; *Biographical Anecdotes of the Founders of the French Republic, and of other Eminent Characters, who have distinguished themselves in the Progress of the Revolution* (London, 1797) 384.
9. Buckman 108–9.
10. Buckman 112.
11. *The Letters of Lafayette and Jefferson*, with introduction and notes by Gilbert Chinard (Paris and Baltimore, 1929) 13; de la Fuye and Babeau 70, 72.
12. *The Marquis de la Fayette's Statement of his own Conduct and Principles, translated from the original French and most respectfully inscribed to the Whig Club* 2nd edn (London, 1793) 22, 34, 38, 43, 64, 79.
13. 24 February 1824 from James Monroe in Marian Klamkin, *The Return of Lafayette* (New York, 1975) 10.
14. Klamkin 12, 16, 18, 20.
15. Klamkin 64, 88–9, 128.
16. Auguste Levasseur, *Lafayette in America in 1824 and 1825; or Journal of a Voyage to the United States* trans. John D. Godman (Philadelphia, 1829) in Klamkin 61.
17. de la Fuye and Babeau 42.
18. *Freemasonry: a Celebration of the Craft*, eds John Hamill and Robert Gilbert (St Albans, 1992) 43, 66, 112; for the stone-laying ceremony on

the site of the Capitol (18 September 1793) when President Washington wore a Masonic apron embroidered by French nuns at Nantes, see Richard M. Ketchum, *The World of George Washington* (New York, 1974) 242–3.

19. Marie Antoinette's remark is recorded in Gaston Maugras, *The Duc de Lauzun and the Court of Marie Antoinette* (London, 1896) 299; for the Franklin-Lalande episode see André Soubiran, *The Good Doctor Guillotin and His Strange Device*, translated Malcolm MacCraw (Aberdeen 1964) 42–6.

20. Claude C. Robin *Nouveau Voyage dans l'Amérique Septentriole, en l'Année 1781* in Simon Schama, *Citizens* (London and New York, 1989) 48; for Freemasons in the French Revolution see, Bernard Fay, *La Franc-Maçonnerie et la révolution intellectuale au xviiie siècle* (Cluny, 1935).

21. For a description of the replica of the Erie Canal running down the centre of the table, and for the Masonic ceremonies at Savannah and Bunker Hill, see Klamkin 60, 135, 171–6.

22. Miss Quincy's diary and Levasseur's journal in Klamkin 171, 136.

23. Klamkin 34; for the visit to Monticello and the University of Virginia, see 102; for the full text of the President's speech and Lafayette's reply, see 190–5.

24. Klamkin 199.

25. de la Fuye and Babeau 315, 328; for full text of the resolution, see Klamkin 200–2. Today the US flag flies on Lafayette's tomb in Paris.

CHAPTER 11 ALLIES IN ARMS

1. *Memoirs of Louis Philippe, Comte de Ségur*, ed. Eveline Cruickshanks (London: Folio Society, 1960) 160, 57.

2. Ségur 127.

3. Ségur 127, 131–2, 135.

4. Ségur 140–1, 147.

5. Ségur 162–3.

6. After his father's execution, Louis Philippe (now Duc d'Orléans) sought refuge in the United States with his two brothers, sailing in 1796 in the aptly named *America*. He would later tell Guizot: 'My three years' residence in America have had a great influence on my political opinions and on my judgment of the course of human affairs.' See T. E. B. Howarth, *Citizen King* (London, 1961) 101. For Louis Philippe's discussion with Lafayette on the suitability for France of the American political model, see Olivier Bernier, *Lafayette: Hero of Two Worlds* (New York, 1983) 310.

7. Gaston Maugras, *The Duc de Lauzun and the Court of Marie Antoinette* (London, 1896) 434.

8. Maugras 468, 478; 28 June 1793 from the Committee of Public Safety, and 10 July 1793 to the Committee of Public Safety in Maugras 490, 493.

9. Maugras 497, 458.

10. Maugras 92; Marie Antoinette asked Lauzun (through an intermediary) for the white heron's plume he had worn with his uniform, and was indiscreet enough to wear it in her head-dress at dinner (Maugras 97).
11. Maugras 196.
12. Maugras 251, 294.
13. *Travels in North America in the years 1780, 1781, and 1782 by the Marquis de Chastellux translated by an English gentleman who resided in America at that period* 2 vols (London, 1787) I 36, 41, 44–5.
14. Chastellux I 73, 113–14, 124, 137, 140–1.
15. Chastellux I 161, 227, 230.
16. Chastellux I 248, 267, 259–60, 289, 334.
17. Chastellux I 332, 322, 323, 366, 431; Franklin's words were: 'I consent, Sir, to this Constitution because I expect no other, and because I am not sure that it is not the best. The opinions I have had of its errors, I sacrifice to the public good.'
18. Chastellux II 9, 30, 41–2, 44–6, 49.
19. Chastellux II 66, 57, 91, 177–8, 180.
20. Chastellux II 199, 201, 204, 208.
21. Chastellux II 228, 238, 259, 265.
22. Chastellux II 337; see chapter 12 for details of the prize essay competition; the title of the pamphlet by Chastellux is: *Discours sur les avantages ou les désavantages qui résultent pour l'Europe de la découverte de l'Amérique* (London and Paris, 1787).

CHAPTER 12 ARMCHAIR PHILOSOPHY

1. Paine, *A Letter Addressed to the Abbé Raynal* in *Complete Works of Thomas Paine: Political and Controversial* (London, 1850) 185; for the development of Raynal's ideas see J. H. M. Salmon, 'The Abbé Raynal 1713–1796, An Intellectual Odyssey' *History Today* XXVI (February 1976).
2. Paine, *Complete Works* 185, 187–9, 205, 209; G. T. P. Raynal, *The Revolution of America* (London, 1781) 92.
3. *Revolution of America* 144, 152, 4–5, 6.
4. *Revolution of America* 13, 33.
5. *Revolution of America* 79, 80, 83, 88–9; Paine 210.
6. *Revolution of America* 172–3, 180–1, xi. The future Marquis de Chastellux wrote (though he says he did not submit) an entry for the competition. It was published in London in 1787 as *Discours sur les avantages ou les désavantages qui résultent, pour l'Europe, de la découverte de l'Amérique* (see chapter 11).
7. Raynal, *A Philosophical and Political History of the Settlements and Trade in the East and West Indies* trans. J. Justamond 5 vols (London, 1776) I ix.
8. *Revolution of America* iii; *Philosophical and Political History* IV 296.
9. Raynal *History* IV 303, 338, 346.
10. *History* IV 372–3, 394.

11. *History* IV 406; V 506.
12. *History* IV 412–13, 418.
13. *History* V 422; Raynal, *History* 10 vols (Geneva, 1781) I 205–6.
14. *History* 5 vols (London, 1776) IV 482, 491, 503; for Diderot's role in the *History* see P. N. Furbank, *Diderot: a Critical Biography* (London, 1992) 415–20.
15. *History* (1776) IV 437, 441, 442, 449; V 56, 124; the reference to Greek and Roman orators echoes Charlevoix (see chapter 1 above). Jedediah Morse in his *American Geography* 2nd edn (London, 1792) 63, referring to Buffon's theory, comments: 'This new and unsupported theory has been applied by the Abbé Raynal to the race of whites transported from Europe. Mr Jefferson has confuted this theory; and by the ingenuity and abilities which he has shown in doing it, has exhibited an instance of its falsehood.'
16. *History* (1776) V 203, 138–9, 136.
17. *History* V 228–9.
18. *History* V 236, 239, 241, 253–5.
19. *History* V 285; 359, 361; for Voltaire on Locke and Carolina, see chapter 1 above.
20. *History* V 305, 327, 351, 353; for the humming-bird see chapter 13 below.
21. *History* V 361, 397, 398.
22. *History* V 403–4, 414, 418, 431, 419.
23. *History* V 448, 449, 515, 555, 569.
24. *History* V 571, 573, 577–9, 581, 586.
25. *History* V 604.

CHAPTER 13 AMERICAN FARMER

1. The original is in the library of the Pennsylvania Historical Society at Philadelphia; for an extract, see Hector St John Crèvecoeur *Letters from an American Farmer* (London: Dent Everyman 1912) 242; correspondence between Crèvecoeur and Franklin in *Life and Writings of Benjamin Franklin*, ed. A. H. Smyth 10 vols (New York 1905–7) VIII 308 and Crèvecoeur *American Farmer* 243–5; for Raynal see chapter 12 above.
2. For Brissot's remark in the original French (here, my translation) see foreword to Clarissa S. Bostelman's translation of Crèvecoeur *Voyage dans la Haute Pensylvanie et dans l'Etat de New-York* 3 vols (Paris, 1801) published as *Journey into Northern Pensylvania and the State of New York* (University of Michigan, 1964) viii.
3. For the title-page of the *Letters* and the publisher's advertisement, see Dent Everyman edn 1, 3; for Jefferson's *Notes on Virginia*, see chapter 3 above.
4. *Letters* 96–7, 92–4.
5. *Letters* 143, 212, 24, 5; for Southey, see chapter 15 below.
6. *Letters* 87, 91, 110, 90, 112, 138.

7. *Letters* 159, 170, 172–3. Crèvecoeur employed slaves on his own northern farms, but in his *Journey* he vehemently attacks slavery.

8. *Letters* 179; G. T. F. Raynal, *Philosophical and Political History of the Settlements and Trade of The Europeans in the East and West Indies* 5 vols (London, 1776) V 321; *Letters* 5–6.

9. *Letters* 43–5, 182, 194–5, 191, 187, 230. Crèvecoeur writes: '*He* is an American, who, leaving behind all his ancient prejudices and manners, receives new ones from the new mode of life he has embraced, the new government he obeys and the new rank he holds.' (*Letters* 43.) Bartram was not French, as Crèvecoeur believed, though his remote ancestors may have been Norman.

10. *Letters* 41, 209, 211.

11. *Letters* 227; for pantisocracy see chapter 15 below.

12. *Letters* xviii.

13. J. P. Brissot, *Correspondance et Papiers*, ed. with biographical introduction by C. Perroud (Paris, 1912) 136 (my trans.); for the Gallo-American Society see chapter 9 above.

14. *Journey* xiii.

15. *Journey* 137–8.

16. *Journey* 303–4, 308.

17. *Journey* 245, 251.

18. Friedrich Melchior Baron Grimm, *Correspondances littéraires, philosophiques et critiques, par Grimm, Diderot, Raynal, Meister, etc*, revue sur les textes originaux, ed. Maurice Tourneux 16 vols (Paris, 1877–82) XIV 88; the hostile pamphlet was by Rev. Samuel Ayscough (see *Letters* Everyman edn 236); for emigrant families, see 66–86 and 213.

19. *Journey* II 62 in notes to *Letters* (Everyman edn) 236; Franklin, *Information to Those Who Would Remove to America* (Passy, 1782) in *Works of Dr Benjamin Franklin Consisting of Essays, Humorous, Moral and Literary*...(London, 1819) 274; for Franklin, see also chapter 2 above.

20. 23 January 1784, 15 July 1784 and 10 July 1790 to Jefferson in *Letters* 247–8; 28 August 1781 to Franklin in *Letters* 243; for Lafayette, see chapter 10 above.

CHAPTER 14 WOMEN AND EMIGRANTS

1. Mary Wollstonecraft, *Vindication of the Rights of Woman* (London, 1792: Penguin bicentenary edn, 1992) 152; William Godwin, *Memoirs of Mary Wollstonecraft*, ed. W. Clark Durant with preface, supplement and bibliographical note (London and New York, 1927) 237.

2. Ralph M. Wardle, *Mary Wollstonecraft: A Critical Biography* (University of Kansas, 1951) 177; *Memoirs* 222.

3. *Analytical Review* XI (September 1791) 44; for Brissot's *Travels*, see chapter 9 above; for Brissot's letters (on Imlay's behalf) to the Committee of General Defence, see *Memoirs* 234–6; a translation of Imlay's *Mémoire sur Louisiana* appears in *American Historical Review* (April 1898).

4. *Four New Letters of Mary Wollstonecraft and Helen Maria Williams*, ed. B. P. Kurtz and Carrie C. Aubrey (Berkeley, 1937) 41; Wardle 201.

5. Wollstonecraft, *An Historical and Moral View of the Origin and Progress of the French Revolution and the Effect it has Produced in Europe* (London, 1794) 2nd edn (1796) v–viii.

6. Wollstonecraft, *French Revolution* 161.

7. Reviews in *Monthly Review* new series XVI (1795) 393–402 and *British Critic* VI (1795) 29–36; the author of the reports in the *New Annual Register* that Mary was accused of plagiarizing was none other than her future husband William Godwin, who for a decade contributed the historical section of the journal; Zoltán Haraszti, *John Adams and the Prophets of Progress* (Harvard, 1952) 187, 195, 211.

8. Wollstonecraft, *Vindication of the Rights of Men, in a Letter to the Right Honourable Edmund Burke* (London, 1790) 7, 94, 144; *Rights of Man* in *Complete Works of Thomas Paine: Political and Controversial* (London, 1850) 290.

9. For Richard Price, see chapter 6 above.

10. Wardle 94; *Posthumous Works of the Author of a Vindication of the Rights of Woman*, ed. William Godwin 4 vols (London, 1798) IV 77; *Analytical Review* XI (October 1791); see also Claire Tomalin, *Life and Death of Mary Wollstonecraft* (London: revised Penguin edn, 1992) 94n.

11. Wollstonecraft, *Rights of Woman* (London, 1792) viii; for Wollstonecraft, *Thoughts on the Education of Daughters with Reflections on Female Conduct in the More Important Duties of Life* (London, 1787), see Wardle 49; *Rights of Woman* (London: Penguin 1992) 79, 130, 240, 304; see 175–94 for criticism of Rousseau.

12. *Memoirs* 216–17; 16 February 1793 Aaron Burr to Theodosia Prevost Burr in Linda K. Kerber, *Women of the Republic: Ideology in Revolutionary America* (Chapel Hill, 1980) 224.

13. Gilbert Imlay, *A Topographical Description of the Western Territory of North America* (London, 1792) 155, 1, 31.

14. *Topographical Description* 33, 39–40, 118.

15. *Topographical Description* 44, 94, 52, 217.

16. *Topographical Description* 60, 156, 158; for the relevant part of *Notes on Virginia*, see *Life and Selected Writings of Thomas Jefferson*, ed. Adrienne Koch and William Peden (New York, 1944) 234–7.

17. *Topographical Description* 186–8, 191, 201; *Notes on Virginia* in *Life and Selected Writings* 256–62; for a modern (and more strident) variation on Imlay's attack on Jefferson, see the intemperate words of Conor Cruise O'Brien in *The Long Affair: Thomas Jefferson and the French Revolution* (London etc, 1996) especially chapter 7.

18. *Topographical Description* 134–7.

19. *Topographical Description* 139; for the complete first version of Coleridge's sonnet, see Coleridge *Poems*, ed. John Beer (London and Vermont, 1993) 23; for Coleridge, Southey and America, see chapter 15.

20. *Topographical Description* 143–5, 149, 139.

21. Imlay, *The Emigrants, &c, or the History of An Expatriated Family, Being A Delineation of English Manners, Drawn from Real Characters* 3 vols (London, 1793); for the preface to the 1793 edn, see *Memoirs* 238; the

long extract comes from the facsimile reproduction of the one-volume (Dublin, 1794) edition, with introduction by Robert Hare (Gainsville, Florida, 1964) 2.

22. For discussion of Mary's probable authorship, see Hare's introduction in *Emigrants* (1794) xiii; for the source of the additional topographical scenes, see Thomas Hutchins, *A Topographical Description of Virginia, Pennsylvania, Maryland and North Carolina* (London, 1778).

23. *Memoirs* 76, 73; for the text of Mary's *Short Residence in Sweden* see *Mary Wollstonecraft and William Godwin*, ed. Richard Holmes (London, New York etc., 1987), which also contains the text of the *Memoirs*. The editor's introduction examines Imlay's connection with Backman.

24. *Memoirs* 98, 129; 10 September 1797 to Thomas Holcroft in Peter H. Marshall, *William Godwin* (Yale, 1984) 190; for Godwin's sexual relations with Mary, see William St Clair, *The Godwins and the Shelleys: the Biography of a Family* (London, 1989: paperback edn 1991) 497–503; for Southey's remark, see St Clair 224; *Monthly Review* XXVII (1798) 321–2; the *Anti-Jacobin Review* commented on Mary's relationship with Imlay: 'Among other advantages, which this just woman planned from her amour, was a trip to America, where she might have eluded her creditors... The moral sentiments and moral conduct of Mrs Wollstonecraft, resulting from their principles, exemplify and illustrate JACOBIN MORALITY.' in I (July 1798) 97–8.

CHAPTER 15   POETS' UTOPIA

1. Coleridge to Charles Heath, September 1794 in *Collected Letters of Samuel Taylor Coleridge*, ed. Earl Leslie Griggs 6 vols (Oxford, 1956) I 97; 22 August 1794 Southey to Horace Bedford in *New Letters of Robert Southey*, ed. Kenneth Curry 2 vols (New York, 1965) I 72; Mrs Henry Sandford, *Thomas Poole and his Friends* 2 vols (London, 1888) I 98–9.

2. 'Religious Musings' lines 354–6 in Coleridge, *Poems*, ed. John Beer (London and Vermont: Everyman, 1993); Richard Holmes *Coleridge: Early Visions* (London etc 1989) 63.

3. 13 November 1793 Southey to Horace Bedford in *Life and Correspondence of Robert Southey*, ed. C. C. Southey 6 vols 2nd edn (London, 1849–50) I 194; for Raynal, see chapter 12 above.

4. John Williams, *Farther Observations on the Discovery of America* (London, 1792) iii; Kenneth Curry, *Southey* (London, 1975) 160; Gwyn A. Williams 'Frontiers of Illusion' in *History Today* XXX (January 1980); for Southey's *Madoc*, see *Poems of Robert Southey*, ed. M. H. Fitzgerald (Oxford, 1909) 460–608.

5. For the Godwin sonnet, see Coleridge *Poems* 23–4; Peter H. Marshall, *William Godwin* (Newhaven and London, 1984) 48; Godwin, *History of the Internal Affairs of the United Provinces* (London, 1787) 345; Godwin, *Enquiry concerning Political Justice and its influence on General Virtue and Happiness* 2 vols (London, 1793) I 186, II 576

6. *Political Justice* I 71–2; for Mary Wollstonecraft and Gilbert Imlay, see chapter 14.

7. For Brissot, see chapter 9 above and for Cooper see chapter 8; Coleridge to Southey, and to Heath in *Collected Letters* I 99, 97.

8. J.-P. Brissot, *New Travels in the United States of America* (London, 1792) 65, 260–1; Sandford I 97.

9. Sandford I 112; 11 November 1793 Southey to Grosvenor Bedford in *Life and Correspondence* I 189

10. For the lecture as reprinted in *The Friend* see *Collected Works of Samuel Taylor Coleridge*, ed. Kathleen Coburn and others 16 vols (Princeton 1969–) IV (1) 328; for the original version, see *Coleridge's Writings: on Politics and Society*, ed. John Morrow (Princeton, 1991) 27; Brissot *Travels* xvi and xvii; original version of the lecture in Morrow 26–36; the lecture was republished as the Introductory Address in *Conciones ad Populum* (1795), but the Brissot quotation was omitted from a revised version of the Address printed in *The Friend* (1818).

11. 18 September 1794 to Southey in *Samuel Taylor Coleridge: Selected Letters*, ed. H. J. Jackson (London, 1987) 8; for a possible connection between Imlay's *Topographical Description* and Coleridge's sonnet, see chapter 14.

12. *Selected Letters* 8; *Collected Letters* I 122, 119.

13. *Collected Letters* I 112.

14. *Collected Letters* I 132, 165.

15. Morrow 26–7.

16. Morrow 30–2, 35; Godwin, *Political Justice* II 576; Coleridge, *Collected Works* I lxx; for a critique of Coleridge's so-called 'Jacobinism', see Stuart Andrews 'Pitt's Gold: Jacobinism and Anti-Jacobinism' in *History Today* XLVIII (1998).

17. 1 October 1803 to Sir George and Lady Beaumont in *Collected Letters* II 1000–1, and [February 1795] to George Dyer in I 152; Coleridge, *Poems* 97.

18. Coleridge, *The Plot Discovered or an Address to the People against Ministerial Treason* (Bristol, 1795) 9, 19–21; [Godwin], *Considerations on Lord Grenville's and Mr Pitt's Bills, concerning, Treasonable and Unlawful Assemblies, by a Lover of Order* (London, 1795) 22; for an assessment of the Bristol lectures, see Stuart Andrews 'Bristol, Coleridge and Revolution' in *Coleridge Bulletin* new series no. 7 (Spring 1996) 11–25.

19. *Collected Works* II 375; *Poems* 281–3; the poem appeared under its original title in the *Morning Post* (April 1798).

20. William Wordsworth *Poetical Works*, ed. Thomas Hutchinson (Oxford, 1936: reset 1950) 17. This is the original version written 1791–2 and published 1793; for the reworked version which appeared in the 1850 edn, see *Poetical Works* 481.

21. 17 December 1796 to Thelwall and 13 December 1796 to Poole in *Collected Letters* I 277, 275; John Cornwell, *Coleridge: Poet and Revolutionary* (London, 1973) 146–7, 152.

22. For the 'Spy Nozy' story, see *Biographia Literaria* (London and New York: Everyman, 1965) 106–8, and Nicholas Roe, *Wordsworth and*

Coleridge: The Radical Years (Oxford, 1988) 248–58; see also E. H. Stuart Jones, *The Last Invasion of Britain* (Cardiff, 1950); for 'Ruth', see Wordsworth *Poetical Works* 153.

23. *Correspondence of Robert Southey with Caroline Bowles*, ed. Edward Dowden (Dublin, 1881) 52; 6 November 1794 Coleridge to George Coleridge *Collected Letters* I 126; *New Letters of Robert Southey* I 30–5.

CHAPTER 16   NORTH AMERICAN NATURALISTS

1. William Bartram, *Travels Through North and South Carolina, Georgia, East and West Florida, the Cherokee Country, the Extensive Territories of the Muscogulges or Creek Confederacy, and the Country of the Chactaws* (London, 1791) 1, 78, 152, 273; Joseph Kastner, *A World of Naturalists* (London, 1978) 107. For Bartram's sketches of birds, animals and plants, see J. I. Meritt III in 'William Bartram in America's Eden' *History Today* XXVIII (November 1978) 712–21.During the Napoleonic Wars, Sir Joseph Banks would scrupulously send back to the royal gardens in Paris, parcels of botanical specimens captured at sea by the British.

2. Samuel Taylor Coleridge, *Biographia Literaria* (London and New York: Everyman 1956) 275; for Coleridge's debt to Bartram, see Kastner 110–11.

3. Bartram, *Travels* 109, 209–210, 211.

4. *Travels* 306, 349, 355, 483, 487; for 'Ruth', see William Wordsworth, *Poetical Works*, ed. Thomas Hutchinson (Oxford, 1936: reset, 1950) 153.

5. John Chancellor, *Audubon* (New York, 1978) 26.

6. Francis Hobart Herrick, *Audubon the Naturalist: a History of his Life and Time* 2 vols (New York, 1968) I 65.

7. Robert Buchanan, *Life and Adventures of Audubon the Naturalist* (London, Toronto and New York: Everyman, 1915) 9; Herrick I 111–12.

8. Herrick I 151; Buchanan 19.

9. Maria R. Audubon, *Audubon and His Journals* 2 vols (London, 1898) I 28

10. Chancellor 55; Herrick I 196; Bartram, *Travels* 284–94; Buchanan 22.

11. Buchanan 23; Chancellor 66; Buchanan 26–7.

12. Herrick I 260; Chancellor 85.

13. Herrick I 317; John James Audubon, *The Birds of America* double elephant folio (London 1827–38); plate xxi reproduced in the Natural History Museum's publication *Audubon's Birds* (Ware, 1991) 75.

14. Herrick I 323; Buchanan 79.

15. Buchanan 79, 80, 82, 83–6.

16. J. J. Audubon, *Ornithological Biography* 5 vols (Edinburgh 1831–9) I xi; Buchanan 89–91.

17. Buchanan 93–4; Herrick I 350; Buchanan 99; for the turkey, see Herrick I facing 358.

18. Buchanan 100; *Etudes sur la Littérature et les Moeurs des Anglo-Américains au XIXe siècle* (Paris, 1851) English trans. in Herrick I 359.

19. Buchanan 105–6; 22 January 1827 in Herrick I 367; Scott refused to
     give Audubon a testimonial, pleading that his inadequate knowledge of
     natural history disqualified him, but adding: 'I am a sincere believer in
     the extent of your scientific attainments.' (Buchanan 113).
20. Buchanan 115.
21. Herrick I 377; Buchanan 119–20.
22. Buchanan 124–5; 137–8.
23. Herrick I 411.
24. Buchanan 143; Herrick I 426, 429–30
25. Herrick I 436.
26. Buchanan 314; see also Robert Elman, *The Living World of Audubon
     Mammals* (New York, 1976); for Audubon echoes in Walt Whitman see
     Richard Gravil ' "The Discharged Soldier" and "the Runaway Slave":
     Wordsworth and the Definition of Walt Whitman' in *Symbiosis* I. 1
     (April 1997) 52, 61.

Bibliography

INTRODUCTION

Letters and Texts

Account of the European Settlements in America 5th edn 2 vols (London, 1770).

Bradford, W. *History of the Plymouth Plantation*, ed. H. C. Syrett (New York, 1960).

Buffon, Comte de, *Les Epoques de la nature* (Paris 1779: *edition critique* Paris 1962).

Charlevoix, P. *Letters to the Duchess of Lesdiguières giving an Account of a Voyage to Canada and Travels through that Vast Country, and Louisiana, to the Gulf of Mexico* (London, 1763).

Chateaubriand, F.-R. de, *L'essai historique, politique et moral sur les révolutions anciennes et modernes considerées dans leurs rapports avec la révolution française* (London, 1797) and *Voyage en Amérique* (Paris, 1840).

Chateaubriand, F. -R. de *The Memoirs of Chateaubriand*, selected, translated and with introduction by R. Baldick (London, 1961).

Chauncy, C. *Seasonable Thoughts on the State of Religion in New England* (Boston, 1743) and *Civil Magistrates must be Just, Ruling in the Fear of God* (Boston, 1747).

De Pauw, C. *Recherches philosophiques sur les Américains ou Mémoires intéressants pour servir à l'Histoire de l'Esèpce humaine.* 2 vols (Berlin, 1768).

Edwards, J. *The Works of Jonathan Edwards* 14 vols ed. Perry Miller et al. (Yale, 1957–97) V (1971).

Genty, L. *L'Influence de la découverte de l'Amérique sur le bonheur du genre humaine* (Paris, 1788).

Greene, J. P. (ed.) *Selling a New World: Two South Carolina Promotional Pamphlets*, (Columbia: University of South Carolina 1989).

The First Colonists: Hakluyt's Voyages to North America, modern version with introduction by A. L. Rowse, and illustrations (London: Folio Society 1986).

Kalm, P. *Travels into North America Containing its Natural History, and a circumstantial Account of its Plantations and Agriculture in General, with the Civil, Ecclesiastical and Commercial state of the country, the manners of the Inhabitants and Several curious and Important Remarks on various subjects.* 2nd English edn 2 vols (London, 1772).

Lough, J. (ed.) *The Encyclopédie of Diderot and D'Alembert* (selected articles), (Cambridge, 1969).

Rousseau, J.-J. *The Social Contract and Discourses* (London: Dent Everyman, 1913) and *La Découverte du Nouveau Monde* in *Oeuvres Complètes: La Nouvelle Héloïse, Théatre, Poésies, Essais Littéraires* (editions Gallimand-Pléiade: Dijon, 1964).

Smith, A. *Inquiry into the Nature and Causes of the Wealth of Nations* (Oxford: World Classics 1993).

Voltaire, F. M. A. de *Essai sur les Moeurs* 2 vols (Paris, 1961–3), *Dictionnaire Philosophique* (London [Geneva] 1764) and *Letters on the English* (*Lettres Philosophiques*), ed. N. Cronk (Oxford and New York, 1994).

Secondary works

Barr, M. M. H. *Voltaire in America – 1744–1800* (London and Baltimore, 1941).

Bloch, R. H. *Visionary Republic: Millenial themes in American thought* (Cambridge, 1985).

Boorstin, D. J. *The Americans: The Colonial Experience* (New York, 1964).

Clark, J. C. D. *The Language of Liberty 1660–1832: Political discourse and social dynamics in the Anglo-American World* (Cambridge, 1994).

Echeverria, D. *Mirage in the West* (Princeton, 1957).

Gay, P. 'The Enlightenment' in *A Comparative Approach to American History*, ed. C. Van Woodward (Voice of America, 1968).

Godechot, J. *France and the Atlantic Revolution of 1770–1799* (New York and London, 1965).

Green, V. H. H. *The Young Mr Wesley* (London, 1961).

Halévy, E. *The Growth of Philosophic Radicalism* (London, 1949).

Hatch, N. O. *The Sacred Cause of Liberty: Republican Thought and the Millenium* (Newhaven, 1977).

Hook, A. *Scotland and America* (Glasgow and London, 1975).

L'Amérique des Lumières: Partie Littéraire du Colloque Bicentenaire de l'Indépendance Américain (Geneva, 1977).

Mellor, G. R. 'Emigration from the British Isles to the New World, 1765–75' in *History* February/June 1955 (New Series XL nos 138 and 139).

Middlekauff, R. *The Glorious Cause: The American Revolution 1763–1789* (Oxford, 1982).

Palmer, R. R. *The Age of the Democratic Revolution: A Political History of Europe and America 1760–1800* 2 vols (Oxford, 1959 and 1964).

Perry, R. B. *Puritanism and Democracy* (New York and Evanston, 1964).

Robbins, C. *The Eighteenth-Century Commonwealthman* (Cambridge, Mass., 1959).

Rowse, A. L. *The Elizabethans and America* (London, 1959).

Sale, K. *The Conquest of Paradise* (London, 1991).

Schama, S. *Patriots and Liberators: Revolution in the Netherlands 1780–1813* 2nd edn (London, 1992).

Scher R. B. and J. R. Smitten, *Scotland and America in the Age of the Enlightenment* (Edinburgh 1990).

Simmons, R. C. *The American Colonies from Settlement to Independence* (London, 1976).

Smith, J. E. *Jonathan Edwards: Puritan, Preacher, Philosopher* (Notre Dame University Press, 1992).

Sowerby, E. M. *Catalogue of the Library of Thomas Jefferson* (Washington, 1952).

Tuchman, B. *The First Salute* (London, 1989).

FOUNDING FATHERS IN EUROPE

Letters and Texts

Warren-Adams Letters. Being chiefly a correspondence among John Adams, Sam Adams and James Warren 2 vols (Boston: The Massachusetts Historical Society, 1917 and 1925).

Adams, C. F. (ed.) *The Works of John Adams, Second President of the United States, with a Life of the Author*, 10 vols (Boston, 1851–6).

Adams, C. F. (ed.) *Familiar Letters of John Adams and his wife Abigail during the Revolution*, (Boston, 1876).

Adams, J. *A Defence of the Constitutions of Government of the United States of America against the attack of M. Turgot in his Letter to Dr Price dated the twenty-second day of March 1778* 3 vols (London, 1794).

Adams, J. *Letters of John Adams, Addressed to his Wife* ed. C. F. Adams (Boston, 1841).

Adams, J. *Diary and Autobiography of John Adams*, ed. L. H. Butterfield 4 vols (Harvard, 1961).

Butterfield, L. H., M. Friedlander and M. J. Kline (eds.) *The Book of Abigail and John: Selected Letters of the Adams Family*, (Harvard, 1975).

Cappon, L. J. (ed.) *The Adams-Jefferson Letters. The Complete Correspondence between Thomas Jefferson and Abigail and John Adams* 2 vols (Chapel Hill, 1959).

Chinard, G. (ed.) *Letters of Lafayette and Jefferson*, (Baltimore and Paris, 1929).

Franklin, B. *Works of Benjamin Franklin Consisting of Essays Humorous, Moral and Literary with His Life Written by Himself* (London, 1819).

Franklin, B. *The Writings of Benjamin Franklin*, ed. A. H. Smyth 10 vols (New York, 1905–7).

Franklin, B. *The Autobiography of Benjamin Franklin*, ed. L. W. Labaree et al. (Yale, 1964).

Franklin, B. *The Papers of Benjamin Franklin*, ed. L. W. Labaree et al. 29 vols (Yale, 1959–92).

Franklin, B. *Benjamin Franklin: His Life as He Wrote it*, ed. E. Wright (Harvard, 1990).

Hamilton, A., J. Madison and J. Jay, *The Federalist or the New Constitution*, ed. Sir Max [now Lord] Beloff (Oxford, 1948) and another edn *The Federalist*, ed. J. E. Cooke (Cleveland and New York: Meridian, 1961).

Jefferson, T. *Papers of Thomas Jefferson*, ed. J. P. Boyd et al. 26 vols (Princeton, 1950–95).

Koch, A. (ed.) *The American Enlightenment: The Shaping of the American Experiment and a Free Society* [extracts from the writings and correspondence of Franklin, Adams, Jefferson and Madison] (New York: George Braziller, 1965).

Koch, A. and W. Peden (eds) *The Life and Selected Writings of Thomas Jefferson*, (New York: Random House, 1944).

Locke, J. *The Second Treatise of Civil Government* ed. J. W. Gough (Oxford, 1948).

Morison, S. E. (ed.) *Sources and Documents Illustrating the American Revolution 1764–1788 and the Formation of the Federal Constitution*, (Oxford, 1965)
Wharton, F. (ed.) *The Revolutionary Diplomatic Correspondence of the United States*, 6 vols (Washington, 1889).

Secondary Works

Aldridge, A. O. *Benjamin Franklin: Philosopher and Man* (Philadelphia and New York, 1965).
Bailyn, B. *The Ideological Origins of the American Revolution* (Harvard, 1967).
Cohen, B. I. *Science and the Founding Fathers: Science in the Political Thought of Jefferson, Franklin, Adams and Madison* (London and New York, 1995).
Davis, R. B. *Intellectual Life in Jefferson's Virginia* (Chapel Hill, 1964).
Dunn, J. 'The politics of Locke in England and America in the eighteenth century' in *John Locke: Problems and Perspectives*, ed. J. W. Yolton (Cambridge, 1969).
Fay, B. *Esprit révolutionnaire* (Paris, 1925).
Haraszti, Z. *John Adams and the Prophets of Progress* (Harvard, 1952).
Jennings, F. *Benjamin Franklin, Politician: The Mask and the Man* (New York and London, 1996).
Kassirer, E. *The Philosophy of the Enlightenment* (Boston, 1955).
Lopez, C.-A. *Mon cher papa: Franklin and the Ladies of Paris* (Yale, 1990).
Mount Vernon China (Mount Vernon Ladies' Association of the Union, 1962).
Nock, A. J. *Jefferson* (New York, 1960).
Schaeper, T. J., *France and America in the Revolutionary Era: the Life of Jacques–Donatien Leray de Chaumont 1725–1803* (Oxford and Providence, 1995).
Smith, P. *John Adams* 2 vols (New York, 1962).
Spurlin, P. M. *Montesquieu in America 1760–1801* (Louisiana State University, 1940).
Van Doren, C. *Benjamin Franklin* (New York: new Viking Press edn, 1964).
Walsh, C. M. *The Political Science of John Adams* (New York, 1915).
Wills, G. *Inventing America: Jefferson's Declaration of Independence* (London, 1980) and *George Washington and the Enlightenment* (London, 1984).

TRANSATLANTIC CITIZENS

Letters and Texts

Bentham, J. *The Works of Jeremy Bentham, Published under the supervision of his Executor, John Bowring* 11 vols (Edinburgh, 1843).
Bentham, J. *A Fragment on Government and an Introduction to the Principles of Morals and Legislation* ed. with introduction by Wilfrid Harrison (Oxford: Blackwell, 1948).
Burke, E. *Reflections on the Revolution in France* (London: Dent Everyman, 1910).

Cobbett, W. *Observations on the emigration of Dr J. Priestley, and on the several addresses delivered to him on his arrival in New York* (London, 1794).

Cooper, T. *Letters on the Slave Trade* (Manchester, 1787).

Cooper, T. *A Reply to Mr Burke's invective against Mr Cooper and Mr Watt, in the House of Commons on the 30th April 1792* (Manchester, 1793).

Cooper, T. *Some Information Respecting America* (London, 1794).

Cooper, T. *Account of the Trial of Thomas Cooper* and *Political Essays* 2nd edn (both Philadelphia, 1800).

Cooper, T. *The Opinion of Judge Cooper on the Effect of a Sentence of a Foreign Court of Admiralty* (Philadelphia, 1808) and *Narrative of Proceedings against Thomas Cooper Esquire, President Judge of the 8th Judiciary District of Pennsylvania on a charge of official misconduct* (Lancaster, 1811).

Cooper, T. *On the Constitution of the United States and the questions that have arisen under it* (Columbia, South Carolina, 1826) and *Consolidation, An Account of Parties in the the United States* (Columbia, 1830).

Fortescue, J. B. *The Manuscripts of J. B. Fortescue Preserved at Dropmore* 10 vols (London, 1892–1927).

Monroe, J. *Writings of James Monroe* 7 vols (New York, 1898–1903).

Morse, J. *American Geography* 2nd edn (London, 1792).

Paine, T. *The Age of Reason* with biographical introduction by John M. Robertson (London, 1912).

Paine, T. *Complete Works of Thomas Paine: Political and Controversial* (London, 1850).

Paine, T. *The Complete Writings of Thomas Paine*, ed. Philip S. Foner 2 vols (New York, 1945).

Peach, B. (ed.) *Richard Price and the Ethical Foundations of the American Revolution* (Duke University Press, 1979).

Price, R. *A Discourse on the Love of Our Country* 5th edn (London, 1790).

Price, R. *Observations on the Nature of Civil Liberty, the Principles of Government and the Justice and Policy of the War with America* (London, 1776) and *Additional Observations on the Nature and Value of Civil Liberty and the War with America* (London, 1777). Both in Peach (ed.).

Price, R. *Observations on the Importance of the American Revolution and the Means of Making it a Benefit to the World. To which is Added a Letter from M. Turgot, Late Comptroller-General of France* (London, 1785) in Peach (ed.).

Priestley, J. *Essay on the First Principles of Government* 2nd edn (London, 1771).

Priestley, J. *A Discourse on the Death of Dr Price* (London, 1791).

Priestley, J. *Memoirs of Dr Joseph Priestley* (London, 1806).

Priestley, J. *Memoirs of Dr Joseph Priestley with a Journal of his travels* with introduction and notes by J. Lindsay under the title *Autobiography of Joseph Priestley* (Bath, 1970).

Priestley, J. *Joseph Priestley: Selections from His Writings*, ed. I. V. Brown (Pennsylvania State University Press, 1962).

Rutt, J. T. (ed.) *Theological and Miscellaneous Works of Joseph Priestley LL. D., FRS etc* 25 vols (London, 1817–31).

Rutt, J. T. (ed.) *Life and Correspondence of Joseph Priestley LL. D., FRS*, 2 vols (London, 1831).

Walker, T. *Review of the Political Events in Manchester* (Manchester, 1794).

Wansey, H. *Journal of an excursion to the United States of North America in the Summer of 1794* (Salisbury, England, 1796) [contains addresses presented to Priestley on his arrival in New York in 1794 together with Priestley's replies].

Wilson, D. A. (ed.) *Peter Porcupine in America: Pamphlets on Republicanism and Revolution*, (London and New York: Cornell University Press, 1994) [Contains a shortened version of *Observations on the emigration of Dr J. Priestley...*].

Secondary Works

Conway, M. D. *The Life of Thomas Paine* 2 vols (New York, 1892).

Hawke, D. F. *Paine* (New York, London etc, 1974).

Keane, J. *Tom Paine: A Political Life* (London, 1995).

Malone, D. *The Public Life of Thomas Cooper 1783–1839* (Yale and Oxford, 1923).

Park, M. C. *Priestley and the Problem of Pantisocracy* (University of Pennsylvania 1947).

Powell, D. *Tom Paine: The Greatest Exile* (London and Sydney, 1985).

Smiles, S. *Lives of the Engineers* 5 vols (London, 1874).

Smith, F. *Tom Paine, Liberator* (New York, 1938).

Woodward, W. E. *Tom Paine: America's Godfather, 1737–1809* (London, 1945).

FRENCHMEN IN AMERICA

Letters and Texts

Brissot de Warville, J.-P. *Examen critique des Voyages dans l'Amérique septrionale de M. le marquis de Chastellux, dans laquelle on réfute principalement ses opinions sur les Quakers, sur les nègres, sur le peuple et sur l'homme* (London, 1786).

Brissot, J.-P. *Plan de conduite des députés du peuple aux Etats Généraux de 1789* (Paris 1789).

Brissot, J.-P. *New Travels in the United States of America performed in 1788* (London, 1792).

Brissot, J.-P., *The Life of J. P. Brissot, Deputy from Eure and Loire to the National Convention. Written by himself* (London, 1794).

Brissot, J.-P. *Correspondance et Papiers*, ed. with a biographical introduction by C. Perroud (Paris 1912).

Chastellux, Marquis de, *An Essay on Public Happiness* 2 vols (London 1774: reprinted New York, 1969).

Chastellux, Marquis de *Discours sur les avantages ou les désavantages qui résultent, pour l'Europe, de la découverte de l'Amérique* (Paris, 1787).

Chastellux, Marquis de *Travels in North America in the Years 1780, 1781 and 1782* 2 vols (London 1787).

*The Marquis de la Fayette's Statement of his own Conduct and Principles,
translated from the original French and most respectfully inscribed to the
Whig Club* 2nd edn (London, 1793).

*Biographical Anecdotes of the Founders of the French Republic, and of other
Eminent Characters, who have distinguished themselves in the Progress of the
Revolution* [including Lafayette] (London, 1797).

Levasseur, A. *Lafayette in America in 1824 and 1825; or Journal of a Voyage to
the United States*, trans. J. D. Godman (Philadelphia, 1829).

Quincy, E. S., *Memoir of the Life of E. S. M. Quincy* [Part I An Autobiography.
Part II Memoir of E. S. M. Quincy by E. S. Quincy] privately printed
(Boston, 1861).

Robin, C. C., *Nouveau Voyage dans l'Amérique Septentriole, en l'Année 1781:
et campagne de l'armée de M. le comte de Rochambeau* (Philadelphia,
1792).

Ségur, Comte de *Memoirs of Louis Philippe, Comte de Ségur*, ed. E. Cruickshanks (London: Folio Society, 1960).

Secondary Works

Bernier, O. *Lafayette: Hero of Two Worlds* (New York, 1983).

Buckman, P. *Lafayette* (New York and London, 1977).

de la Fuye M. and Babeau, E. *The Apostle of Liberty: a Life of Lafayette*, trans.
E. Hyams (London, 1956) Fay, B. *La Franc-Maçonnerie et la révolution
intellectuelle au xviiie siècle* (Cluny, 1935).

Hamill, J. and R. Gilbert (eds) *Freemasonry: a Celebration of the Craft*, (St
Alban's, 1992).

Ketchum, R. *The World of George Washington* [illustrated] (New York, 1974).

Klamkin, M. *The Return of Lafayette* (New York, 1975).

Loth, D. *Lafayette* (London, 1952).

Maugras, G. *The Duc de Lauzun and the Court of Marie Antoinette* (London,
1896).

Schama, S. *Citizens* (London and New York, 1989).

Soubiran, A. *The Good Doctor Guillotin and His Strange Device*, trans. M.
MacCraw (London, 1964).

Woodward, W. E. *Lafayette: a biography* (London, 1939).

IMAGES AND VISIONS

Le Clerc, G.L. Comte de Buffon, *Les Epoques de la nature*, édition critique by
J. Roger (Paris, 1962).

Coleridge, S. T. *Collected Letters of Samuel Taylor Coleridge*, ed. E. L. Griggs
6 vols (Oxford, 1956).

Coleridge, S. T. *Biographia Literaria* (London and New York: Dent Everyman,
1965).

Coleridge, S. T. *Collected Works of Samuel Taylor Coleridge*, ed. K. Coburn et
al. 16 vols (Princeton, 1969–).

Coleridge, S. T. *Samuel Taylor Coleridge: Selected Letters*, ed. H. J. Jackson (London, 1987).

Coleridge, S. T. *Coleridge's Writings: on Politics and Society*, ed. J. Morrow (Princeton, 1991).

Coleridge, S. T. *Poems*, ed. John Beer (London and Vermont: Dent Everyman, 1993).

Crèvecoeur, H. St John de *Letters from an American Farmer* (London; Dent Everyman, 1912).

Crèvecoeur, H. St John de *Journey into Northern Pennsylvania and the State of New York* [*Voyage dans la Haute Pensylvanie et dans l'Etat de New-York* 3 vols (Paris, 1801)], trans. C. S. Bostelman 3 vols (University of Michigan, 1964).

Godwin, W. *History of the Internal Affairs of the United Provinces* (London, 1787).

Godwin, W. *Enquiry concerning Political Justice and its influence on General Virtue and Happiness* 2 vols (London, 1793).

Godwin, W. *Considerations on Lord Grenville's and Mr Pitt's Bills, concerning Treasonable and Unlawful Assemblies, by a Lover of Order* (London, 1795).

Godwin, W. *Posthumous Works of the Author of a Vindication of the Rights of Woman* 4 vols (London, 1798).

Godwin, W. *Memoirs of Mary Wollstonecraft*, ed. W. Clark Durant, with preface, supplement and bibliographical note (London and New York, 1927).

Imlay, G. *Mémoire sur Louisiana*, English translation in *American Historical Review* (April, 1898).

Imlay, G. *A Topographical Description of the Western Territory of North America* (London, 1792).

Imlay G. [and Mary Wollstonecraft?], *The Emigrants, &c, or the history of An Expatriated Family, Being a delineation of English Manners, Drawn from Real Characters* 3 vols (London, 1793) and 1 vol (Dublin, 1794). See facsimile of one-volume Dublin edn, ed. with an introduction by R. Hare (Gainsville, Florida, 1964).

Paine, T. *A letter Addressed to the Abbé Raynal* in *Complete Works of Thomas Paine: Political ad Controversial* (London, 1850).

Raynal, G. T. P. *The Revolution of America* (London, 1781).

Raynal, G. T. P. *A Philosophical and Political History of the Settlements of Trade of the Europeans in the East and West Indies*, trans. J. J. Justamond 2nd edn 5 vols (London, 1776).

Raynal, G. T. P. *Philosophical and Political History etc* 10 vols (Geneva, 1781).

Southey, R. *Life and Correspondence of Robert Southey*, ed. C. C. Southey 2nd edn 6 vols (London 1849–50).

Southey, R. *Correspondence of Robert Southey with Caroline Bowles*, ed. E. Dowden (Dublin, 1881).

Southey, R. *New Letters of Robert Southey*, ed. K. Curry 2 vols (New York, 1965).

Wollstonecraft, M. *Thoughts on the Education of Daughters with Reflections on Female Conduct in the More Important Duties of Life* (London, 1787).

Wollstonecraft, M. *Vindication of the Rights of Men, in a Letter to the Right Honourable Edmund Burke* (London, 1790).

Wollstonecraft, M. *An Historical and Moral View of the French Revolution and the Effect it has Produced in Europe* (London, 1794: 2nd edn, 1796).

Wollstonecraft, M. *Four New Letters of Mary Wollstonecraft and Helen Maria Williams*, ed. B. P. Kurtz and C. C. Aubrey (Berkeley, California, 1937).

Wollstonecraft, M. *Vindication of the Rights of Woman* (London, 1792: bicentenary edn, 1992).

Wollstonecraft, M. *Letters written during a Short Residence in Sweden, Norway and Denmark* in *Mary Wollstonecraft and William Godwin*, ed. R. Holmes (London, New York etc., 1987).

Williams, J. *Farther Observations on the Discovery of America* (London, 1792).

Wordsworth, W. *Poetical Works*, ed. T. Hutchinson (Oxford, 1936: reset, 1950).

Secondary Works

Ashton, R. *The Life of Samuel Taylor Coleridge: A Critical Biography* (Cambridge, Mass. and Oxford, 1996).

Audubon, M. *Audubon and His Journals* 2 vols (London, 1898).

Buchanan, R. *Life and Adventures of Audubon the Naturalist* (London, Toronto, New York: Dent Everyman, 1915).

Chancellor, J. *Audubon: A Biography* (New York, 1978).

Cornwell, J. *Coleridge: Poet and Revolutionary* (London 1973).

Curry, K. *Southey* (London, 1975).

Elman, R. *The Living World of Audubon Mammals* (New York, 1976).

Furbank, P. N. *Diderot: a Critical Biography* (London, 1992).

Herrick, F. H. *Audubon the Naturalist: a History of His Life and Time* 2 vols (New York, 1968).

Kastner, J. *A World of Naturalists* (London, 1978).

Holmes, R. *Coleridge: Early Visions* (London etc., 1989).

Kerber, L. K. *Women of the Republic: Ideology in Revolutionary America* (Chapel Hill, 1980).

Lefebure, M. *The Bondage of Love: A Life of Mrs Samuel Taylor Coleridge* (New York, 1987; paperback edn 1989).

Marshall, P. *William Godwin* (Yale, 1984).

Roe, N. *Wordsworth and Coleridge: The Radical Years* (Oxford, 1988).

Sandford, Mrs H. *Thomas Poole and his Friends* 2 vols (London, 1888).

St Clair, W. *The Godwins and the Shelleys: the Biography of a Family* (London, 1989; paperback edn 1991).

Stuart-Jones, E. H. *The Last Invasion of Britain* (Cardiff, 1950).

Tomalin, C. *The Life and Death of Mary Wollstonecraft* (London: revised Penguin edn 1992).

Wardle, R. M. *Mary Wollstonecraft: A Critical Biography* (University of Kansas, 1951).

Williams, G. 'Frontiers of Illusion' in *History Today* XXX (January 1980).

Index

Published works (with date of publication and abbreviated title) appear under author's name. Exceptions are: newspapers, and other works where no author is known, where the reference is an isolated one, or where an individual's name (other than the author's) appears in the title. Page references in bold type relate to illustrations.

256   *Index*